WEST ORANGE LIBRARY
46 MT. PLEASANT AVENUE
WEST ORANGE, NJ 07052
(973) 736 – 0198
10/22/2007

TURNING BACK
THE CLOCK

Also by UMBERTO ECO

The Mysterious Flame of Queen Loana

Baudolino

The Island of the Day Before

Foucault's Pendulum

The Name of the Rose

Postscript to the Name of the Rose

Five Moral Pieces

Kant and the Platypus

Serendipities

How to Travel with a Salmon

Misreadings

Travels in Hyperreality

Semiotics and the Philosophy of Language

A Theory of Semiotics

The Open Work

UMBERTO ECO

TURNING BACK THE CLOCK

Hot Wars and Media Populism

Translated from the Italian
by Alastair McEwen

HARCOURT, INC.

Orlando   Austin   New York   San Diego   London

© 2006 RCS Libri SpA/Bompiani-Milano
English translation copyright © 2007 by Alastair McEwen

All rights reserved. No part of this publication may be reproduced
or transmitted in any form or by any means, electronic or mechanical,
including photocopy, recording, or any information storage and retrieval
system, without permission in writing from the publisher.

Requests for permission to make copies of any part of the work should be
submitted online at www.harcourt.com/contact or mailed to the following
address: Permissions Department, Harcourt, Inc., 6277 Sea Harbor Drive,
Orlando, Florida 32887-6777.

www.HarcourtBooks.com

This is a translation of *A Passo di Gambero*

Umberto Eco's introduction to Will Eisner's *The Plot: The Secret Story of
the Protocols of the Elders of Zion* is copyright © 2005 by Umberto Eco,
English translation is copyright © 2005 by W.W. Norton & Company, Inc.

Library of Congress Cataloging-in-Publication Data
Eco, Umberto.
[A passo di gambero. English]
Turning back the clock: hot wars and media populism/Umberto Eco;
translated from the Italian by Alastair McEwen.
p.   cm.
A collection of previously published articles.
1. Eco, Umberto—Political and social views.   I. McEwen, Alastair.
II. Title.
PQ4865.C6A62613   2007
854'.914—dc21   2007022472
ISBN 978-0-15-101351-7

Text set in Bodoni Book
Designed by Linda Lockowitz

Printed in the United States of America
First edition
K J I H G F E D C B A

Contents

III. THE RETURN OF THE GREAT GAME

IV. THE RETURN OF THE CRUSADES

V. THE *SUMMA* AND THE REST

TURNING BACK
THE CLOCK

Steps Back

This book is a collection of articles and speeches written between 2000 and 2005.

The period was a momentous one. It began with anxieties over the new millennium; September 11 was followed by the wars in Afghanistan and Iraq; and in Italy, we saw the rise to power of Silvio Berlusconi.

So I have decided to leave out many articles on various topics and include only those pieces that deal with the events in the world of politics and the media that occurred in those six years. This criterion was suggested to me by one of the last pieces in my previous collection of articles (published in Italy as *La bustina di Minerva*): "Il trionfo della tecnologia leggera" ("The Triumph of Light Technology").

In the form of a fake review of a book attributed to a certain Crabe Backwards, I observed that recent times had witnessed technological developments that represented authentic steps back. I noted that "heavy communication" had entered a crisis toward the end of the seventies. Until then, the main means of communication was the color television, an enormous, cumbersome box that in the darkness emitted sinister flashes of light and enough sound to disturb the entire neighborhood. The first step toward "light communication" came with the invention of the remote control, thanks to which the viewer could not only turn down but even switch off the volume. The same device also made it possible to eliminate color and "surf" from one channel to another.

Skipping through dozens of debates, sitting in front of a black-and-white screen with the volume off, the viewer entered a state of creative liberty known in Italy as the "Blob phase," after a television program ("Blob") made up of hundreds of short clips cut and pasted to form a completely new narrative. Furthermore, old television, which broadcast events live, made us dependent on their linearity. Emancipation from live television came with the VCR, which not only marked the evolution of Television into Cinema but also enabled the viewer to rewind cassettes, thus completely freeing him from his passive and repressed role in the event being related.

At this point it would have been possible to eliminate the sound altogether and coordinate the random sequence of images with a pianola soundtrack synthesized by computer; and—given that TV channels, under the pretext of helping the hearing-impaired, had taken to inserting written captions commenting on the action—it would not have been long before we had programs in which a couple kissed in silence while viewers saw a word bubble with "I love you" inside it. And so light technology would have invented the silent films of the Lumière Brothers.

The next step was the elimination of movement from the images. With the Internet the user could save neural effort by receiving only low-definition stills, often in black and white, and no sound was needed, since the information appeared on the screen in alphabetical characters.

A further stage in this triumphal return to the Gutenberg Galaxy would have been—as I said at the time—the radical elimination of the image. We would have invented a box that emitted only sound and didn't even require a remote: you could surf simply by turning a knob. I was under the illusion that I had invented the radio, but I was only predicting the advent of the iPod.

That transmission over the airwaves, with all its attendant physical disturbances, was superseded by pay-per-view TV and the Internet, which marked the beginning of the new era of transmission via telephone cable, so we moved from wireless telegraphy to wired telephony, thus sidestepping Marconi and returning to Alexander Graham Bell.

Playful as these observations were, they were not so far-fetched. That things were going backward had already emerged clearly after the fall of the Berlin Wall, when the political geography of Europe and Asia was radically changed. Publishers of atlases had to pulp all their stock (made obsolete by the presence of the Soviet Union, Yugoslavia, East Germany, and similar monstrosities) and fall back into line with atlases published before 1914, complete with Serbia, Montenegro, the Baltic states, and so on.

But the history of steps back doesn't stop here, and the beginning of this millennium has provided a generous number of examples. Let's take a quick look at a few. After fifty years of cold war, Afghanistan and Iraq have marked the return of hot war, which has even included the replay of memorable nineteenth-century attacks launched by the "wily Afghans" on the Khyber Pass. The Crusades have also made a comeback with the clash between Islam and Christianity—complete with the Assassins, the suicide killers of the Old Man of the Mountains—and such medieval glories as the Battle of Lepanto. In fact, some successful political pamphlets of recent years could be summed up by the old cry from the days of the Barbary corsairs: *Mamma li turchi!* ("Oh Mother, the Turks are coming!").

The resurgence of the anti-Darwinian polemic marks the reappearance of a Christian fundamentalism that seemed to belong to the chronicles of the nineteenth century, while the ghost of the yellow peril has risen again (albeit only in demographic and economic form). For some time now our families have once more been employing colored servants, as in *Gone with the Wind,* while great migrations are once more under way, as in the first centuries after Christ. And in Italy, some rituals and customs of the late Roman Empire are enjoying a revival.

Anti-Semitism has re-emerged vigorously with its *Protocols,* and in Italy we now have some Fascists (post-Fascists, if you will, but many are no different) in the government. As I correct these proofs, I learn that a football player gave the Fascist salute to a cheering crowd of fans. Exactly as I used to do as a member of a Fascist youth group almost seventy years ago—except for the fact that I had to. Then there is the problem of devolution, which would bring Italy back to the days before Garibaldi.

Also in Italy, the old row about church and state has come up again, and many other things are returning, like undeliverable mail—various forms of the Christian Democratic Party, for example.

Almost as if history, breathless after the leaps forward made in the last two millennia, is drawing back into itself, returning to the comfortable splendors of tradition.

Many such backward phenomena will emerge from the articles in this book, enough of them to justify the title if nothing else. But there is no doubt that something new has happened, something unprecedented: the establishment in Italy of a government based on a populism conveyed by the media and perpetrated by the interests of private enterprise. This experiment, new at least on the European scene, is far shrewder and technologically more aggressive than the populist movements of the Third World.

This theme lies at the heart of many of these articles, which sprang from disquiet and indignation about the advance of the new order, an advance that we still don't know how to stop. If it can be stopped at all.

The second section of the book takes its title from the phenom-

enon of regime by media populism, and I have no hesitation in talking about a "regime," at least in the sense in which the people of
the Middle Ages (who were not communists) spoke of *de regimine
principum.*

In this regard I decided to open the second section with an appeal
that I had written before the 2001 elections and that was much reviled. A right-wing pundit, but one who evidently doesn't dislike me
altogether, was pained and surprised that a "good" man like me
could deal so scornfully with that half of his fellow countrymen who
had not voted for the same party as he had. Recently, and not from
a right-wing source either, the kind of commitment I advocated was
called arrogant—an attitude that makes much of opposition culture
look disagreeable.

As I have many times been accused of trying to be agreeable at
all costs, the discovery that I am disagreeable fills me with pride
and virtuous satisfaction.

But this accusation is curious, as if in their day Italian political
figures such as Rosselli, Gobetti, Salvemini, and Gramsci, not to
mention Matteotti (if I may compare the small with the great), had
been accused of disrespect to their adversaries.

If someone fights for a political preference (and, here, civic and
moral preferences as well), apart from his duty to be prepared to
change his mind one day, in that moment he must believe he is in
the right and must vigorously expose the error of those in opposition.
I cannot imagine any electoral campaign that could be waged under
the banner of "You are all in the right, but vote for one who is in the
wrong." Criticism of the adversary must be severe and ruthless, in
order to convince the undecided, if no one else.

Further, many criticisms deemed disagreeable are those of social mores. And the critic of social mores (who in railing against the
vices of others rails against his own, or his own temptations) must

be caustic. In other words, if I may refer once more to the great, if you want to chastise social mores, you must be like Horace; if you are like Virgil, then you write a poem, maybe even a beautiful one, in praise of the ruling deity.

But the times are murky, the mores corrupted, and even the right to criticize, when not smothered by censorship, elicits popular disapproval.

I therefore present these writings in the name of the positive disagreeability I claim for myself.

In each text, I refer to the source, but many pieces have been reworked. I revised not for the purpose of updating them, or to insert prophecies that later came to pass, but to prune them of repetitions (it's hard to avoid returning doggedly to the same topics), to correct the style, or to eliminate a few references too bound up with the current events of the time, by now forgotten by the reader and thus incomprehensible.

I

WAR, PEACE, AND OTHER MATTERS

Some Reflections on War and Peace

In the early sixties I contributed to the establishment of the Italian Committee for Atomic Disarmament and took part in several peace marches. I declare myself to be a pacifist by vocation and am to this day. Nonetheless, here I must say bad things not only about war but also about peace. So I ask the reader to bear with me.

I have written a series of articles on war, starting with the Gulf War, and now I realize that each article modified my ideas on the concept of war. As if the concept of war, which has remained more or less the same (aside from the weapons used) from the days of Ancient Greece till yesterday, needed to be rethought at least three times over the last ten years.[1]

---

1. I return to some topics dealt with in an essay from *Five Moral Pieces* (New York: Harcourt, 2001), when I reflected on the first Gulf War, but even the things said at that time take on new meaning when considered from the standpoint of successive events.

Talk given at a conference held in Milan at the Communità di Sant'Egidio, July 2002.

From Paleowar to Cold War

In the course of the centuries, what was the purpose of that form of warfare we shall call paleowar? We made war in order to vanquish our adversaries and thus profit from their defeat; we tried to achieve our ends by taking the enemy by surprise; we did everything possible to ensure that our adversaries did not achieve their ends; we accepted a certain price in human lives in order to inflict upon the enemy a greater loss of life. For these purposes it was necessary to marshal all the forces at our disposal. The game was played out between two contenders. The neutrality of others, the fact that they suffered no harm from the conflict and if anything profited from it, was a necessary condition for the belligerents' freedom of action. Oh yes, I was forgetting; there was a further condition: knowing who and where the enemy was. For this reason, usually, the clash was a frontal one and involved two or more recognizable territories.

In our times, the notion of "world war," a conflict that could involve even societies with no recorded history, such as Polynesian tribes, has eliminated the difference between belligerents and neutral parties. Whoever the contenders may be, atomic energy ensures that war is harmful for the entire planet.

The consequence is the transition from paleowar to neowar via the cold war. The cold war established what we might call belligerent peace or peaceful belligerence, a balance of terror that guaranteed a remarkable stability at the center and permitted, or made indispensable, forms of paleowar on the periphery (Vietnam, the Middle East, African states, and so on). At bottom, the cold war guaranteed peace for the First and Second Worlds at the price of seasonal or endemic wars in the Third World.

Neowar in the Gulf

The collapse of the Soviet empire marked the end of the conditions of the cold war but left us faced with the problem of incessant warfare in the Third World. With the invasion of Kuwait, people realized that it was going to be necessary to go back to a kind of traditional warfare (if you recall, reference was made to the origins of the Second World War: if Hitler had been stopped as soon as he invaded Poland, and so on . . .), but it immediately became evident that war was no longer between two sides. The scandal of the American journalists in Baghdad in those days was equal to the (far greater) scandal of the millions and millions of pro-Iraqi Muslims living in the countries of the anti-Iraqi alliance.

In wars of the past potential enemies were interned (or massacred), and compatriots who from enemy territory spoke in favor of the enemy's cause were hanged at the end of the war. You might remember John Amery, who attacked his country on Fascist radio and was hanged by the English. Ezra Pound, thanks to his renown and the support of intellectuals of many countries, was saved, but at the cost of a full-blown mental illness.

What are the characteristics of neowar?

The identity of the enemy is uncertain. Were all Iraqis the enemy? All Serbs? Who had to be destroyed?

The war has no front. Neowar cannot have a front because of the very nature of multinational capitalism. It is no accident that Iraq was armed by Western industry, and likewise no accident that Western industry armed the Taliban ten years later. This falls within the logic of mature capitalism, which eludes the control of individual states. And here it is worth mentioning an apparently minor but significant detail: at a certain point it was thought that Western aircraft had destroyed a cache of Saddam's tanks or aircraft, only to find out later that they were decoys produced and legally sold to Saddam by an Italian factory.

Paleowars worked to the advantage of the armaments industries of each of the belligerents, but neowar works to the advantage of multinationals whose interests lie on both sides of the barricades (if real barricades still exist). But there is more. While paleowar enriched arms dealers, and such gains compensated for the temporary cessation of certain other forms of trade, neowar not only enriches the arms dealers but also creates a worldwide crisis in air transport, entertainment and tourism, the media (which lose commercial advertising revenue), and in general the entire industry of the superfluous—the backbone of the system—from the building sector to the car industry. Neowar brings some economic powers into competition with others, and the logic of their conflict outweighs that of the national powers.

I noted in those days that neowar would typically be short, because prolonging it would benefit no one in the long run.

But if individual states must submit to the industrial logic of the multinationals, they also must submit to the needs of the information industry. In the Gulf War we saw, for the first time in history, the Western media voicing the reservations and the protests not only of the representatives of Western pacifism, the pope first and foremost, but also of the ambassadors and journalists of those Arab countries that supported Saddam.

Information services continually permitted the adversary to speak (whereas the aim of all wartime politics is to block enemy propaganda) and demoralized the citizens of the combatant countries with regard to their own government (whereas Clausewitz pointed out that a condition for victory is the moral cohesion of a country).

Every war of the past was based on the principle that the citizenry, holding it to be just, were anxious to destroy the enemy. But now the media were not only causing the citizens' faith to waver, they also impressed on them the death of their enemies—no longer a vague, distant event but an unbearable visual record. The Gulf War was the first one in which the belligerents sympathized with their enemies.

In the days of Vietnam, some sympathy was evident, even though it took the form of discussion, held on highly specific, often marginal occasions by groups of American radicals. But we didn't see the ambassadors of Ho Chi Minh or General Giap speechifying on the BBC. Nor did we see American journalists transmitting news from a hotel in Hanoi the way Peter Arnett did from a hotel in Baghdad.

The media puts the enemy behind the lines. The Gulf War established that in modern neowar, the enemy is among us. Even if the media were muzzled, new communication technologies would maintain the flow of information—a flow that not even a dictator could block, because it uses minimal infrastructures that not even he can do without. This information carries out the functions performed by the secret services in traditional warfare: it rules out any sneak attack. How can you have a war in which you cannot surprise your enemy? Neowar has institutionalized the role of Mata Hari and thus made "enemy intelligence" generally available.

By putting so many conflicting powers into play, neowar is no longer a phenomenon in which the calculations and intentions of the main actors determine the issue. This multiplication of powers (which actually began with globalization) means that their respective influence was unpredictable. The outcome may prove convenient for one of the contenders, but in principle neowar is a loss for everyone involved.

To state that a conflict has shown itself to be advantageous for someone at a given moment suggests an equation of the momentary advantage with the final advantage. You would have a final moment if war were still, as Clausewitz put it, the continuation of policy by other means—that is, the war would be over upon the attainment of a state of equilibrium that permitted a return to politics. But the two great wars of the twentieth century made it clear that postwar politics always continue (by any means) the premises posed by war. However the war goes, because it causes a general reorganization that does not correspond fully with the will of the contenders, it must be extended by dramatic political, economic, and psychological instability for decades to come, a process that can only produce the politics of war.

On the other hand, were things ever any different? Deciding that classic wars have produced reasonable results—a final equilibrium—derives from a Hegelian prejudice according to which history has a direction. There is no scientific (or logical) proof that the political order in the Mediterranean after the Punic Wars or the political order in Europe after the Napoleonic Wars was one of equilibrium. It could be, instead, an imbalance that would not have come about if these wars had not occurred. The statement that for thousands of years humanity has made war as a solution to states of imbalance can no more be proved than the statement that during the same period humanity solved psychological imbalance by turning to alcohol and other drugs.

That these reflections of mine at the time were not pipe dreams is shown by the events following the Gulf War. The Western forces liberated Kuwait but did not proceed to the annihilation of the enemy. The resulting state proved no more balanced than the one that led to the conflict, so the question of destroying Saddam Hussein was repeatedly tabled.

The fact is that the Gulf neowar led to the emergence of a problem that was absolutely new, not only to the logic and dynamics of paleowar but also to its governing psychology. The aim of paleowarfare was to destroy as many of the enemy as possible, accepting that many of one's own men had to die too. After a victory, the great military leaders of the past would pass by night through battlefields sown with thousands and thousands of dead, and they weren't surprised that half of them were their own soldiers. The commemoration with medals and moving ceremonies of the death of one's own soldiers gave rise to the cult of the hero. The death of the others was publicized and gloried in, and civilians at home were expected to rejoice at their elimination.

The Gulf War established two principles: (1) none of our men should die and (2) as few enemies as possible should be killed. Re-

garding the death of our adversaries we saw some hypocrisy, because a great number of Iraqis died in the desert, but the very fact
that no one emphasized this detail is an interesting sign. In any case
neowarfare typically tries to avoid killing civilians, because if you
kill too many of them, you run the risk of condemnation by the international media.

Hence the employment and celebration of smart bombs. After
fifty years of peace due to the cold war, such sensitivity might strike
many young people as normal, but can you imagine this attitude in
the years when the V1s were destroying London and Allied bombs
were razing Dresden?

As for our own soldiers, the Gulf War was the first conflict in
which the loss of a single man seemed unacceptable. The country at
war would not have tolerated the paleomilitary logic that required
thousands and thousands of its sons to be prepared to die in order
to win the day. The loss of a Western aircraft was perceived as extremely painful, and we even came to lionize, on television, those
captured soldiers who, in order to save their lives, agreed to act as
mouthpieces for enemy propaganda. "Poor souls," people said,
"they were tortured into doing this"—forgetting the sacred principle that a captured soldier must not talk even under torture.

The logic of paleowarfare would require such men to be held up
to public scorn—or at least a compassionate veil would have been
drawn over their misfortune. Instead they were accorded understanding, enveloped in a warm sense of solidarity, and rewarded, if
not by the military authorities, by media curiosity, because after all
they had managed to survive.

In brief, neowar became a media product, so much so that Bau-
drillard was able to say, paradoxically, that it didn't actually take
place but was merely shown on television. By definition, the media
sell happiness and not suffering: they had to take the logic of war
and maximize the good—or at least minimize the sacrifice. A war

that involves little sacrifice and strives to safeguard the principle of maximum happiness must necessarily be brief. And so it was with the Gulf War.

But it was so short, it was largely useless, otherwise the neocons would not have been obliged to urge both Clinton and Bush to give Saddam no quarter. Neowar was by then at loggerheads with the very logic that had fueled it.

Neowar in Kosovo

With the war in Kosovo, all the characteristics of neowarfare that had emerged at the time of the Gulf War reappeared in an even more intense form.

Not only did Western journalists stay on in Belgrade, the Italian government was sending aircraft to Serbia and at the same time keeping up diplomatic and commercial relations with Yugoslavia. The television stations of the NATO countries told the Serbs hour by hour which NATO aircraft were leaving the Italian base at Aviano; Serbian agents supported their government's position—and we heard and saw them doing so on our television screens. But we weren't the only ones to have the enemy in our backyard. The Serbs were in the same position.

Many Italians will remember that a Serbian journalist, Biljana Srbjanović, sent in anti-Milošević pieces to Italy's newspaper *Re-pubblica* on a daily basis. How can you bomb a city whose inhabitants were sending letters of friendship to the enemy and showing hostility toward their own government? Of course, in 1944 the city of Milan was full of anti-Fascists waiting for aid from the Allies, but this did not prevent the Allies—for irreproachable military reasons—from launching ruthless bombing raids on Milan. Nor was there any protest from the dissidents, because they thought that this was right. But the bombardment of Belgrade was marked by a form of persecution complex on Milošević's part, on the part of the anti-Milošević Serbs, and on the part of the Westerners who were doing the bombing. Hence the publicity accorded to the use of smart bombs, even when they proved to be not smart at all.

Again, during this second neowar, no one was meant to die. In any event, fewer died than in Iraq, because Serbs are as white and as European as the people who were bombing them, and then they had to be protected from the Albanians, although the conflict had begun to protect the Albanians from the Serbs. This war certainly had no front: the contending parties were separated not by a straight line but by a series of interwoven zigzags.

There had never been a war based so much on the principle of maximum happiness and minimum sacrifice, which is why this war too was very brief.

Afghanistan

September 11 turned the logic of war on its head once more. It is worthy of note that this event did not mark the beginning of the war in Afghanistan but the confrontation, still in progress, between the Western world—more specifically, the United States—and Islamic terrorism.

If September 11 was the start of a conflict, in this new phase of neowar the front completely vanished. Even those who see the Western world and the world of Islam clearly set against each other know that the conflict is no longer territorial. The infamous rogue states may be hotbeds of terrorism, but terrorism has no borders. It is also present in Western countries. This time the enemy really is behind the lines.

At the time of the conflicts in the Gulf and in Kosovo, the enemy agents acting on our home ground were known (and in fact they made television appearances), but the strength of international terrorists is that (1) they remain unknown, (2) our media cannot monitor them the way Peter Arnett monitored life in Baghdad during the Western bombing raids, and (3) they are not only people from foreign backgrounds who have infiltrated our territory but also our own countrymen. The envelopes containing anthrax were most likely put into circulation not by Muslim kamikazes but by Yankee sectarian groups, neo-Nazis, or other fanatics.

Moreover, the role played by the media was very different from that played in the two preceding neowars, where at most they gave voice to the opinions of the adversary.

All terrorist acts are carried out to launch a message that, obviously, spreads terror or at least anxiety. The terrorist message destabilizes even when its impact is minimal, particularly when the target is a "strong" symbol. What was bin Laden's aim in striking the Twin Towers? To create "the world's greatest catastrophe," one never even imagined by catastrophe movie makers, to give a visual impression of the attack on the very symbols of Western power, and to show that even the most important sanctuaries of that power could be violated.

Bin Laden's aim was to impress world public opinion with that image, and accordingly the mass media talked about it, showed the dramatic rescue operations, the excavations, and the mutilated skyline of Manhattan. Did they have to repeat this news item every day, for at least a month, with photographs, film clips, and the endless eyewitness reports, broadcasting over and over the images of that wound before the eyes of all? It is hard to give an answer. Sales of newspapers with those photos went up, television channels that offered continuous repeats of those film clips enjoyed improved ratings, the public wanted to see those terrible scenes replayed, perhaps to feed its indignation, perhaps sometimes to indulge an unconscious sadism. Maybe it was impossible to do otherwise, but the fact remains that in this way the media gave bin Laden billions of dollars' worth of free publicity, showing every day the images he had created, sowing bewilderment among Westerners, and giving his fundamentalist supporters a reason for pride.

Hence while the mass media reproved bin Laden, they were also his best allies, because it was with their help that he won the first round.

Attempts to censure or tone down the communiqués that bin Laden sent through Al Jazeera failed. The global information network was stronger than the Pentagon, and so it reestablished the fundamental principle of neowarfare, whereby the enemy talks to you in your own home.

In this case, neowar placed not two native lands in opposition but several powers in competition with one another. In the two preceding neowars, these powers worked to shorten the conflict; this time they risked prolonging it.

In an interview with *Repubblica* some months ago, the ex-director of the CIA said that the enemy to bombard ought to have been offshore banks, like those in the Cayman Islands, and perhaps the banks of the great European cities.

A few days before, on an Italian TV program hosted by Bruno Vespa, member of parliament Gustavo Selva, when faced with a challenge of this kind (but weaker, coming not from the former director of the CIA but from a member of the antiglobalization movement), reacted indignantly, saying that it was insane and criminal to think that the great Western banks were playing the terrorists' game. Which shows how a politician well over retirement age cannot conceive of the true nature of neowar. Someone in Washington did understand it, and we know that in the first phase, from September 11 to the beginning of operations in Afghanistan, the United States considered waging the conflict as if it were a great spy war, by paralyzing the economic centers of terrorism. But it was necessary to assuage immediately the feelings of the American public, who had been deeply humiliated, and the only way to do that was by paleowar.

Hence the war in Afghanistan was one based again on territory, involving pitched battles and traditional tactics, to the extent that it was reminiscent of the nineteenth-century British campaigns in the Khyber Pass, thus returning to some of the principles of paleowarfare:

1. That the media were not allowed to undermine the effectiveness of military operations from the inside led to something very much like censorship. But the global information system made sure that what the Americans wouldn't say was said by an Arab television station, proving that paleowarfare is not really possible in the age of the Internet.

2. The enemy may have won the first round symbolically but had to be physically destroyed. The principle of sparing innocent civilians was preserved (hence the use of smart bombs yet again), but it was accepted that whenever the local forces of the Northern Alliance took over from the Western forces, a few massacres could not be avoided—but they were glossed over.

3. Once again it was accepted that the lives of one's own soldiers would be lost, and the nation was asked to prepare itself for new sacrifice. George W. Bush, like Churchill in the Second World War, promised his people final victory but also blood and tears, something his father had not done at the time of the Gulf conflict.

The Afghan paleowar may have solved the problem it set itself (i.e., the Taliban were driven from power), but it didn't solve the problems of the third-phase neowar from which it sprang. The aim of the Afghan war may have been to eradicate Islamic international terrorism and neutralize its operational centers, but clearly they continued to exist elsewhere, and the problem then was where to make the next move. Or if the aim was to eliminate bin Laden, it is by no means clear that that was accomplished; and even if it had been, we might have discovered that bin Laden was a charismatic figure but not the solution to fundamentalist Islamic terrorism.

Shrewd men like Metternich knew that sending Napoleon to die on Saint Helena would not eliminate Bonapartism, so Metternich tried to get the most out of Waterloo through the Congress of Vienna, but it wasn't enough, as the history of the nineteenth century demonstrated.

The neowar that began on September 11 was neither won nor lost by the Afghan war—and I honestly couldn't tell you whether or how Bush could have done anything differently, but this is not the point under discussion. The point is that, when it comes to neowars, there may be no military leaders capable of winning them.

The contradiction is now at its peak, as is the ensuing confusion. On the one hand, the conditions that make it possible to wage a war have ceased to exist, given that the enemy is completely hidden. On the other hand, to show that in some way we are still engaging the enemy, we must construct simulacra of a paleowar, which allow our citizens to think that the country stands firm and to forget that the enemy is not where we are bombing but right here among us.

Faced with this bewilderment, public opinion (of which demagogues have made themselves the interpreters) is trying desperately to dust off the image of paleowar, and the metaphor it has found is that of the Crusade, the clash between cultures, a new battle of Lepanto between Christians and infidels. If the little Afghan war was won, why can't we win the global neowar by turning it into a global paleowar, we whites against the Moors? Put in these terms, it's like something out of a comic book, but the success of Oriana Fallaci's books tells us that it is a comic book read by many adults.

The supporters of the Crusade have not realized that a Crusade is still a form of paleowar, which cannot be waged in a world that has created the conditions and the contradictions of neowar.

Scenario for a Crusade

We imagine a global confrontation between the Christian and Muslim worlds—a frontal clash, therefore, as in the past. But in the past the borders of Europe were well defined: the Mediterranean lay between Christians and infidels, and the Pyrenees ensured the isolation of the Western part of the continent that was still partly in Arab hands. The clash could take two forms: attack or containment.

The attack was the Crusades, but we know what happened. The only Crusade that led to an effective conquest (with the establishment of Frankish kingdoms in the Middle East) was the first. After less than a century, Jerusalem fell once more into the hands of the Muslims, and the following one and a half centuries witnessed another seven Crusades, none of which solved anything.

The only successful military operation came later, the Reconquest of Spain, but this was a struggle for national reunification and not an overseas expedition. Nor did it eliminate the clash between the two worlds; it merely shifted the border between them. As for containment, the Turks were stopped at the gates of Vienna, the Christians won the battle of Lepanto, towers were erected along the coastline to keep a lookout for Saracen pirates—but the confrontation remained.

Then, after waiting for the East to grow weak, the West colonized it. As such operations go, that was certainly a success, and one that lasted a long time, but the results can be seen today. The confrontation has not been eliminated; it has been sharpened.

If we were to revive the frontal clash today, in what way would it differ from those of the past? In the days of the Crusades, the military power of the Muslims was not unlike that of the Christians: both sides had swords and siege engines. Today the West is in the lead as far as military technology is concerned. It is true that Pakistan, in the hands of fundamentalists, could use nuclear weapons, but at best it could raze Paris to the ground, and its nuclear reserves would be instantly destroyed. If the Americans lose a plane, they can make another; if the Syrians lose a plane, they will have trouble buying another from the West. The East razes Paris, and the West drops an atom bomb on Mecca. The East spreads botulism by mail, and the West poisons the entire Arabian desert by spraying, as one sprays pesticides over the boundless fields of the Midwest, and even the camels die. This wouldn't take long, a year at most, then everyone would carry on with stones, unless one side, getting the worst of it, gave up.

There is another difference with respect to the past. In the days of the Crusades, the Christians did not need Arab iron for their swords, nor did the Muslims need Christian iron. Today even our most advanced technology depends on oil, and they have the oil— most of it, at any rate. Left to their own devices, if their oil wells were bombed, they would be unable to extract it, but we would be without it too. The West therefore should restructure all its technology to eliminate the dependency on oil. Since we still haven't managed to make an electric motor vehicle that can do over 80 km/h and doesn't need a whole night to recharge its batteries, I don't know how long such a conversion would take. Even if we used atomic energy to drive our planes and tanks and feed our electric power stations, without taking into account the vulnerability of these technologies, the process would take a long time.

It will be interesting to see if the Seven Sisters go along with this.[2] I wouldn't be surprised if some Western oilmen—provided they can carry on making a profit—would be prepared to accept an Islamized world.

But that's not the whole story. In the good old days the Saracens stayed in their lands overseas, and the Christians in theirs. But today's Europe is full of Muslims, who speak our languages and study in our schools. If some of them have already taken sides with the fundamentalists of their original countries, imagine what it would be like if a global conflict broke out. It would be the first war in which the enemy not only lives in your own country but also has the right to national health insurance.

Note, however, that the Islamic world will face the same problem, because its lands contain Western industries and even Christian enclaves, as in Ethiopia.

---

2. The Seven Sisters here are major oil companies in the 1970s (the phrase was popularized by the Italian oil tycoon Enrico Mattei): Exxon (Esso), Shell, BP, Gulf, Texaco, Mobil, Socal (Chevron).

Since the enemy is bad by definition, all the Christians living overseas must be given up for lost. War is war. Right from the start, they are as good as dead. Then we'll canonize them all in St. Peter's Square.

But what do we do at home? If the conflict sharpens and another two or three skyscrapers fall, or even St. Peter's, then a Muslim hunt will begin. A kind of St. Bartholomew's Night, or the Sicilian Vespers: people will grab anyone with a mustache and swarthy complexion and cut his throat. Millions of people would have to be killed, but the mob will see to that without any need to trouble the armed forces.

Reason might prevail. No one gets his throat cut. But when the Second World War began, even the highly liberal Americans, albeit most humanely, put all their Italian and Japanese residents into concentration camps, even those born in the United States. So (and let's not bother too much about the subtleties) you identify everyone who might be Muslim—if they are Ethiopian Christians, never mind, God will take care of his own—and you put them somewhere. Where? With all the non-EU immigrants now loose in Europe, to set up prison camps will require space, organization, surveillance, food and medical care, all at an unaffordable price, not to mention the fact that such camps would be powder kegs.

Or you take them, all of them (not easy, but you can't leave one behind, and it must be done in one fell swoop), you put them on a fleet of merchant ships, and you unload them . . . where? "Excuse me, Mr. Gadhafi, excuse me, Mr. Mubarak, will you please take these three million Turks I'm kicking out of Germany?"

The only solution is the one commonly adopted by certain unsavory types who run illegal immigrants into Italy by boat: you toss them in the sea. A final solution reminiscent of Hitler's Germany. Millions of corpses afloat in the Mediterranean. I want to see the government that could do such a thing. The *desaparecidos* would be nothing in comparison. Even Hitler massacred in stages, and in secret.

As an alternative, because we are civilized, we let them live peacefully in our country but have a secret police keep an eye on each and every one. Where do we find all these agents? Should we recruit them from among the non-EU immigrant community? And what if you begin to suspect—as happened in the United States, where airlines intent on cutting costs put airport security in the hands of Third World immigrants—that these workers are not trustworthy?

Naturally a reasonable Muslim on the other side of the fence might make all these reflections. The fundamentalist front could not be entirely victorious; a series of civil wars would lead to much bloodshed and horrible massacres in their countries; the economic repercussions would hit them too; having even less food and medicines than the little they have today, they would die like flies. But if we are considering a frontal clash, we mustn't worry about their problems but our own.

Within the ranks of the West, pro-Islamic groups would be formed not out of faith but out of opposition to the war, and new sects would arise that reject the West, Gandhians who would put down their tools and refuse to collaborate with their governments, fanatics like the Davidians in Waco who (without being Muslims) would unleash terror campaigns to purify the corrupt Western world. In the streets of Europe, processions would form of desperate, passive supplicants waiting for the Apocalypse.

But such lunatic fringes aside, would everyone accept a reduction of electrical energy without even being able to fall back on oil lamps? A disastrous blackout of communications and therefore no more than one hour of television a day? Travel by bicycle rather than by car, the closing of movie theaters and nightclubs, long lines at McDonald's for a daily ration consisting of a slice of bran bread topped by a lettuce leaf? In other words, the cessation of an economy of prosperity and waste? What would an Afghan or Palestinian refugee care about living in a war economy; for them nothing would change. But what about us? What crisis of collective depression and lack of motivation would we find ourselves up against?

How much would the blacks of Harlem, the underprivileged of the Bronx, or the Chicanos of California still identify with the West?

Finally, what would the Latin American countries do, where many people, not Muslims, feel resentment against the gringos? And in fact, after the Twin Towers fell, there were some down there who whispered that the gringos had it coming to them.

In short, the global war could reveal an Islam less monolithic than we think, but it would also reveal a fragmented and neurotic Christendom, where only a tiny few would offer themselves as the new Templars or kamikazes of the West.

This is a science fiction scenario that I would never want to see come to pass. But it's worth describing in order to demonstrate that, if a global war were to happen, no one would win. Hence a third-phase neowar, even by transforming itself into a global paleowar, would lead to no result other than its perennial continuation against a desolate backdrop straight out of *Conan the Barbarian*.

In the era of globalization, a global war is impossible—that is, it would lead to defeat for everyone.

Peace

When I was writing my reflections on the neowar in the Gulf, the conclusion that war had become impossible brought me to the idea that perhaps the moment had come to make war universally taboo. But now I realize, after what followed, that this was a pious hope. Today my impression is that, since neowar has no victors and no vanquished and paleowar settles nothing except on the level of the psychological satisfaction of the temporary winner, the result will be a form of permanent neowar with lots of peripheral paleowars forever breaking out and forever being ended temporarily.

I imagine that this notion will not please many people, because we are all fascinated by the ideal of peace. That the uselessness of neowar might lead to a serious consideration of peace was a fine thought but unrealistic. The fact is that the very concept of neowar makes us reflect upon the equivocal nature of peace.

When we talk of peace and wish for peace, we always think (to the extent permitted by our intellectual capacities) in universal, global terms. We wouldn't talk of peace if we thought of it only for a few, otherwise we'd go live in Switzerland or enter a monastery, as people used to do in the dark days of endless invasions. Either peace is proposed as global, it seems, or it's not worth thinking about.

The second way of thinking about peace, complementary to the first, is that it is an original state. From the idea of an Edenic society to that of a golden age, peace has always been advocated as the restoration of a primal condition of humanity (which even contemplated peace between the human and the animal worlds) that was at a certain point corrupted by some act of hatred and injustice. But let's not forget that, with regard to the myths of the golden age, Heraclitus was rational enough to say that "struggle is the rule of the world and war is the father of all and the king of all." He was followed by Hobbes and his *homo homini lupus* and Darwin and his "struggle for life."

So let's try to imagine that the general curve of entropy is dominated by conflict, destruction, and death and that the isles of peace are those that Prigogine calls dissipative structures, moments of order, pretty little blips in the overall entropic fall, exceptions to war that need a lot of energy to survive.

Moving from science to metaphor (as far as I know, no science of peace exists), I would say that peace is not a state that has already been given to us and so all we need to do is restore it; it is an energy-sapping struggle like trench warfare, a few yards at a time and at the cost of many lives.

The great peaces we have known in history, the ones that involved large territories, such as the Pax Romana or in our time the Pax Americana (but there was also a Pax Sovietica that for seventy years curbed areas that are now in turmoil and seething with mutual conflicts), and that great and blessed Pax of the First World known as the cold war, whose passing we all now regret (but perhaps we could also talk of a Pax Ottomana or a Pax Sinae) were the result of continuous military pressure and conquest that maintained a certain order and reduced conflict at the center at the cost of many small paleowars on the periphery. The great peaces were the result of military power.

This arrangement might please those who stand in the eye of the hurricane, but those at its margins suffer from the paleowars that serve to maintain the equilibrium of the system. As if to say that if there is peace, it is always ours, never that of others. Give me one example of peace in the world, at least in the last few millennia, which does not comply with this rule, a rule that may not be golden but is certainly iron. If there is anything valid about the antiglobalization movement, it is the idea that the advantages of peaceful globalization are paid for by the suffering of those who live on the periphery of the system.

Will this rule of peace change with the advent of neowars? I would say not, because, to sum up what I have tried to say so far, from paleowar to third-phase neowar the following developments have taken place:

1. Paleowar created a state of transitory equilibrium between two contenders, leaving an imbalance on a border occupied by neutral parties.
2. The cold war produced a frozen equilibrium at the center of the two First Worlds, at the cost of many transient imbalances in all the peripheral areas, which were plagued by many minor paleowars.
3. Third-phase neowar promises a constant imbalance at the center, a region now marked by daily anxiety and constant terrorist attacks and contained through continual bloodletting via a series of peripheral paleowars, of which Afghanistan is only the first example.

Thus it may be concluded that we are worse off than before, given the collapse of the illusion, provided by the cold war, that there was a state of peace at least at the center of the two First Worlds. It was the loss of that peace that the Americans experienced firsthand on September 11, hence their shock.

I don't believe that on this earth men, who are wolves preying on their fellow men, will attain global peace. Basically, Fukuyama was thinking about this peace with his idea of the end of history, but recent events have shown that history repeats itself, and always in the form of conflict.

Local Peace

If global peace is the result of war—and the more war becomes self-consuming and unable to solve the problems that caused it, the more peace becomes impossible—what is left for those who believe that peace is a war and not an inheritance to be claimed through divine grace?

There remains the possibility of working gradually for peace, creating whenever possible situations of peace in that immense periphery where paleowars continue to erupt, one after another.

If universal peace can result only from a military victory, local peace can spring from a cessation of belligerence. It is not necessary to make war to attain local peace. It is established when combatants are weary and a negotiating agency offers to mediate. For such mediation to be effective, the paleowar must be marginal, so that a long time after its beginning, the media no longer follow it with much interest. In that way those who accept mediation do not lose face in the eyes of international public opinion.

The peripheral nature of the conflict and the short memory of the media are essential conditions for peace negotiation. These days, no negotiation or mediation seems able to remedy a central imbalance, especially if that imbalance no longer depends on the will of any government. We cannot therefore foresee a peace process for third-phase neowar, only for each of the paleowars that it produces.

A succession of local peaces might lead to a long-term decrease in the tension that keeps neowar alive. This means (if reducing the process to an example does not involve the risk of losing sight of its flexibility and applicability to situations that are very different) that a peace made today in Jerusalem would certainly contribute to a reduction in tension throughout the epicenter of global neowar.

Even if we do not always achieve this end, a peace realized like a small blip in the general entropic curve to chaos—neither the final goal nor a stage in the path toward any goal—would still serve as an example, a model.

Peace as an example. This may be, if you will, a very Christian concept, but I would argue that it would have been accepted by many pagan sages. Let's make peace between us two, even if only between the Montagues and the Capulets; it will not solve the problems of the world, but it will show that negotiation is still possible.

The work of reducing local conflicts inspires us with the confidence that one day it will also be possible to solve global conflicts. A foolish hope, but sometimes you have to lie by example. If you lie with words, you lie badly, but if—through action—you let it be thought that others may act likewise, then you lie well, making people believe that a particular proposition (some ps make qs) can be transformed into a universal proposition (all ps make qs).

But this is why ethics and rhetoric are not part of formal logic. Our only hope is to work on local peace.

Love America and March for Peace

Evil leads to evil. I am not saying anything new when I observe that the principal aim of every terrorist action is to destabilize the camp of those it strikes. Destabilization also means putting others in a state of agitation, rendering them unable to react calmly, and making them suspicious of one another. All things considered, neither right-wing terrorists nor their left-wing counterparts managed to destabilize Italy, for example. Which is why they were defeated, at least after their first and most formidable offensive.

Bin Laden's terrorism (in any event, that of the vast range of fundamentalist groups that he represents) is clearly far more able, widespread, and efficient. After September 11, this brand of terrorism managed to destabilize the Western world, raising ancient specters of the struggle between civilizations, wars of religion, and the clash between continents. But now it is achieving a far greater result: having deepened the rift between the West and the Third World, it is now creating deep rifts within the Western world. There is no sense in fooling ourselves: conflicts are looming (not armed but certainly moral and psychological) between America and Europe,

---

This article appeared in la Repubblica, *February 2003.*

and a series of rifts within Europe itself. Latent French anti-Americanism makes itself heard, and (could we ever have imagined this?) in America the term "Frogs" to indicate the French comes back into fashion.

These rifts do not pit the Americans against the Germans or the British against the French. As we watch the protests against the war on both sides of the Atlantic, let's try to remember that "All Americans want war" is no more true than "All Italians want peace." Formal logic teaches us that if even a single inhabitant of the Earth hates his mother, we cannot say, "All men love their mothers." We can say, "Some men love their mothers," where "some" may mean few but also ninety-nine percent. Even ninety-nine percent amounts to "not all." There are few cases in which you can use the universal "all": perhaps only in the statement "All men are mortal," because even the two men who are believed to have been resurrected, Jesus and Lazarus, at a certain point ceased to live and entered the tunnel of death.

So the rifts are not between all people on the one side and all those on the other. They are always between some of the two (or three, or four) parties. It seems like a cavil, but without qualifications of this kind you slip into racism.

At the heart of these painful but not yet bloody rifts, you hear statements every day that lead inevitably to racism, of the type "All those against the war are allies of Saddam," but also "All those who think the use of force is justified are Nazis." Shall we try to think about this?

Some time ago an English reviewer spoke, all in all in a fairly favorable way, of my little book *Five Moral Pieces,* which had recently been translated into English. But when he got to the page where I write that war should become a universal taboo, he commented sarcastically: "Tell that to the survivors of Auschwitz." Implying that if everyone held war in horror, Hitler would not have been defeated and the Jews in the death camps (alas, only some of them) would not have been saved.

Now, this argument at the very least strikes me as unjust. I can maintain (and I do maintain) that homicide is an inexcusable crime, and I would never ever want to kill anyone. But if a man with a knife broke into my home wishing to kill me or any of my dear ones, I would do everything possible to stop him, and use all possible violence. Likewise, war is a crime, and the criminal who unleashed the Second World War was Hitler: once he started it, the Allies went into action and opposed violence with violence, and they did well, because it was a question of saving the world from barbarism. This takes nothing away from the fact that the Second World War was an atrocious business that cost fifty million lives, and it would have been better if Hitler had not started it.

A less paradoxical form of the objection: "So you admit that it was a good thing when the United States intervened militarily to save Europe and to prevent the Nazis from setting up death camps in Liverpool or Marseilles?" Certainly, I reply, they did well, and I can still remember the thrill I felt when as a thirteen-year-old I went to greet the first regiment of American liberators (a black regiment, too) as it arrived at the little town to which I had been evacuated. I immediately made friends with Corporal Joseph, who gave me my first chewing gum and my first Dick Tracy comics. But, after my answer, this version of the objection is followed by another: "So the Americans did well to nip the Nazi-Fascist dictatorship in the bud!"

The truth is that neither the Americans nor the British nor the French nipped the two dictatorships in the bud. They tried to contain Fascism, to tame it, and even to accept it as a mediator until early 1940 (with a few demonstrative moves such as sanctions, but little more), and they allowed Nazism to expand for some years. The United States intervened only after the Japanese attack on Pearl Harbor. What's more, many forget that Germany and Italy, after

Japan, declared war on the United States and not vice versa (I realize that younger people might find this hard to believe, but that's how it went). The United States waited before engaging in a terrible conflict, despite the moral pressure to do so, out of caution, because the Americans didn't feel they were sufficiently prepared, and because even in their midst there were some (famous) Nazi sympathizers, and Roosevelt had to play his cards right to lead his people into that episode.

Were France and Britain wrong to wait, still hoping to check German expansionism, while Hitler invaded Czechoslovakia? Perhaps, and Chamberlain's desperate maneuvers to save the peace have given rise to much irony. This tells us that sometimes you can err out of prudence, but that everything possible must be tried in order to save the peace. In the end it became clear that Hitler was the one who had started the war and who therefore bore all the responsibility.

So I regret the front page of the American newspaper that showed photographs of a cemetery full of brave Yankees who died to save France (and they did) and that accused France of forgetting this debt. France, Germany, and all those who consider the war being waged now in Iraq premature are not turning their backs on the United States in this time of international terrorism. They are merely maintaining, as many people of good sense do, that attacking Iraq will not defeat terrorism but probably (in my view, definitely) strengthen it, swelling the terrorist ranks with many who were confused before or in doubt. Terrorism is gaining supporters who live in the United States and in European countries, and if their money cannot be deposited in Baghdad banks, the fighters in Iraq can still receive weapons, chemical or otherwise, from other countries.

Suppose that, before the Normandy landings, de Gaulle had dug in his heels, given that his troops were located overseas, and insisted on a landing at the Côte d'Azur. The Americans and the British would have opposed this for various reasons: there were still German troops in the Tyrrhenian who controlled the Italian coast at least in the Gulf of Genoa, and by landing in the north the Allies had Britain at their backs and it was safer to transport invasion troops across the Channel than have them sail around the Mediterranean. Would we have said that the United States was stabbing France in the back? No, in such a case America would have expressed its strategic dissent, and I believe it was in fact wiser to land in Normandy. They would have used all their influence to persuade de Gaulle not to attempt a futile and dangerous operation.

Another objection in circulation is this one, made to me recently by a very important gentleman who has been recognized for his peace mission efforts over many years: "But Saddam is a ferocious dictator and his people are suffering under his bloody rule. Shouldn't we think of the poor Iraqis?" We do think of them, but do we think of the poor North Koreans? Of those who live under the heel of many African or Asian dictators? Or of those who have suffered tin-pot right-wing dictators who were supported to prevent left-wing revolutions in South America? Did we ever think of taking up arms to liberate the poor Russian, Ukrainian, Estonian, or Uzbek citizens whom Stalin sent to the gulags? No, because if we were to make war on every dictator, the price—in terms of lives and the risk of atomic attack—would be enormous. And so, as is always the case in politics, which is realistic even when inspired by ideals, we played for time, trying to accomplish the maximum with nonviolent means. A winning strategy, it turned out: in the end the Western democracies managed to eliminate the Soviet dictatorship without launching missiles. It took time, and meanwhile people lost their lives, and this grieves us, but we were also spared a few hundred million deaths.

These few observations are sufficient, I hope, to suggest that the situation in which we find ourselves, precisely because of its gravity, does not admit of clear-cut divisions or condemnations of the kind "If that's what you think, then you're the enemy." This too is fundamentalism. You can love the United States, as a tradition, as a people, as a culture, and with the respect due to those who won on the field the rank of the world's most powerful country. You can be deeply touched by the injury America suffered in 2001, but without denying the need to warn Americans that their government is making a mistake and that they should see our position not as a betrayal but as frank dissent. Not warning them means trampling on the right to dissent—the exact opposite of what we learned, after years of dictatorship, from our liberators of 1945.

The Prospects for Europe

This article does not spring from any personal decision of mine. Some time ago Jürgen Habermas approached colleagues in various European countries asking them to publish, on the same day, an article of theirs in an important local daily newspaper. Apart from an exchange of a few messages in which Habermas communicated his intentions, as I write I don't know anything precise about the content of the pieces published today by Habermas and Jacques Derrida (a joint article that will appear simultaneously in the *Frankfurter Allgemeine* and in *Libération*), by Fernando Savater (*El pais*), Gianni Vattimo (*La Stampa*), Adolf Muschg (*Neue Zürcher Zeitung*), and Richard Rorty (as a voice from overseas but in the *Süddeutsche Zeitung*). It may be that a debate will result from a comparison of the various contributions. In any case Habermas asked his friends and colleagues to voice their opinion on the current state of the European Union, and to send a request to the respective national governments and to what amounts to a European government (of which there is now a fair bit but not enough).

This article appeared in la Repubblica, *May 2003.*

This seems a poor moment to speak of the future of a united Europe: the various positions taken up with regard to the conflict in Iraq have revealed a divided Europe, while the entry of Eastern European nations into the union has brought together ancient democracies, not fully prepared to reassess their national sovereignty, and younger democracies, bent on reinforcing a form of national government only just created, even if that means forging a system of alliances that extends beyond the frontiers of Europe.

In this picture we can say that, on the one hand, there exist a European consciousness and identity; on the other hand, a series of events are tending to break up that unity.

I know that Habermas will also make this point: the fundamental principles of the so-called Western world, the Greek and Judeo-Christian inheritance, the ideas of liberty and equality born with the French Revolution, the legacy of modern science handed down by Copernicus, Galileo, Kepler, Descartes, and Francis Bacon, capitalism, the secularization of the state, Roman law or common law, the idea of justice realized through the class struggle—these typically European things are today no longer the patrimony of Europe alone. They have been established, diffused, and developed in America, Australia, and in many places in Asia and Africa. We can talk of Western civilization (which tends to see itself as the successful model in the process of globalization) without saying that it represents Europe.

In the meantime, a European identity is growing more and more noticeable. Perhaps this identity is not evident when we Europeans visit another European country, because the visit triggers rather a perception of the differences—but differences are also perceived by a Milanese who goes to Palermo or by a Calabrian who visits Turin. The sense of identity prevails, however, when we come into contact with a non-European culture, American culture included: there are moments, during a conference, in an evening spent with friends from different countries, or even in the course of a tourist outing, in which we sense a common sentiment. The points of view, behavior, and tastes of a Frenchman, a Spaniard, or a German are more familiar to us than those of non-Europeans.

On opening a peace conference in Paris in December 2002, the philosopher and cabinet minister Luc Ferry observed (and his was certainly no discovery, but he made his point in a dramatic manner) that by now a Frenchman finds the idea of war with Germany quite inconceivable (and of course the same holds for an Englishman regarding Italy or a Spaniard regarding Flanders), whereas conflicts of this kind were the norm for two thousand years. It is a historically new situation, unthinkable only fifty years ago, yet one that perhaps does not always impinge on our awareness. It now accompanies our every act, even when less cultivated Europeans go on holiday, calmly crossing frontiers that their forefathers once crossed with rifles in their hands.

There are many reasons a Frenchman still feels he is different from a German, but today both are the heirs of experiences that left a mark on them and on their respective nations. We have in common a concept of welfare developed through trade union struggles and not thanks to the homeostasis of an individualistic ethic of success; we have all seen the failure of colonialism and the loss of empire; we have all been subjected to dictatorships and can now recognize their warning signs, and perhaps we have been vaccinated against them (or most of us, at least).

We have all known war in our homelands, the situation of continuous danger, and I daresay that if two jets had crashed into Notre Dame or Big Ben, the reaction would have been fear, grief, and indignation, but it would not have been accompanied by the amazement, depression, and impulse to react immediately and at all costs that seized Americans, struck for the first time in modern history on their own soil.

In short, Europeans have a lot in common: joys and suffering, pride and shame, traditions to defend and remorse to be digested. Every European country, unlike others, has had relations with Asia and Africa, with which it has sometimes traded and sometimes fought but from which it is not separated by an ocean.

Is all this enough to create a truly united Europe? It seems not to be, and we see proof of this every day, despite the euro and the fact that many countries would like to join this community: it seems that all of them want to belong and are prepared to give up something—but not everything. And new conflicts are triggered. Take the various positions on the war in Iraq, for example.

But the unity Europe cannot find within itself is being imposed upon it. During the cold war, having just emerged from the Second World War and divided between East and West, Europe was obliged to live behind the shield of another power, the United States or the Soviet Union. Each of these great powers played a role in Europe.

For the United States, China was not yet a formidable adversary as it was struggling to maintain its internal stability, and China's immediate problem was not America but Russia. The Americans could allow a stalemate in Korea and a defeat in Vietnam, because their real game was played in Europe, and it was in Europe that they won it, with the collapse of the Soviet empire.

Located at the center of this global game, the European nations had to model their foreign policies on those of the two blocs with which they identified; they accepted a unified military defense (NATO or the Warsaw Pact).

The picture changed after the fall of the Berlin Wall, but new problems emerged, for example, when the Americans showed a limited interest in the Balkan question. Having defeated their enemy of fifty years, they found themselves faced with a new enemy whose territory was poorly defined but lurking in the Muslim world, both in the Middle and the Far East, and it was against this enemy that they turned their military power, from Kabul to Baghdad and beyond. This new commitment prompted them to shift their military bases. They no longer saw NATO as a reliable support (largely because they realized that for historical and geographic reasons, the European states were bound to have relationships with the Arabs that conflicted with American interests).

Meanwhile the United States is clearly preparing to take on China. There is nothing to suggest war, but there will be an economic and demographic struggle. All you need do is visit an American university to see how study grants, research posts, and leadership within the student community are more and more in the hands of Asian students. (Genetic considerations aside, Asian students are culturally far more prepared than their counterparts of European origins to work eighteen hours a day in order to win top-flight positions.) American scientific development will be more and more due to the import not of European brains but of Asian ones, from India to China and Japan.

America's attention will shift from the Atlantic to the Pacific, just as for years now the great centers of production and research have been moved to, or have arisen on, the Californian coast. Eventually New York will become an American Florence, still a center of fashion and culture but less and less a place where the decisions are made.

That America is on its way to becoming not an Atlantic but a Pacific country affects Europe. While the Wasps of the twenties cultivated the legend of Paris, the new Americans who count will live in places where the *New York Times* (a great Atlantic newspaper) doesn't arrive, or if it does, it arrives on the following day and only in certain locations. Increasingly Americans will know little or nothing about Europe, and when they do learn something, they won't understand the logic of this continent that is far more distant, exotic, and mysterious than Hawaii or Japan.

With an America that is shifting its attention to the Middle East and the immense Pacific, Europe might not count anymore. And how can the United States be expected to lose sleep over a continent that no longer runs the risk of being conquered either by Nazi panzers or by Cossacks anxious to slake their horses' thirst in the holy water stoups of St. Peter's?

Hence Europe, in obedience to the quasi-Hegelian decree by which events unfold as reality, which is rational, must either become European or disintegrate.

The hypothesis of disintegration seems unlikely, but it's worth outlining: Europe becomes Balkanized, or South Americanized. The new world powers (in a distant future, the dominant power might be China instead of the United States) will use the small European states to their own advantage. It may suit them to have a base in Poland or Gibraltar, or Helsinki or Tallin because of the polar routes. And the more Europe is divided and the less competitive the euro becomes on the world market, the more convenient.

Unless Europe finds the energy to establish itself as a third player between the United States and the Orient, which could be Beijing or, who knows, Tokyo or Singapore.

To establish itself as a third player, Europe must not only create customs and monetary unity but also have its own unified foreign policy and its own defense system—even if only a small one, as it is unlikely that Europe would invade China or fight the United States—sufficient to give it the security capability that NATO can no longer guarantee.

Will the governments of Europe sign such agreements? Habermas suggests that such a goal is not possible now with an enlarged Europe, one that includes Estonia, Turkey, Poland, and maybe one day Russia. But the project might interest the nucleus of countries that established the European Union. If a proposal were forthcoming from that nucleus, little by little other states might fall into line.

Utopia? Well, perhaps a utopia made necessary by the new global equilibrium. It's this way or no way. Europe, if you will, is condemned, in order to survive, to find common defense and foreign policy instruments. Otherwise, and I mean to offend no one, it will become Guatemala.

This is the appeal that some European citizens have made to the governments of the continent in which they were born and in which they would like to continue to live, proud of belonging to it.

The Wolf and the Lamb:
The Rhetoric of Oppression

I don't know if it's worth saying what I have to say, because I'm talking to a bunch of complete idiots who won't understand a thing.

Do you like this beginning? It's an example of *captatio malevolentiae*—that is, the use of a rhetorical figure that does not and cannot exist, whose aim is to alienate the audience and turn them against the speaker. I thought I had invented *captatio malevolentiae* years ago, to define the typical attitude of a friend, but then—after checking on the Internet—I saw that many sites mention it. I don't know if they are the result of my proposal's spreading or of literary polygenesis (when the same idea occurs to different people in different places at the same time).

I could have started this way: "I don't know if it's worth saying what I have to say, because I'm talking to a bunch of idiots, but I'll say it for the two or three of you in this room who are not." This would be a case (albeit an extreme and dangerous one) of *captatio benevolentiae,* because all of you would automatically think you

A paper given at a conference held at the University of Bologna on May 20, 2004, for the series "Nel segno della parola," organized by La Permanenza del Classico research center. A slightly different version appears in Nel segno della parola, *edited by Ivano Dionigi (Milan: BUR, 2005).*

were one of those two or three and, with scorn for all the others, follow me with fond complicity.

As you have guessed, *captatio benevolentiae* is a rhetorical device to win over the person you are addressing. More common forms of *captatio* are opening remarks such as: "It is an honor for me to speak before such a learned audience." It is also customary to use (and may sometimes spill over into irony): "As you yourself have taught me . . . ," where, in telling someone of a thing he doesn't know or has forgotten, you suggest that you are embarrassed to say what the person should have been the first to know.

Why is *captatio benevolentiae* taught in rhetoric? As we know, rhetoric is not the employing of useless words or overemotional appeals. Nor is it, as a deplorable commonplace would have it, a sophistical art—the Greek sophists who practiced it were not the scoundrels often presented to us by badly written textbooks. The great master of rhetoric was Aristotle himself, while Plato, in his dialogues, used highly refined rhetorical devices, and he used them precisely in order to dispute with the sophists.

Rhetoric is a technique of persuasion, and persuasion is not a bad thing, even though, reprehensibly, you can persuade someone to act against his own interests. This technique has been worked out and studied, because the use of apodictic argument allows you to convince a listener about only a few things. Once we have established the nature of an angle, a side, an area, and a triangle, no one can doubt Pythagoras's theorem. But, for most everyday matters, we discuss things about which different opinions are held. Ancient rhetoric was divided into judiciary (debating in court whether a clue has weight or not), deliberative (debating in a parliament or assembly whether or not to construct a railroad tunnel through a mountain, have a new elevator installed in our condominium, or vote for Tom rather than Dick), and epidictic—that is, in praise or blame of something, and we all agree that no mathematical law exists that establishes that Gary Cooper is more attractive than

Humphrey Bogart, Omo washes whiter than Dash, or Condoleezza Rice has more feminine allure than Rue Paul.

Since most of the debates in this world involve arguing about questions that are open to discussion, the art of rhetoric teaches us how to find the opinions with which most of the audience will agree, to work out arguments that are hard to confute, to use the language best suited to convince others of the goodness of our proposals, and also to arouse in the audience those emotions appropriate to the triumph of our arguments, including the use of *captatio benevolentiae*.

Naturally there are convincing arguments easily taken apart by arguments more convincing, showing their limitations. The approach "Eat shit, millions of flies can't be wrong" is occasionally used to oppose the notion that the majority is always right. The rejoinder is to ask if the flies eat shit for its taste or out of necessity. The next question is, if the fields and the streets were spread with caviar and honey, whether the flies might not prefer these substances, and the speaker will remark that the premise "All who eat something do so because they like it" is contradicted by innumerable cases in which people are obliged to eat what they do not like, as happens in prisons, hospitals, the army, during famines and sieges, and when one is on a diet.

At this point it is clear why *captatio malevolentiae* cannot be a rhetorical device. Rhetoric aims at obtaining a consensus and so cannot allow opening remarks that immediately create dissent. Also, rhetoric is a technique that can flourish only in free, democratic societies, including the democracy—albeit imperfect—of ancient Athens. If I can impose something by force, why ask for a consensus? Robbers, rapists, looters, and Auschwitz camp guards have never needed to use rhetoric.

It would be simple therefore to draw a line: there are cultures and nations in which power is based on consensus, and in such places techniques of persuasion are applied, and there are despotic countries ruled solely by the laws of force and oppression, in which it is unnecessary to persuade anyone. But life is not always that simple, and that's why I speak now about the rhetoric of oppression.

If, as it says in the dictionary, *oppression* means "abusing power to gain an advantage" and "crossing the limits of the lawful," it often happens that the oppressor, knowing that he is such, wishes in some way to legitimize his actions and even—as occurs in dictatorial regimes—to obtain the consensus of those he is oppressing, or to find someone who will justify it. And so you can oppress and use rhetorical arguments to justify that abuse of power.

A classic example of the pseudorhetoric of oppression comes to us in Phaedrus's fable of the wolf and the lamb:

> A wolf and a lamb, driven by thirst, came to the same stream. The wolf stopped upstream, the lamb much farther downstream. So that scoundrel, in his insatiable hunger, sought a pretext for a quarrel.
>
> "Why," said he, "are you muddying the water I'm drinking?"
>
> Fearfully, the lamb replied: "I'm sorry, but how could I do that? I am drinking the water that has passed first by you."

As we can see, the lamb has no lack of rhetorical ability, overturning the wolf's weak argument on the basis of the opinion shared by sensible people whereby water carries detritus and impurities from upstream down and not vice versa. Faced with the lamb's confutation, the wolf falls back on another argument:

> And he, defeated by that fact, said, "Six months ago, you talked about me behind my back."
>
> The lamb replied, "But I wasn't even born yet!"

Another good move on the lamb's part, to which the wolf responds by changing his justification again:

> "By Hercules, then it was your father who spoke badly of me," said the wolf. And he pounced on the lamb and killed it

unjustly. This fable has been written for those men who oppress the innocent under false pretexts.

The fable tells us two things. That the oppressor tries first to justify himself. If justification is refuted, he opposes rhetoric with the
nonargument of force. The fable recounts nothing untrue. In this article I show how such situations recur in history, albeit in more refined form.

Phaedrus's fable offers us a caricature of the oppressor as
rhetorician, because the wolf uses only weak arguments, but at the
same time it gives us a good picture of the oppressor. The falsity of
the wolf's arguments is evident, but arguments can be subtler when
they seem to be based on an opinion shared by the majority (a device known as *endoxa* in Greek rhetoric). The oppressor may also
use the technique of *petitio principii,* or begging the question, where
the thesis yet to be proved is used instead as the argument or where
one disproves an argument on the grounds that the argument has
been disproved.

Let's take a look at this passage:

From time to time our illustrated papers publish, for the edi-
fication of the German philistine, the news that in some quarter or other of the globe, and for the first time there, a Negro
has become a lawyer, a teacher, a pastor, even a grand opera
tenor or something of that kind. While the bourgeois block-
head stares with amazed admiration at the notice that tells
him how marvelous are the achievements of our modern educational system, the more cunning Jew sees in this fact evidence in support of the theory with which he wants to infect
the public, namely that all men are equal. It does not dawn on
the dull bourgeois mind that the published fact is a sin
against reason itself, that it is an act of criminal insanity to
train a being anthropoid only by birth until the pretense can
be made that the being has been turned into a lawyer—while

millions who belong to the most civilized races have to remain in positions unworthy of their cultural level. The bourgeois mind does not realize that it is a sin against the will of the eternal Creator to allow hundreds of thousands of highly gifted people to remain floundering in the swamp of proletarian misery while Hottentots and Zulus are drilled to fill positions in the intellectual professions. For here we have the product only of a drilling technique, just as in the case of the performing dog. If the same amount of care and effort were applied among intelligent races, each individual would become a thousand times more capable in such matters. . . . It is indeed intolerable to think that year after year hundreds of thousands of young people without a vestige of talent are deemed worthy of a higher education, while other hundreds of thousands who possess high natural gifts have to go without any sort of higher schooling at all. The practical loss to the nation is incalculable.[1]

Who wrote this passage? Bossi, Borghezio, or some other Northern League xenophobe? A minister of the Italian government? It seems possible, but the excerpt is taken from Adolf Hitler's *Mein Kampf*. In the preparation of his racist campaign, Hitler found himself obliged to refute a strong argument against the inferiority of certain races: that if an African is given the opportunity to learn, he will show himself to be as receptive and capable as a European, thereby proving that his race is not inferior. How does Hitler deal with this argument? By saying that, since it isn't possible for an inferior being to learn, he has only been trained like a circus animal. Hence the argument that aims to demonstrate that blacks are not animals is refuted by resorting to the opinion, which his readers shared in full, that blacks *are* animals.

---

1. This passage is based on the translation by James Murphy (1939). —Trans.

But let's return to our wolf. In order to devour the lamb, it seeks a casus belli—that is, it tries to convince the lamb, or the onlookers, and maybe even itself, that it may eat the lamb because the lamb has wronged him. This is the second form of a rhetoric of oppression. The history of the casus belli has witnessed rather shrewder wolves. A typical example is the casus belli that led to the First World War.

The Europe of 1914 had all the preconditions for war. First and foremost of them was the keen economic competition among the strongest powers: the progress made by the German empire in the great markets worried Great Britain; France was concerned about German encroachment in her African colonies; Germany suffered from an encirclement complex and felt that her international ambitions were being smothered; Russia, having appointed herself the protector of the Balkan countries, was at loggerheads with the Austro-Hungarian Empire. Hence an arms race, and nationalist uprisings and interventionist movements in the individual countries. Each country had an interest in a war, but none was justified. Since whichever country that declared war would look as if it were defending national interests while riding roughshod over those of the other nations, a pretext was needed.

Then, in Sarajevo on June 28, 1914, a Bosnian student called Gavrilo Princip assassinated the heir to the Austro-Hungarian Empire, Franz Ferdinand, along with his wife. Obviously, the act of one fanatic does not involve an entire country, but Austria seized the opportunity. In agreement with Germany, it placed the entire responsibility for the bloodshed on the Serbian government, and on July 23 a tough ultimatum was sent to Belgrade with the accusation of an anti-Austrian plot. Russia immediately assured Serbia of its support. The Serbs responded to the ultimatum in a fairly conciliatory manner but also announced a general mobilization. At that point Austria declared war on Serbia, not waiting for a mediation proposal presented by Great Britain. Within a short time all the European states were at war.

Until the Second World War with its fifty million dead, the first set a record among all the tragic follies of history.

Austria, a civil, enlightened country, had a pretext: Princip's act, the assassination of the crown prince, was not isolated; it was instigated by the Serbian government. An unprovable argument but one that carried a certain emotional impact. Which brings us to another form of justification of oppression, the conspiracy syndrome.

One of the first arguments used to start a war or set persecution in motion is that we must stop a plot hatched against us, against our group, country, or culture. *The Protocols of the Elders of Zion*, the pamphlet that served as a justification for the extermination of the Jews, is a typical example of the conspiracy syndrome. But the syndrome is far older than that. Let's take a look at what Karl Popper had to say about what he defined as the social theory of conspiracy:

> . . . the theory, more primitive than many forms of theism, is like the one found in Homer. For Homer, the power of the gods meant that everything that happened on the plain before Troy was merely a reflection of the many plots being woven on Olympus. The social theory of conspiracy is actually a version of this theism, i.e., of the belief in divinities whose whims or desires underpin all things. As such it is a consequence of the end of god as a point of reference, and of the subsequent question: "Who is there in his place?" That place is now occupied by various powerful men and groups—sinister lobbies, which may be accused of having organized the Great Depression and all the ills we suffer from. The social theory of conspiracy is widespread, and there is little truth in it. Only when conspiracy theorists come into power does it assume the nature of something that describes real events. For example, when

Hitler took power, believing in the myth of the conspiracy of the Elders of Zion, he tried to do no less with his own counter-conspiracy.[2]

In general, in order to maintain popular support for their decisions, dictatorships point the finger at a country, group, race, or secret society that is plotting against the people under the dictator. All forms of populism, even contemporary ones, try to obtain consensus by talking of a threat from abroad, or from internal groups. Hitler wasn't the only one who used conspiracy theory to justify his own casus belli—and we must remember that the alleged Jewish conspiracy formed the basis not only of his massacre of the Jews but also of his entire politics of conquest against what the Italian press called the "Demo-Judaic Plutocracies"—Mussolini was another skilled practitioner when it came to blending casus belli and conspiracy theory.

An excellent example is the speech of October 1935 in which il Duce announced the beginning of the conquest of Ethiopia. Shortly after Unification, Italy had tried to emulate the other European states by obtaining some colonies. We will not judge the worth of this action, which was not questioned in the nineteenth century, when the dominant ideology was that of Kipling's "white man's burden" and his civilizing mission. Having established herself in Somalia and Eritrea, Italy made several attempts to subjugate Ethiopia, called Abyssinia at that time, but there she found herself up against a country with an ancient Christian tradition, a land Europeans had once identified with the fabled empire of Prester John, and a country that—in its own way—was trying to open the door to Western civilization.

---

2. "Per una teoria razionale della tradizione." *Congetture e confutazioni: Lo sviluppo della conoscenza scientifica.* Bologna: Mulino, 1972.

In 1895 the Italians were defeated at Adua, and after that Italy had to recognize the independence of Ethiopia, over which she maintained a sort of protectorate while retaining a few bridgeheads in Ethiopian territory. But in the days of Fascism, Ras Tafari had already tried to develop his country, leading it from a still-feudal situation toward more modern forms, and after him Haile Selassie understood that the only chance of saving Africa's last sovereign state was modernization. To combat the penetration of Italian experts, he called in advisers and experts from France, Great Britain, Belgium, and Sweden for the reorganization of the army and for training in the use of new weaponry and aviation. As far as Fascism was concerned, it was not a question of civilizing a country that was already making its laborious way along the path to Westernization (and, I repeat, there wasn't even the religious pretext of sending a Christian mission to an idolatrous culture): it was merely a matter of defending economic interests. Hence the decision to invade Ethiopia could only spring from a casus belli.

This arose from the area of Ual-Ual, fortified by the Italians to control a score of wells, an essential resource for the nomadic peoples of the Ogaden. The possession of the area was not recognized by Ethiopia, and it also worried Great Britain, which had neighboring colonies. In short, an incident occurred: on November 24, 1934, a mixed Anglo-Ethiopian commission approached the wells, accompanied by hundreds of armed Ethiopians, who demanded that the position be abandoned. Italian forces intervened, including the air force. The British protested and left, but the Ethiopians remained, and there was a clash. Three hundred Ethiopians and twenty-one *dubats,* Italian colonial troops, were killed, and about a hundred Italians were injured. Like many frontier clashes, this one too could have been resolved by diplomatic means (in terms of deaths, the Italy-Ethiopia ratio was fourteen to one), yet Mussolini found the excuse he had been looking for for some time.

Consider the rhetoric he used to legitimize his actions before the
Italian people and the world, in a speech of October 2, 1935, given
from the balcony of Palazzo Venezia, Rome:

> Black shirts of the Revolution! Men and women of all Italy! Ital-
> ians scattered throughout the world, beyond the mountains and
> overseas: listen! A solemn hour is about to strike in the history
> of the Motherland. *Twenty million men* are at this moment oc-
> cupying the squares of all Italy. A more gigantic spectacle has
> never before been witnessed in the history of humankind.
> Twenty million men: one heart, one will, one decision.
>
> For many months *destiny's wheel,* driven by our calm de-
> termination, is turning toward its goal. . . . It is not only an
> army striving to attain its objectives but an entire people of
> forty-four million souls, against whom an attempt has been
> made to commit the blackest of injustices: that of *robbing us* of
> a little place in the sun.
>
> When in 1915 Italy ventured to throw its lot in with the Al-
> lies, how our courage was extolled and how many promises
> were made! But, after the common Victory, to which Italy made
> the supreme contribution of 670,000 dead, 400,000 mutilated,
> and one million injured, around the parsimonious table of
> peace Italy's share in the rich colonial loot was no more than a
> few *scant crumbs.*
>
> We have been patient for thirteen years, during which the
> circle of selfishness that smothers our vitality has grown ever
> tighter. *We have kept patience with Ethiopia for forty years!*
> *Enough!* . . .
>
> But let it be said yet again, and in the most categorical
> manner: in this very moment I make a sacred commitment be-
> fore you that we will do everything possible to ensure that this
> colonial conflict *does not* assume the character and scope of a
> European conflict. . . .

Never as in this historic epoch has the Italian people shown the *quality of its spirit* and the strength of its character. And it is to this People that humanity owes some of its greatest conquests, *and it is against this People of poets, artists, heroes, saints, navigators, and those who cross the oceans, it is against this People that they dare talk of sanctions!*

Let's read again the salient points of this speech (the italics are mine). First of all, it is legitimization by *popular will*. Mussolini has decided on his own, but the presumed presence of twenty million Italians assembled in the various city squares means that the decision for the conflict has been shifted onto them. In the second place, the decision has been made because this is the will of *destiny*. Il Duce, and the Italians with him, are merely interpreting destiny's decree. In the third place, the desire to take possession of the Ethiopian colony is presented as resisting a *theft*: others want to steal our little place in the sun. In truth, those others (i.e., the European countries that imposed sanctions on Italy) didn't want Italy to take what wasn't hers. Let's forget about the national interests of other countries in their opposition to the Italian invasion. The fact remains that they did not want to steal property from us: they opposed our stealing it from someone else.

Then the appeal to the conspiracy syndrome. Proletarian Italy is being starved by the Demo-Pluto-Judaic powers, inspired naturally by Jewish capitalism. This is followed by an appeal to *nationalistic frustration*, with the harking back to the theme of a desecrated victory. We won a world war, and we didn't get what was our due.

In reality Italy made war to get back Trent and Trieste, and they were returned to her. But let that pass. It is only through an appeal to a common frustration (the conspiracy syndrome always involves a persecution complex) that the final coup de théâtre becomes emotionally necessary and comprehensible: we have kept patience with Ethiopia for forty years, and that's long enough. One might wonder whether it wasn't Ethiopia that had been patient with Italy, given that Italy was the one that marched into Ethiopia's backyard while that country had neither the idea nor the possibility of marching into hers. But no matter, the coup de théâtre works, and the crowd erupts into roars of satisfaction.

In conclusion—and this is an original rhetorical move in that the *captatio benevolentiae* appears not at the beginning but at the end. This persecuted and scorned people whose will must legitimize the invasion has qualities of spirit and strength of character. It is par excellence a people of poets, artists, heroes, saints, and navigators. As if Shakespeare, the builders of the Gothic cathedrals, Joan of Arc, and Magellan had all been born between Bergamo and Trapani.

Mussolini and Hitler were not the last to make use of the conspiracy syndrome. I know that at this moment many Italian readers will be thinking of Silvio Berlusconi, but he is merely a pale repeater of the theory. Far more worrying is the resurgence of the *Protocols* and of the Jewish conspiracy to justify Arab terrorism.

To cheer you up, I cite an umpteenth variation of the theory, which I came across in an article by Massimo Introvigne, an expert in sects of all kinds, published in *il Giornale* on September 17, 2004: "Pokémon? A Judeo-Masonic Plot." It would appear that the Saudi Arabian government banned Pokémon in 2001. Now a lengthy fatwa issued by Sheikh Yusuf al-Qaradawi in December 2003 explains the reasons behind the Saudi ban of 2001. Exiled by Nasser in the seventies, al-Qaradawi lives in Qatar, where he is considered one of the most authoritative preachers who speak on Al Jazeera. What's more: many people in the highest echelons of the Catholic world consider him an indispensable interlocutor in the dialogue with Islam.

Now this religious authority states that Pokémon should be condemned because "they evolve," in other words in certain conditions they transform into characters with greater powers. In this way, al-Qaradawi assures us, "Darwinian theory is inculcated in the minds of young people," all the more so because the characters struggle "in battles where the survivors are those who adapt better to the environment: another of Darwin's dogmas." Moreover, the Koran forbids the representation of imaginary animals. Pokémon also figure in a card game, and these games are forbidden by Islamic law as "vestiges of pre-Islamic barbarism."

But in Pokémon you also see "symbols whose meaning is well known to those who produce them, such as the six-pointed star, the emblem of Zionists and Masons, which has become the symbol of the cancerous usurper state of Israel. There are other signs, such as triangles, which are a clear reference to Masonry, as well as symbols of atheism and Japanese religion." These symbols can only corrupt Muslim children, and this is their purpose. It is even possible that certain Japanese expressions spoken rapidly in the cartoons mean, "I am a Jew" or "Become a Jew": but the point is controversial, and al-Qaradawi does not state this with certainty.

In any event, for fanatics the plots and conspiracies of the Other lurk everywhere.

In the First World War and the invasion of Ethiopia, the casus belli existed, albeit deliberately overstated. But there are cases in which it is created *ex novo*. I don't want to take part—out of respect for the diverse opinions of my readers—in the current debate as to whether Saddam actually had the WMDs that justified the attack on Iraq. I'd rather take a look at some texts by those American lobbyists known as neoconservatives or simply neocons, which maintain, not without reason, that as the United States is the world's most powerful democratic nation, it not only has the right but the duty to intervene in order to guarantee what is commonly referred to as the Pax Americana.

Now, in the various documents drawn up by the neocons the idea had been gaining ground for some time that the United States showed weakness when, in the days of the first Gulf War, it did not go on to occupy all Iraq and depose Saddam. Especially after the

tragedy of 9/11, it was held that the only way to curb Arab fundamentalism was to make a show of force to demonstrate that the
world's greatest power was capable of destroying its enemies. Consequently, the occupation of Iraq and the toppling of Saddam became indispensable, not only to defend American oil interests in
that area but also to give an example of a power to be dreaded.

I don't intend to discuss this thesis, which is also motivated by
Realpolitik. But here's the letter sent to President Clinton on January 26, 1998, by the top exponents of the Project for the New American Century, the spearhead of the neocons, and signed by, among
others, Francis Fukuyama, Robert Kagan, and Donald Rumsfeld:

> We can no longer depend on our partners in the Gulf War
> coalition to continue to uphold the sanctions or to punish Sad-
> dam when he blocks or evades UN inspections. Our ability to
> ensure that Saddam Hussein is not producing weapons of mass
> destruction, therefore, has substantially diminished. Even if
> full inspections were eventually to resume . . . experience has
> shown that it is difficult if not impossible to monitor Iraq's
> chemical and biological weapons production. The lengthy pe-
> riod during which the inspectors will have been unable to
> enter many Iraqi facilities has made it even less likely that
> they will be able to uncover all Saddam's secrets. . . . The only
> acceptable strategy is one that eliminates the possibility that
> Iraq will be able to use or threaten to use weapons of mass de-
> struction. In the near term, this means a willingness to under-
> take military action. . . . In the long term, it means removing
> Saddam Hussein and his regime from power. . . . We believe
> the U.S. has the authority under existing UN resolutions to
> take the necessary steps, including military steps, to protect
> our vital interests in the Gulf.

The text strikes me as unequivocal. In brief, it says, "To protect
our interests in the Gulf, we must intervene; in order to intervene,

we need to prove that Saddam has WMDs. This can never be proved with certainty, so we'll intervene anyway." The letter doesn't say that the proof must be fabricated, because the signatories are men of honor.

This letter, received by Clinton in 1998, had no direct influence on American policy. But on September 20, 2001, some of the same signatories wrote to President Bush, and by that time one of them had become Defense Minister:

> It may be that the Iraqi government provided assistance in some form to the recent attack on the United States. But even if evidence does not link Iraq directly to the attack, any strategy aiming at the eradication of terrorism and its sponsors must include a determined effort to remove Saddam Hussein from power in Iraq.

Two years after, the dual protest about the weapons and the aid given to Muslim fundamentalism was used in the clear awareness that, even if the weapons were there, it was not possible to prove their existence, and that Saddam's dictatorial regime was a lay one and not a fundamentalist one. Yet I repeat, I am not judging the political wisdom of this war but analyzing the ways in which an act of force may be legitimized.

We have examined some cases in which oppression seeks a specific justification, a casus belli. But the last passage of Mussolini's speech conceals another argument, of ancient lineage, that we might sum up as, "We have the right to oppress, because we are the best." As Mussolini's rhetoric was that of a self-educated man, he couldn't avoid falling back on the rather kitsch statement that the Italians were a people of poets, saints, and navigators. There was a far nobler model at his disposal, but he couldn't use it, because it contained praise of detested democracy.

The model was the speech made by Pericles when he was about

to start the Peloponnesian War (as recorded by Thucydides, *The Peloponnesian War*, 2.60–64). This speech is and has been understood over the centuries as a eulogy of democracy. It is a superb description of how a nation may live by guaranteeing the happiness of its citizens, the exchange of ideas, the free deliberation of laws, respect for the arts and education, and a tendency toward equality:

> We have a form of government that does not emulate the laws of our neighbors, for we are more of an example to others than imitators. And since our government is such that civil rights are enjoyed not by a few but by the majority, it is called democracy. As far as concerns private interests, all have the right to be treated equally before the law, and as far as concerns the administration of the state, each man is preferred according to his success in a certain field and not for his social provenance . . . And as far as poverty is concerned, if a man can do something good for the city, he is not prevented from doing so on account of his lowly status. . . . We carry on our private relations without inflicting any reciprocal harm upon ourselves, and in public life it is reverence above all that prevents us from breaking the law: obedience to those who are in command, and to the institutions that protect those who suffer injustice, and in particular to those laws that—albeit unwritten—bring upon all those who break them a shame recognized by all men. . . .
>
> And we have fed our spirit by relief from labor, by habitually establishing games and festivities throughout the year, and by having fine, elegant private houses, which form a daily source of the pleasure with which we banish sorrow. And thanks to its great size, the city is provided with all kinds of products from all lands, and we enjoy the goods of other men with no less pleasure than our own. . . .

We love beauty, but without extravagance, and we devote ourselves to knowledge, but without weakness; we use wealth more for the possibility of action that it offers than for vain display, and while it is no disgrace for anyone to admit to poverty, disgrace is indeed the fate of those who do not attempt to free themselves of it. We have a care for both public and private affairs, and even though we devote ourselves to other activities, there is no lack of awareness among us with regard to the public interest.

But what is the purpose of this praise of Athenian democracy, idealized to the utmost? To legitimize Athenian hegemony over her Greek neighbors and over foreign peoples. Pericles portrays the Athenian way of life in charming colors in order to legitimize Athens's right to impose its power.

And if our ancestors are worthy of praise, our fathers are even more so: they spared no pains to add the empire that is now ours to the one that had been left to them, and that they bequeathed to us. But the extension of that empire is our work, the work of all of us who are now in our prime and who have enlarged our city to ensure that it is well prepared in every way and self-reliant in peace and war. . . . As for military matters, we are unlike our enemies for the following reasons. Our city is open to all, nor do we drive out foreigners to prevent them from learning or observing anything (while an enemy who might see a certain thing, not hidden, could profit from it). For our trust is placed more in our boldness in action (a boldness that springs from ourselves) than in the preparation of defenses and in trickery. And in education, from early youth other nations try with laborious exercises to attain manliness, while we, though we live as we please, are not prevented by this from facing all perils. Here is the proof of this: not even the Lacedaemonians invade our land by themselves, but together with all their allies, and when we attack our neighbors on our own, we usually have no trouble winning on foreign soil, fighting against men who are defending their own property. So far no enemy has encountered our united forces, for we are busy with our fleet, while on land we send off several units of our troops in many enterprises. If our enemies clash with a small part of our forces and win, they boast that they have beaten off all Athens, whereas if they are vanquished, they boast that they have been beaten by all of us. Yet, though we are habitually more inclined to take things through ease than through toil, we are prepared to face danger with a courage engendered in us not so much by the laws but by our way of acting. From this derive two advantages: we do not weaken ourselves by anticipating the hardships that await us, and, when we face them, we do not show ourselves more timorous than those who have always put themselves to a hard test. Athens is thus worthy of admiration for this and other things.

This is another figure, perhaps the shrewdest, of the rhetoric of oppression: we have the right to impose our might on others because we embody the best form of government in existence. But Thucydides himself offers us another, ultimate example of the rhetoric of oppression, which consists no longer in finding pretexts and a casus belli but in the direct claim that oppression is necessary and inevitable.

In the course of their conflict with Sparta, the Athenians sent an expeditionary force against the island of Melos, a Spartan colony that had remained neutral. The city was small, it had not declared war on Athens, nor had it allied itself with her enemies. It was therefore necessary to justify that attack, and to show above all that the people of Melos didn't accept the principles of rationality and political realism. So the Athenians sent a delegation to the folk of Melos to tell them that they wouldn't be destroyed as long as they submitted. The people of Melos refused, out of pride and a sense of justice (today we would say: a sense of international law), and in 416 BC, after a long siege, the island was conquered. As Thucydides put it, "The Athenians killed all the adult males who fell into their hands and made slaves of the women and girls." It is Thucydides himself (in *The Peloponnesian War*) who reconstructs the dialogue between the Athenians and the people of Melos before the final attack.

Let's look at the fundamental points. The Athenians say that they won't indulge in a lengthy discourse, not a very convincing one in any case, by maintaining that they have the right to exercise hegemony because they defeated the Persians or that they have the right to make reprisals because the folk of Melos did them wrong. They decline the principle of *casus belli*, and they don't behave ineptly like Phaedrus's wolf. They simply invite the people of Melos to parley on the basis of each party's real intentions, because the principles of justice hold only between opposing parties of equal strength and that "the mighty do what is possible, and the weak must submit."

Note that in saying this the Athenians are effectively affirming, while denying the fact, that they behave this way because their victories over the Spartans have given them the right to dominate Greece and because the people of Melos are colonists of their adversaries. Instead, with extraordinary lucidity—I should say honesty, but perhaps the honest one is Thucydides in his reconstruction of the dialogue—they explain that they will do what they do because power is legitimized only by might . . .

Since the islanders cannot appeal to justice, they make a reply that follows their adversaries' own logic. Falling back on the criterion of practicality, they try to convince the invaders that, if the

Athenians met defeat in the war against Sparta, they would incur the merciless revenge of a city unjustly attacked, like Melos. The Athenians reply: "We'll run that risk. We intend to show you that we are here to maintain our dominion and that we will now make our proposals for saving your city, because we want to dominate you without effort. Keeping you safe and sound is in your interest as much as it is in ours."

The folk of Melos say, "And how can it be as useful for us to be slaves, as it is useful for you to dominate us?" And the Athenians: "Because instead of suffering the extreme consequences, you would become subjects, and we would gain by not destroying you. . . ." The people of Melos reply, "What if we committed ourselves to stay out of the conflict, allying ourselves with neither of the two parties?" The Athenians retort, "No, because your hostility does not damage us as much as your friendship. Your friendship would be proof of our weakness while your hatred is proof of our strength." In other words they say: We're very sorry, but it's more convenient for us to subjugate you than to let you live. That way everyone will fear us.

The men of Melos say that they don't think they can resist Athenian power but that, despite everything, they are confident that they won't succumb because, being devoted to the gods, they are opposed to injustice. "The gods?" reply the Athenians. "There is absolutely nothing about our requests or our actions that clashes with people's beliefs in divinity. . . . We are convinced that, wherever they hold power, men and gods alike will use it, thanks to an insuppressible natural drive. And we are not the ones who have imposed this law, nor are we the first to enforce it. It already exists. It existed when we inherited it, and it will exist forever. You too, like others, would do exactly as we are doing, if you had our power."

It is reasonable to suspect that Thucydides, while representing with intellectual honesty the conflict between justice and power, agrees in the end that political realism is on the Athenian side. In any event he has portrayed the only true rhetoric of oppression that seeks no justification beyond itself. This conviction can be identified with the *captatio malevolentiae:* "Listen, small fry, like it or lump it."

History would prove to be a long, faithful, and scrupulous imitation of this pattern, even though not all oppressors have had the lucidity and the undoubted sincerity of the good Athenians.

Enlightenment and Common Sense

I have always been passionately interested in debates on the Enlightenment. I was amused by an observation made by Sebastiano Maffettone (with whom I agree about everything else) to the effect that an Enlightenment thinker like Eugenio Scalfari has had little influence on the cultural pages of *la Repubblica*, the well-known Italian daily founded by Scalfari himself. But after a start still inspired by outdated Crocean idealism (in those days Scalfari too was a post-Crocean), the cultural pages have been divided equally between articles on Nietzsche and reevocations of the salons of the eighteenth century, and so they have contained at least something of the Enlightenment. If anything, the cultural page of *Corriere della Sera* leans more toward tradition. But this is not the point. Instead I'd like to say what I think it means today to be an Enlightenment thinker, given that a lot of water has gone under the bridge since the *Encyclopédie* was written and I don't think there's much point in

---

Speech given during a debate on the Enlightenment, opened by Eugenio Scalfari. It appeared in la Repubblica, *January 2001, and was later included in* Attualità dell'illuminismo *(Bari: Laterza, 2001).*

dealing with the work of cabinetmakers, as Diderot felt he had to do at the time.

One indispensable condition for an enlightened intellectual ethic is the willingness to subject all beliefs to criticism, even those that science serves up as absolute truth. But, having said this, I think we ought to identify a few essential conditions so that we can say we are inspired not by the criterion of Strong Reason (à la Hegel) but by human reasonableness. Because this is the fundamental legacy of the Enlightenment: there is a reasonable way to reason. If we keep our feet on the ground, everybody ought to agree with what we say, because even in philosophy you have to pay attention to common sense.

This implies that common sense will be less intrusive than "right reason." All we have to do is avoid burdening our minds with too many metaphysical requirements. And then, as Leibniz suggested, we can sit around a table and say, *"Calculemus."*

So a good Enlightenment thinker is someone who believes that things "go a certain way." This minimalist realism was recently restated by Searle, who doesn't get everything right but sometimes has clear and reasonable ideas. To say that reality goes in a certain way is not the same as saying that we can know it or that we may know it one day. But even if we never knew it, things would go in a certain way and not otherwise. Even those who might think that things go one way today and another way tomorrow, in other words people who think that the world is bizarre, chaotic, and changeable, shifting from one law to the next despite the metaphysicians and cosmologists, would have to admit that this fickleness of the world is precisely the way things go. So it's worth offering a description of these damned things.

Once I said to Gianni Vattimo that maybe there are laws of nature, given that if we cross a dog with a dog, another dog is born, but if we cross a dog with a cat, either nothing is born or we get something we wouldn't like to see wandering around the house. Vattimo replied that today genetic engineering can alter even the rules that govern the species. Correct, I said: if to cross a dog with a cat you need engineering (i.e., an art), then there exists some nature on which this art artificially acts. I am more of an Enlightenment thinker than Vattimo, but I don't think he is bothered by that.

Good sense tells us that in some cases we can all agree about how things go. To say that the sun rises in the east and sinks in the west is not a question of common sense; it's based on astronomical convention. To say that it's not the sun but the Earth that turns would be an even bigger problem, but who knows, maybe the entire Galilean cosmology ought to be called into question again. But to say that we *see* the sun rising in one direction and setting in another is a common sense datum, and it's reasonable to accept that.

As I write, I have just learned of the death of Professor Quine. If ever there was an empiricist, it was he. He even said that, when push comes to shove, the meaning of a word is bound up with our regularity of response to a stimulus. But if ever there was a thinker convinced that all our truths present themselves not alone but within a complex of cultural conventions, it was again he. How to reconcile these two contradictory positions? Because it is by experience that we know drops of water fall on our hands, and by cultural convention that we then say it is probably raining. If, before discussing the meaning of "rain," in a meteorological sense, two people agree that drops of water are falling on their hands, then we have two good minimalist Enlightenment thinkers.

Now I am going to give a freely reworked version of Quine's famous example of the Gavagai. There is an explorer who knows nothing of the native language. When a rabbit passes by in the grass, he points it out to a native, who reacts by exclaiming "Gavagai." Does *gavagai* mean "rabbit" in the native's language? Not necessarily; it might mean "animal," or "rabbit running." Not to worry; we do the test again when a dog passes by, or when the rabbit is standing still.

But what if the native was using *gavagai* to express the movement of the grass due to the passage of an animal? Or to say that a spatiotemporal event was occurring? Or to say that he likes rabbits? Moral: the explorer can only make hypotheses and build his own manual of translation, which may be no better than another (the main thing is that it be reasonably consistent).

The good Enlightenment thinker will therefore be skeptical of all manuals of translation. But he cannot deny that the native said, "Gavagai," and that he didn't say it when looking up at the sky, but only when his eyes were on the spot where the explorer thought he saw a rabbit.

Note that such an attitude works even in the most transcendental debates. It is a cultural issue whether the pope is right to maintain that embryos are human beings or whether Aquinas was right in saying that embryos will not participate in the resurrection of the flesh. But it is a matter of sound empiricism to agree that there are physical differences between an embryo, a fetus, and a newborn baby. After that, *calculemus*.

Is there a transcendent ethic that all good minimalist Enlightenment thinkers should recognize? I believe so. In general, a human being wants to have everything he likes. To do this, he must take from other human beings who like the same things. The easiest way to keep the other from taking them from him is to kill the other. *Homo homini lupus,* and may the best man win. But this law cannot be universal, because if I kill everyone, I will be alone, and man is a social animal. Adam needs at least Eve, not so much to satisfy sexual desire (a goat would suffice for that) but for procreation and increase. If Adam kills Eve, Cain, and Abel, he will be a solitary animal.

Hence man must negotiate goodwill and mutual respect. In other words he must subscribe to a social contract. When Jesus says to love one's neighbor and suggests that we do as we would be done by, he is an excellent Enlightenment thinker (he almost always is, except when he says he is the son of God—because that may have been evident to him but was not to others and thus could not be based on reasonableness, only on faith).

The Enlightenment thinker believes it's possible to work out an ethic, even a very complex one, even a heroic one (it is right, for example, to die to save the lives of one's children), based on the necessary principle of negotiation.

Finally the Enlightenment thinker knows that man has five fundamental needs (right now I can't think of any more): food, sleep, affection (which includes sex but also the need to bond at least with a household pet), play (i.e., doing something for the sheer fun of it), and wondering why. I put them in descending order of priority, but it is certain that even a baby, once he has eaten, slept, played, and learned to identify Mummy and Daddy, starts to ask why about everything. The first four needs are common to animals too, but the fifth is typically human and requires the use of language.

The fundamental why is why things are. The philosopher wonders why there is being instead of nothingness, but he is doing no more than the average man when he wonders who made the world and what there was before its creation. To answer this question, man constructs gods—or discovers them (I don't want to address theological issues here).

Hence the Enlightenment thinker knows that when men talk of gods, they are doing something that should not be taken lightly. He knows that a pantheon is a cultural phenomenon, which can be critiqued, but that the question leading to the establishment of the pantheon is a natural datum, worthy of the utmost respect and consideration.

I would be prepared to recognize an Enlightenment thinker, today, under these inalienable conditions. And if that's all right, I'll sign up.

From Play to Carnival

That the debate on the Enlightenment has engendered, as its own more or less legitimate offspring, a debate on play has irritated me, I confess. In my article I thought it obvious that one of the fundamental human needs, along with food, sleep, affection, and knowledge, is play, and what do I see? My idea is described (and I quote from a headline in *la Repubblica* of January 6) as a "provocation." As if no one had ever noticed that children, kittens, and puppies express themselves above all through play, as if, together with the definition of man as a *rational animal,* the phrase *Homo ludens* had not been around for centuries.

Sometimes we get the impression that the mass media are forever telling us about things we already know (the Italian expression for this is "to discover hot water"). But on mature reflection, you have to admit that telling people about things they already know is one of the fundamental functions of the media. A newspaper can't just suddenly say it's worth reading Manzoni's classic novel *The Betrothed.* It must wait until a new edition of the novel comes out and then run a long piece on it with the headline "Cultural Trends: The

This article appeared in la Repubblica, *January 2001.*

Return of Manzoni." The paper needs to do this, because among its readership are some who have forgotten about Manzoni and many young people who know almost nothing about him. It's as if, given that youngsters today think that hot water comes out of the tap by itself, every now and then you had to find a pretext to remind them about the boiling process.

All right then, let's talk about play. Rereading the various articles published in this newspaper, I realized that in different ways they all point to a profound impending anthropological change. Play, as a moment of carefree exercise, which is good for the body or, as the theologians used to say, removes the *tristitia* of labor, and certainly sharpens our mental capacities, must be parenthetical if it is to be true play. It is a pause in the daily panorama of obligations: not only hard manual labor but also the intense philosophical conversations between Socrates and Cebes.

A positive aspect of the *felix culpa* (or the Fortunate Fall) is that, had Adam not sinned, he wouldn't have had to earn his bread by the sweat of his brow; lounging about in Eden all day long, he would have remained a playful idler. Hence the timeliness of the serpent's arrival.

Nonetheless all cultures have earmarked a few days of the year for total play. A period of license, which we call Carnival and other cultures call something else. During Carnival, play is continual, but if Carnival is to be enjoyable and not fatiguing, it must be brief. And I ask *la Repubblica* not to start another debate about this "provocation," because there is an enormous amount of literature on Carnival.

Now, one of the characteristics of the culture we live in is the total Carnivalization of life. This is not to say that we work less, leaving machines to do it, because providing incentives and organizing free time have unquestionably been on the minds of dictatorships and liberal-reformist regimes alike. The fact is that even work has been Carnivalized.

It's easy and obvious to talk of the Carnivalization of the hours that the average citizen spends sitting in front of a television screen. Apart from the very brief space devoted to news, TV provides first and foremost entertainment, and these days the preferred entertainment is the kind that portrays life as an endless party where jesters and stunningly beautiful women throw not confetti but a shower of millions that anyone can win by playing a game. (And we complain that the Albanians, seduced by this image of Italy, are prepared to do anything to get into this permanent fairground.)

It's easy to talk of Carnival in terms of the time and money spent on mass tourism and its offers of dream islands at charter prices, its invitations to visit Venice—where, after making tourist whoopee, you leave your cans, wastepaper, leftover hot dogs with mustard, as at the end of any Carnival worthy of the name.

But consider the Carnivalization of the workplace, where helpful little robots, doing what you once had to do, make the work hours seem like leisure time.

It's permanent Carnival for the office worker who, unbeknownst to the boss, uses his computer to play video games or visit the *Playboy* Web site. It's also Carnival for those who drive cars that talk to them, tell them which road to take, and expose them to peril by having them press buttons to receive information on the temperature, on how much gas is left, on average speed, and on the time required to make the trip.

The mobile phone (today's equivalent of Linus's blanket, as Stefano Bartezzaghi suggested) is a tool for those whose professions require a fast response, such as doctors or plumbers. It should serve the rest of us only in those exceptional circumstances in which, finding ourselves away from home, we must communicate an unexpected emergency, lateness for an appointment because of a train derailment, flood, or traffic accident. In which case the phone would be used once or—for the unlucky—twice a day. Hence ninety-nine percent of the time spent by those people we see with a phone

clamped to their ear is time spent playing. The imbecile who sits beside us on the train doing financial deals at the top of his voice is in
reality strutting around like a peacock with a crown of feathers and
a multicolored ring around his penis.

We are playing when we spend time in the supermarket or a
highway rest stop, both of which offer you a cornucopia of mostly
useless objects, so that, although you go in to buy a tin of coffee, you
stay for an hour and come out with dog biscuits—you don't have a
dog, but if you did, it would be a Labrador, the most fashionable dog
of all, which is no use as a guard dog, can't be used for hunting or for
finding truffles, and will lick the hand of the person stabbing you, but
it's a wonderful plaything, especially if you put it in the water.

I recall that in the seventies the radical left-wing Potere Operaio group called for a strike—because the triumph of automation
had reduced the need for this hard necessity. At the time the objection was raised that if the working class didn't work, who would
develop automation? In a sense Potere Operaio was right: automation has implemented itself on its own. But the result was no en-
noblement of the working class as it attained the utopian condition
dreamed of by Marx, in which everyone goes fishing, hunting, and
so on. On the contrary, the working class has been employed by the
Carnivalization industry as its average user. It no longer has nothing to lose but its chains. Today, if some act of revolution caused a
blackout, it would lose an episode of its favorite reality show, therefore it votes for the people who provide the show, and it keeps working to offer surplus value to those who serve up amusement.

If it is then discovered that in parts of the world people are not
having much fun, are dying of hunger, our conscience is set to rest
by a grand (playful) charity event to collect funds for African children, paraplegics, and the emaciated.

Sport has been Carnivalized. How? Sport is play par excellence:
how can play be Carnivalized? By becoming not the interlude it was

meant to be (one soccer match a week, and the Olympics only every so often) but an all-pervasive presence; by becoming not an activity for its own ends but a commercial enterprise. The game played doesn't matter anymore (a game, moreover, that has been transformed into an immensely difficult task that requires the taking of performance-enhancing drugs) but the grand Carnival of the before, during, and after, in which the viewers, not the players themselves, play all week long.

Politics has been Carnivalized, and so we now commonly use the expression "the politics of spectacle." As parliament is steadily deprived of power, politics is conducted on television, like gladiatorial games, and in order to legitimize a prime minister you have him meet Miss Italy. And she does not appear dressed like a normal woman but (for all her intelligence) in her pageant costume. The day may come when even the president of the Republic, to legitimize himself, must appear in the costume of president.

Religion has been Carnivalized. There was a time when we smiled at those ceremonies in films where colored men dressed in multicolored vestments, tap-danced while yelling, "Oh yes, oh Jesus!" Today, *absit iniuria,* many of these jubilees played out to the sound of rock music remind us more of the discothèque than anything else. (And good works, what about good works? Those of us with Catholic backgrounds used to ask ourselves. What has happened to good works in these post-Protestant Carnivals of the one dancing faith?)

Some gays believe they have found compensation in the Carnival of Gay Pride for centuries of distressing marginalization. In the end they have been accepted, because on Carnival days everything is accepted, even a singer dancing with her navel on show in the presence of John Paul II. (Don't pretend you have forgotten this. It happened, and only a few felt sorry for that unhappy and venerable old man.)

Since we are playful creatures by definition, and as we have lost sense of the dimensions of play, we have attained total Carnivalization. The species has many resources, perhaps it is undergoing a transformation and will adapt to this new condition, even draw spiritual advantage from it. And maybe it's right that work should no longer be a curse, that we don't have to spend our time preparing for a good death, and that the working class will finally go to paradise laughing all the way. Don't worry, be happy!

Or perhaps History will see to things—a nice world war with lots of depleted uranium, a nice hole in the ozone layer now bigger than ever—and the Carnival will be over. But we need to reflect on the fact that total Carnivalization does not satisfy desire, it sharpens it. Proof of this is found in discothèques, where after all that dancing and all those decibels, kids still want to participate in the high-speed, late-night gymkhana of death on the roads.

Total Carnivalization risks reproducing that situation admirably described in the old joke about the guy who accosts a young lady and in insinuating tones says: "Hey, honey, doing anything after the orgy?"

The Loss of Privacy

The first thing that the globalization of communication through the Internet threatened was the notion of boundaries—a notion as old as the human race, in fact as old as the animal kingdom. Ethology teaches us that every animal recognizes around itself, and its fellows, a bubble of respect, a territorial area within which it feels safe, and that it will see as an adversary whoever steps over that boundary. Social anthropology has shown us how this protective bubble varies according to cultures. In certain cultures, for example, the closeness of another person is an expression of familiarity; in others it is seen as intrusive and aggressive.

On the human level, this area of protection was extended from the individual to the community. The boundary—of the city, region, realm—has always been viewed as a kind of collective enlargement of the individual bubble of protection. We need only think of how obsessed the Latin mentality was with boundaries, so much so that Rome's own foundation myth centers on a territorial violation: Romulus traced a boundary and killed his brother because his brother

---

From a speech given September 2000 in Venice, during a conference on privacy organized by Stefano Rodotà.

did not respect it. In crossing the Rubicon, Julius Caesar felt the same distress that perhaps seized Remus before he violated the boundary marked by his brother. Caesar knew that by crossing that river he was invading Roman territory under arms. That he later established a bridgehead in Rimini and marched on Rome is irrelevant: the sacrilege occurs when you cross the boundary, and it is irreversible. The die is cast. The Greeks knew the boundary of the *polis,* and that boundary was marked by the use of the language— or by its various dialects. The barbarians began where people no longer spoke Greek.

Sometimes the notion of (political) boundaries has been so obsessive as to result in the construction of a wall inside the city itself, to establish who must stay on one side and who on the other. Stepping over an inner-city boundary exposed East Germans to the same punishment inflicted on the legendary Remus. The example of East Berlin tells us something that concerns every boundary: a boundary protects a community not only from attack by outsiders but also from their gaze. Walls both physical and linguistic can help a despotic regime keep its subjects in ignorance of what is happening elsewhere, but in general they guarantee citizens that no intruder will gain knowledge of their customs, riches, inventions, or agricultural systems. The Great Wall of China did not only defend the subjects of the Celestial Empire from invasion, it also safeguarded the secret of silk production. Conversely, people have always paid for this communal privacy by accepting the loss of individual privacy. Inquisitions of various kinds, secular and religious, had the right to watch over the behavior and even the thoughts of subjects, not to mention customs regulations and tax laws, hence it has always been thought just that the private wealth of citizens be known to the state.

With the Internet the very definition of the nation-state is being put into question. The Internet is not only an instrument that enables the establishment of international and multilingual chat lines. The fact is that today a city in Pomerania can pair itself with a town in Estremadura, finding common interests online and doing business independently of the road and rail networks, which still cross frontiers. Today, amidst an unstoppable wave of migration, it is getting easier and easier for a Muslim community in Rome to link up with a Muslim community in Berlin.

This collapse of boundaries has caused two opposite phenomena. On the one hand, there is no longer any nation that can prevent its citizens from knowing what is happening in other countries, and soon it will be impossible to prevent the subject of any dictatorship to know in real time what's going on elsewhere. On the other hand, the strict surveillance that states once maintained over the activities of the citizenry has been shifted to other centers of power technically able (although not always legally) to find out to whom we have written, what we have bought, what trips we have taken, what our encyclopedic curiosities are, and even our sexual preferences. The unhappy pedophile who once, in the closed world of his town, tried to keep his passion a secret, is today encouraged to become an exhibitionist, by exposing the vice online. The big problem facing a citizen's private life is not hackers, which are no more frequent and dangerous than the highwaymen who beset traveling merchants, but cookies and all those other technical marvels that make it possible to collect information about every one of us.

A recent television program showed the world public that a Big Brother situation comes about when some individuals decide (freely if misguidedly) to let themselves be spied on by a mass audience, which is happy to do the spying. But this is not the Big Brother that Orwell wrote about. The Orwellian situation results from a restricted group that spies on every individual act performed by every member of the masses, against the wishes of all. The Orwellian Big Brother is not the television show where millions of voyeurs watch a single exhibitionist; it's Bentham's panopticon, where many unseen guards observe a single condemned man. If in Orwell's novel Big

Brother was an allegory for Stalin, the "little father," the modern Big Brother watching us has no face and is not an individual, it is the global economy in its entirety. Like Foucault's Power, it is not a recognizable entity but the combination of a series of centers that accept the game, backing one another up reciprocally. The member of one center of power who spies on others making purchases in the supermarket will be spied on in turn when he pays his hotel bill with a credit card. When Power no longer has a face, it becomes invincible. Or at least difficult to control.

Let's return to the roots of the concept of privacy. In my hometown every year they put on a show called *Gelindo,* a comic-religious play where the action takes place among the shepherds of Bethlehem in the days of the Savior's birth. But at the same time, the action seems to be set in my own country, among the peasants of the villages around Alessandria. The dialogue is in dialect and plays on textual contaminations whose effect is highly comic—the characters say that to get to Bethlehem they have to cross the river Tanaro, or they attribute to the wicked Herod the laws and regulations of our present government. The characters are portrayed as both obtuse and passionate, thus illustrating the personality of the people of Piedmont, who traditionally are very reserved, jealous guardians of their private life and sentiments.

At a certain point the Wise Men approach Maffeo, one of the shepherds, and ask him the way to Bethlehem. The shepherd, old and a bit simple, says he doesn't know and suggests that they ask his master, Gelindo, who ought to be back soon. When Gelindo returns and meets the Wise Men, one of them asks him if he is Gelindo. At present we are interested not in the dialogue between Gelindo and the Wise Men but in what happens shortly afterward, when Gelindo asks his shepherds how that foreigner knew his name and Maffeo confesses that it was he who told the foreigner. Gelindo, furious, threatens to beat Maffeo because, he says, you don't put a man's name in circulation as if it were money to spend. A name is private property; by making it public, you steal from the person who bears it. Gelindo doesn't know the word *privacy*, but that is precisely the value he defends. If he possessed a richer vocabulary, he would say that he is showing reserve or discretion, that he is defending his private sphere.

Note that the defense of one's name is not only an ancient custom. During the student assemblies in 1968, those who took the floor introduced themselves as Paolo, Marcello, or Ivano, giving no last name. This was sometimes justified by the fear that police agents might be present to take down names. More often, that reserve was a mannerism, inspired by the custom of the wartime partisans, known only by their nicknames to avoid reprisals against their distant families. But a vague desire to protect one's identity is still present in those who call in to radio and TV shows, whether to express an opinion or to answer a quiz-show question. An instinctive embarrassment (and by now a convention encouraged by presenters) prompts them to introduce themselves as Marcella from Pavia, Agata from Rome, or Spiridione from Termoli.

At times the defense of our identity verges on cowardice, an unwillingness to take responsibility, so much so that we may envy those countries where, when someone introduces himself in public, he immediately gives both name and surname. But if the defense of our name can be bizarre and sometimes hard to justify, it is certainly justifiable in our private life. It's in private that we wash not only our dirty linen but our clean linen too, and so some people do not wish to reveal their age, their illnesses, or their income—unless they must do so by law.

Who wants their privacy defended? Those who have secret business dealings, those who wish their personal correspondence to remain personal, those working on research that they do not yet wish to make public. We know all this perfectly well, and laws are enacted to protect the right to privacy. But how many people call for this right? It seems to me that one of the great tragedies of mass society, of the press, television, and Internet, is the voluntary renunciation of privacy. The extreme expression of this renunciation is, at its pathological limit, exhibitionism. It strikes me as paradoxical that someone has to struggle for the defense of privacy in a society of exhibitionists.

Another tragedy of our times has been the transformation of that (mostly beneficial) safety valve: gossip.

Classic gossip, the kind that used to go on in villages, in the porter's lodge or down at the bar, was an element of social cohesion. You never gossiped about people saying they were healthy, lucky, and happy; you gossiped about their faults, mistakes, misadventures. But by so doing, you participated in their misfortune, because gossip doesn't always imply contempt, it may also arouse compassion. Gossip worked as long as the victims were not present and were unaware of their status, or could save face by pretending not to know about it. When they came to know of the gossip and could no longer pretend, there would be a scene ("You ugly gossip, I know you've been going around saying that . . ."). The scene having been made, the rumor became public. The victims had exposed themselves to public ridicule or social censure, and the gossipers were left with nothing to gossip about. Therefore, if the value of gossip as a social safety valve was to remain intact, everyone—gossips, backstabbers, and victims—had to maintain a certain reserve, a zone of secrecy.

What we shall call modern gossip first occurred in the press. At one time there were special publications that gave information about people who, because of their work or status (actors and actresses, singers, exiled monarchs, playboys), voluntarily exposed themselves to photographers and reporters. The ploy was so obvious that the readers knew perfectly well that, if actor so-and-so had been spotted in a restaurant with actress so-and-so, it did not necessarily mean that they had become more than "good friends." The whole thing had probably been cooked up by press agents. But the readers of such publications did not require the truth, merely amusement.

In order to deal with competition from television, on the one hand, and fill a large number of pages and thus live on advertising fees, on the other, the so-called quality press, including the dailies, had to run more and more items about social events and trends, showbiz, gossip, and, when there was no news, they had to invent some. Inventing news doesn't mean providing information about something that hasn't happened; it's making news out of something that wasn't news in the first place: a few words let slip by some politician on vacation, events in the world of show business. In this way gossip became the stuff of generalized information, and it penetrated inner sanctums that had always been shielded from the curious surveillance of the gossip columns: the sanctums of reigning monarchs, political and religious leaders, heads of state, and scientists.

In this transitional phase, gossip, formerly whispered, was shouted and therefore known to the victims, backstabbers, and all those who basically weren't interested in it. It lost the glamor and power of secrecy. But it did produce a new image of the victim, who was no longer someone to commiserate with, having become a victim precisely because he was famous. To be the subject of (public) gossip gradually emerged as a sign of social status.

We moved into a second phase when television came up with programs in which it was no longer the gossips who gossiped about the victims but the victims who gladly appeared in order to gossip about themselves, hoping in this way to acquire the status of a movie star or politician. On television you never speak ill of someone not present: it is the victim who gossips about himself, revealing his private life. Those gossiped about are always the first to know, and everyone knows this. They are not victims of scandal mongering. There are no longer any secrets. And you can't even criticize the victims, because they have had the courage to bare their own weaknesses; nor can you commiserate, because their confessions have brought them an enviable public exposure. Gossip has thus lost its nature as a social safety valve and become pointless exhibition.

There was no need to wait for reality shows like Big Brother, which rightly condemn to this national voyeurism people who are already on the list of those who need a psychologist. For years now, people whom no one considered unstable have been appearing on television to argue with their spouses about reciprocal betrayals, to fight with their mothers-in-law, to make desperate appeals to sweethearts who have left them, to slap each other in public, and to subject their sexual inadequacies to pitiless analysis.

Once, private life was so secret that the secret of secrets was by definition that of the confessional, but now our notion of the confessional has been turned on its head.

And worse has happened. Through the exhibition of their shameful secrets, ordinary men and women amused the public on the one hand and satisfied their personal need to be seen on the other, but now even the character once known as the village idiot is condemned to public exposure. In a spirit of understatement with a hint of the biblical about it, and out of respect for his misfortune, I shall call him the Fool.

The village idiot of times gone by was one who, shortchanged by Mother Nature both physically and intellectually, would frequent the local inn, where cruel fellow townsmen would buy him drinks so that he would get drunk and say unseemly or lewd things. Note that, in such villages, the idiot was vaguely aware that they were treating him like an idiot, but he accepted the game, because it was a way to get free drinks and because a certain exhibitionism was part of his role as a fool.

The latter-day Fool of the global televisual village is not an average person, like the husband who appears on the screen to accuse his wife of infidelity. He is below average. He is invited to talk shows and quiz shows precisely because he is a Fool. He is not necessarily backward. He may be a bizarre soul, like a discoverer of the Lost Ark or the inventor of a new perpetual motion system who for years has been vainly knocking on the doors of newspaper and patent offices, until at last he finds someone who takes him seriously. He may also be a weekend writer who has been turned down by all the publishers and has realized that, instead of doggedly trying to write a masterpiece, he can become a success by pulling his pants down on television and using swearwords in the course of a cultural debate. Or the televisual Fool may be a provincial bluestocking who finds an audience at last as she pronounces difficult words and talks about her extrasensory experiences.

Once, when the company in the inn egged on the village idiot until he behaved in an intolerable manner, the mayor, the chemist or a family friend would step in, take the poor soul by the arm, and lead him home. But no one protects and takes home the Fool of the global televisual village, whose function has become similar to that of a gladiator sentenced to death for the pleasure of the crowd. Society, which tries to keep depressives from committing suicide or drug addicts from the craving that will lead to their death, does not protect the televisual Fool; it encourages him, as it used to encourage dwarfs and bearded ladies to exhibit themselves in fairground freak shows.

This is clearly a crime, but it is not the protection of the Fool that concerns me (though the authorities should not permit this abuse): the problem is that, glorified by his appearance onscreen, the Fool becomes a universal model. If he has managed that, anyone can. The Fool's performance persuades the public that nothing, not even the most embarrassing misfortune, has the right to remain private, and that the display of deformity brings rewards. The dynamics of the ratings ensures that, as soon as the Fool appears on TV, he becomes a famous Fool, and this fame is measured in advertising contracts, invitations to conferences and parties, and sometimes the offer of sexual favors (Victor Hugo does teach us that a beautiful woman can fall for the *Man Who Laughs*). In short, the very concept of deformity is deformed, and everything becomes beautiful, even ugliness, as long as it is elevated to the glory of the TV screen.

Do you remember the Bible? *Dixit insipiens in corde suo: Deus non est.* The televisual Fool proudly states: *Ego sum.*

A similar phenomenon is now under way on the Internet. Exploring home pages shows us that many sites are set up merely to exhibit the site owner's squalid normality, if not abnormality.

Some time ago I found the home page of a man who made available, and maybe still does, a photograph of his colon. As we know, for many years now it has been possible to go to a clinic to have your rectum examined by a probe whose tip is equipped with a tiny TV camera. The patient himself can observe on a color television screen the travels of the probe (and the camera) through his most secret recesses. Usually, a few days after the examination, the doctor gives the patient a highly confidential report complete with a color photograph of his colon.

The problem is that the colons of all human beings (not counting those with terminal tumors) resemble one another. Therefore, while you might be interested in a color photograph of your colon, a photograph of another person's leaves you indifferent. The man I am referring to went to the trouble of setting up a home page to show everyone his. Evidently we are dealing with a person to whom life has given nothing, not heirs to carry on his name, not partners drawn to his looks, not friends to whom he might show slides from his vacations, so he relies on this last desperate exhibition to gain a little visibility. In this, as in other cases of voluntary renunciation of privacy, lies an abyss of desperation that ought to persuade us to take pity and look away. But the exhibitionist (and this is his tragedy) does not allow us to ignore his shame.

———

I could go on giving examples of this joyous renunciation of privacy. The thousands of people we overhear on the streets, in restaurants, or on the train, as they discuss their most private affairs on their cell phones are not prompted by the urgent need to communicate something of importance, otherwise they would talk in low voices, guarding their secrets. Rather, they want everyone to know that they are decision makers in a refrigerator manufacturing company, that they buy and sell on the stock exchange, that they organize conferences, or that their partner has left them. They have paid for a cell phone and the hefty bills that come with it, to flaunt their private lives in the presence of all.

It was not amusement that prompted me to dwell on this parade of psychological and moral monstrosities great and small. The fact is that the authorities who watch over our privacy need to defend not only those who wish to be defended but also those who no longer know how to defend themselves.

It is precisely the behavior of exhibitionists that tells us how much the assault on privacy has become—more than a crime—a social cancer. First and foremost, we should educate children to save them from the corrupting influence of their parents.

But it's a vicious circle. The assault on privacy accustoms everyone to the disappearance of privacy. Already many of us have decided that the best way to keep a secret is to make it public, so people write e-mails or make phone calls in which they say everything openly, certain that no one listening in will find interesting any statement made with no attempt at concealment. Little by little we become exhibitionists, having learned that nothing can be kept confidential anymore and that no behavior is considered scandalous. Those who are attacking our privacy, seeing that the victims themselves consent, will no longer stop at any violation.

What I wanted to say is that the defense of privacy is not only a judicial problem but also a moral and social one. We must learn to work out, spread, and reward a new sensibility toward reserve, to educate people about reserve for themselves and toward others. I think that the best example of reserve toward others comes from Manzoni's *The Betrothed*. Obliged to admit finally that, by accepting the advances of the perverse Egidio, the Nun of Monza was plunged into debauchery and crime, and reluctant to violate the privacy of that poor woman yet unable to conceal her sin from the reader, Manzoni tells us simply that "the unfortunate girl replied"—where a more inconsiderate writer would have spent pages and pages describing voyeuristically what poor Gertrude had done. A splendid example of religious compassion, and of a secular respect for another's intimacy.

Regarding respect for our own privacy, I'd like to quote the last phrase from the brief note left by Cesare Pavese before he committed suicide: "Don't gossip too much."

On Political Correctness

I believe that the term "politically correct" is now used in a politically incorrect sense. In other words, a movement of linguistic reform has given rise to lamentable linguistic usage. If you take a look at the article that the online encyclopedia *Wikipedia* has on *PC* (as it is now known when there is no risk of confusion with personal computers or police constables), you will find the history of the term. It seems that in 1973, the Supreme Court of the United States (in a case known as *Chisholm v. Georgia*) argued that mention was made too frequently of a State instead of the People, for whose good the State exists, and that therefore it was not correct, in a toast, to talk of the United States instead of "the People of the United States."

Then the movement gained a footing in American university circles in the early eighties during the last century, as (and I quote again from *Wikipedia*) an alteration of language in order to prevent discrimination (real or claimed) and to avoid giving offense, with a view to finding euphemistic replacements for words having to do with differences in race, gender, sexual orientation, disability, religion, and political opinions.

This article appeared in la Repubblica, *October 2004.*

We all know that the first battle waged by the PC movement was fought to eliminate offensive epithets regarding colored people, not only the infamous "nigger" but also "Negro," which evoked the days of slavery. Hence the adoption of "black," followed by the subsequent correction "African American."

This business of correction is important, because it underlines a fundamental element of PC. The idea is not to decide (we who are talking) what to call others but to let the others decide what they want to be called. And if the new term persists in upsetting them, to accept a third term.

If you are not in a certain situation, you can't know which term will upset or offend those who are in it; therefore you must accept what they propose. A typical case is that of using *visually challenged* instead of *blind.* One might argue that there is nothing offensive about the term *blind* and that its use does not diminish, in fact it reinforces, the feeling of respect and solidarity due to those belonging to this category (there has always been a certain nobility in speaking of Homer as the great blind seer); but if members of this category feel easier with *visually challenged,* we have to respect their wishes.

Was the term *street cleaner* offensive to those who did this honest job? Well, if the group prefers it, we will use *ecological operative.* For the love of paradox, when the day comes that lawyers feel unhappy with *lawyer* (maybe because of the echo of expressions with pejorative connotations such as *Philadelphia lawyer* or *advocate of lost causes*) and ask to be called *legal operatives,* it would be polite to use that expression.

Why would lawyers never dream of changing their title (can you imagine Gianni Agnelli asking to be called a legal operative)? Because, obviously, they enjoy prestige and excellent financial status. The point here is that politically correct decisions can represent a way of avoiding unresolved social problems, disguising them with a more polite use of language. If we stop calling people in wheelchairs *handicapped* or even *disabled* (they are *differently abled*) but fail to build them access ramps to public areas, we have clearly—and hypocritically—got rid of the word but not of the problem. The same may be said of the replacement of *unemployed* with *involuntarily leisured.*[1]

This explains why a category requests a change of name and after a while, conditions remaining unchanged, wants a new name, in a sort of race "back to the future" that might never end unless the thing is changed as well as the name. There have even been steps backward, where a group requests a new name yet in its own private language preserves the old one, or goes back to it, out of defiance (*Wikipedia* observes that in some African American juvenile gangs the kids make brazen use of the term *nigger,* but naturally you're in trouble if you use it when you're not one of them—a bit like jokes about Jews, Scots, or the Irish, which can be told only by Jews, Scots, or the Irish).

Sometimes PC language can verge on latent racism. I remember very well, in the postwar period, that while many Italians still distrusted the Jews, they didn't want to appear racist, so if they wanted to say that someone was a Jew, after the briefest of pauses, they would say that he was an *Israelite.* They didn't know that Jews were proud of being Jews, even though (and in part precisely because) the term had been used as an insult by their persecutors.

Another embarrassing case was that of lesbians: for a long time those who wished to appear correct were afraid to use this word, just as they avoided the usual pejoratives for homosexuals, and they would timidly talk of *Sapphists.* Then it was discovered that, although homosexual men wanted to be called *gays,* homosexual women had no problem with *lesbians* (also because of that term's literary pedigree), so it was perfectly fine to call them that.

Sometimes PC has really changed, and without much trauma,

1. See Edoardo Crisafulli, *Igiene verbale* (Florence: Vallecchi, 2004).

linguistic usage. It is more and more common, when making general examples, to avoid the masculine singular pronoun in favor of *they*. Many American professors no longer say, "When a student comes to me . . . ," but either talk of "students" (in English this works fine, but doesn't quite in Italian) or introduce gender variation in their examples, sometimes using *he* and sometimes *she*; and by now substitutions such as *chairperson* or *chair* for *chairman* have been accepted. Although those who joke about PC have suggested changing *mail man* to *person person* (playing on the homophones *mail* and *male*).

These satires indicate that, once PC became established as a democratic and "liberal" movement—that is, one associated with the left (at least in the sense of the American left)—it occasionally degenerated. Some said *mankind* was sexist, because of the prefix *man-*, thus excluding women, and so it was decided to replace the word with *humanity*. But this was etymologically ignorant, given that the word *humanity* also derives from *homo* (and not from *mulier*). Albeit purely in a spirit of provocation, certain fringes of the feminist movement have proposed that we no longer speak of *history* but of *herstory* (perhaps sometimes without knowing that *history* derives from the Greek, where the prefix *his-* lacks the pronominal sense it has in English).

The exportation of PC to other countries has produced new contortions. In Italy there are (ongoing) debates about whether it is more respectful to call a female lawyer *avvocatessa* (feminine) or *avvocato* (masculine). Whereas in America people question whether it is PC to call a woman poet a *poetess,* in Italy the term *poetessa* is accepted just as much as the longer established *professoressa,* but *banchieressa* or *banchiera* (possible feminine forms of *banchiere,* or banker) would sound bizarre and even insulting.

Another case of difficult transposition is the change from *negro* to *nero*. In America the shift from the highly charged *Negro* to *black* was a radical move, but in Italian the shift from *negro* to *nero* sounds a little strained. All the more so because the term *negro* has its own legitimate history and is to be found in many literary sources: we all remember that the translations of Homer we read in school mentioned *negro vino* ("black wine"), and some French-speaking African writers talk of *négritude.*

In America the degeneration of PC has encouraged a plethora of false but highly entertaining PC dictionaries in which beyond a certain point you can't tell whether an entry was really proposed or only invented for satirical purposes. Alongside replacements currently in use, you find *socially separated* for *convict, bovine control functionary* for *cowboy, geological correction* for *earthquake, residentially flexible* for *hobo, erectionally challenged* for *impotent, horizontally accessible* for *woman of easy virtue, follicularly challenged* for *bald,* and even *melanin-deprived* for a person who is white.

On the Internet you will find publicity for STUPID (Scientific and Technical University for Politically Intelligent Development), on which campus the road signs are not only in five languages but also in Braille, and where they offer courses on the contributions made to quantum mechanics by Australian aborigines and the Indians of the Aleutian Islands; on how being short (*vertically challenged*) encouraged the scientific discoveries of Newton, Galileo, and Einstein; and on feminist cosmology, which replaces the male chauvinist and ejaculatory metaphor of the Big Bang with the theory of Gentle Nurturing, according to which the birth of the universe occurred through lengthy gestation.

You can also find on the Internet PC versions of "Little Red Riding Hood" and "Snow White" (and I leave to your imagination what a follower of PC would do with the Seven Dwarfs). I came across a long discussion on how you might translate into PC "the fireman propped a ladder up against the tree, climbed up, and rescued the cat." Apart from the obvious changing of the fireman into a fireperson, the translation runs on for many lines, because it is a matter of clarifying that in this specific case the fireperson was a man but could easily have been a woman, that he acted against the freedom of the cat, which had the right to go where it wanted to, that with the ladder he jeopardized the well-being of the tree, that he took for granted that the cat was the property of its masters, and that by climbing with such ease he might offend the sensibilities of phys-ically disabled persons, and so on.

Apart from such exaggerations and the humor produced by them, from the start PC caused a violent reaction in conservative circles, who see it as a case of left-wing bigotry and a curtailment of free speech. Reference is often made to Orwell's newspeak and (sometimes directly) to the official language of Stalinism. Many of these responses are equally bigoted, and in fact there is a right-wing form of PC, just as intolerant as the left-wing brand. Think of the abuse hurled against those who talk of the Iraqi "resistance."

Nor should we blur the distinction between moral proposals and legal obligations. It's one thing to say that it is ethically incorrect to call homosexuals *faggots,* and if the person who does so is cabi-net minister of the Berlusconi government (the post-Fascist Mirko Tremaglia), writing this moreover on ministry letterhead, then we can only talk of wretched incivility. But, aside from Tremaglia's vul-garity, because there seems to be no law that assigns months or years in prison for those who say *street cleaner* instead of *ecological operative,* all this is still a matter of personal responsibility, good taste, and respect for other people.

That said, television shows have been penalized by loss of adver-tising revenue, or even discontinued, for making politically incorrect use of language, and there is no shortage of university scandals in which lecturers have been dismissed for not employing politically correct language. We can see, therefore, how the controversy involves not only liberals and conservatives gunning for each other, but may often unfold along highly problematic lines of division.

Not long ago, the *Los Angeles Times* decided that its editorial policy would be to use the term *antiabortion* instead of *pro-life,* given that this second term implies an ideological judgment. On checking an article written by a colleague reviewing a show, an editor found the term *pro-life*, but used in the completely different sense of "life-affirming," and changed it to *antiabortion*. In response to the subsequent outcry, the paper apologized and gave the name of the editor responsible for the blunder, but this led to a new complaint: the editor's right to privacy had been violated when the newspaper made his name public.

Gradually, however, especially in America, there has been a shift from the merely linguistic problem (calling others as they wish to be called) to the problem of the rights of minorities. In certain universities, non-Western students want courses on their own cultural and religious traditions and on their own literature. An African student, say, might want a course on Shakespeare to be replaced with one on African literature. Such curriculum decisions, when made, may have respected African American identity but they also deprive students of knowledge that is useful for those wishing to live in the Western world.

We have forgotten that schools must teach not only what students want to learn but also, and sometimes exactly, what they don't want or don't know they want. Otherwise in all primary and middle schools teachers would no longer teach math or Latin, only video games. It's like the fireman letting the cat run along the highway, because that is what it naturally wants to do.

Which brings me to my final point. More and more, every political stance in favor of understanding other races and religions, or of listening to an adversary's arguments, is called political correctness. The most significant case occurred during an American TV show, when the host Bill Maher took issue with a remark made by Bush describing the terrorists who attacked the Twin Towers on September 11 as cowards. Maher observed that you can say what you like about a kamikaze but not that he lacks courage. The program's advertising revenue fell, and the show was axed. The Maher case had nothing to do with PC, neither from a left- nor a right-wing stand-point. Maher could have been criticized for voicing an opinion un-pleasant to a public still suffering from the terrible wounds of September 11; it could have been pointed out, as someone did, that there is a difference between moral and physical cowardice; it could have been said that the mind of a kamikaze is so clouded by fanati-cism that you can no longer talk either of courage or of fear . . . Nev-ertheless, Maher was expressing his own idea, a provocative one if you will, but he wasn't using politically incorrect language.

Here in Italy too, people occasionally wax ironic about an ex-cess of PC on the part of those who sympathize with the Palestini-ans, call for the withdrawal of our troops from Iraq, or appear overindulgent toward the demands of non-EU minorities. In such cases PC just doesn't enter into it, it's a question of an ideological or political position, which everyone has the right to object to; this has nothing to do with word choice. The problem is that the dis-credit heaped upon PC in conservative circles makes the accusation of PC a tool with which to silence those you disagree with. In this way it becomes a dirty word, as is happening with *pacifism.*

A complicated business, as you can see. Let us at least agree that it is politically correct to use words, including PC terms, in their proper way and in accordance with common sense (so I would not call Berlusconi a *vertically challenged person trying to avoid fol-licular regression*). And let us stick to the fundamental principle that it is humane and civilized to eliminate from current usage all those words that make our fellow beings suffer.

On Private Schools

The Italian writer Pitigrilli once said that every morning he used to read the editorial of his paper in order to know what he was supposed to think. This is a principle I don't share, at least not always. But it's certainly true that sometimes we write articles in order to know what to think. It's a way of putting our ideas in order. This is why I'd like to say a few things about private schools—without going into the technical-parliamentary details of the situation here in Italy.

Ask people whether they think it is right in a democratic country for anyone to establish a private school, and for families to choose the form of teaching they consider most suitable for their children, and the answer must be yes, otherwise what kind of democracy would we be living in?

Now let's ask whether a person who has spent a fortune to buy a Ferrari has the right to go 150 mph on the highway. Sadly for anyone who has made such an investment, and for Ferrari CEO Luca Cordero di Montezemolo, the answer is no. And if I spend all my savings to buy a little house by the sea, am I entitled to forbid people

This article appeared in la Repubblica, *August 2001.*

to sit on the beach in front of my house, make noise, and leave rub-
bish and empty Coke cans all over the place? The answer is no, I
have to grant them right of way because there is a strip of beach that
is open to everyone (at most I can call the police and report these
people for littering).

The fact is that in a democracy we all have the right to enjoy our
freedoms as long as we do not infringe on the freedoms of others.
I would even say that people have the right to commit suicide—
provided the percentage of suicides remains negligible. If there
were an epidemic of suicides, the state would have to step in, to
curb a practice that might hurt society as a whole.

What does this have to do with private schools? Take a country
like the United States, where the state guarantees its citizens every
possible liberty, including the right to bear arms (though some
Americans are beginning to wonder if that right isn't detrimental to
the rights of others). In America you can choose whether to send
your children to a public or a private school. Friends of mine, non-
practicing Jews, sent their daughter to a school run by Catholic
nuns. It was expensive, because the school promised to teach the
girl who Julius Caesar was, whereas the public school curricula
went back only to George Washington at best. Naturally, after at-
tending a good school, that girl went on to Harvard, whereas children from the public schools didn't, because the teaching had to be
kept at the level of the students in the class who had difficulty
speaking English.

And this is the situation in the United States: those with money
can buy their children a good education; the children of those without money are condemned to semi-illiteracy. Hence the American
state does not provide its citizens with equal opportunities. If the
universities, both public and private, are excellent in general, it is
because they must compete in the educational market. In higher education this holds true for Italian universities too, especially after
they were given autonomy. All the state does is recognize the de-

grees awarded by some private universities, and establish national commissions for the awarding of chairs. If you graduate from a good private institution like Milan's Bocconi University, you're guaranteed a job. If you graduate from a private university whose reputation is not so good, then the market will determine where you go, or you will have to sit the various public examinations for the magistracy, the bar, the teaching profession, and so on.

But neither public competition nor the market have any control over kindergarten, primary, and middle schools. One person attends a school for the underprivileged and never knows it (because he is culturally clueless); another attends an excellent school and becomes a member of the ruling class. Is this democratic?

Solution: let the state recognize the right of private individuals to teach at primary- and middle-school levels but give a voucher of the same value to all citizens. Catholics will be free to send their children to the Scolopian Fathers and angry lay people can send theirs to the local state school. In a democracy parents have the right to decide on their children's education. But private schools, no matter how excellent, must not add additional tuition fees to the voucher; otherwise, obviously, to attract wealthy, cultivated parents, they would try to keep out the children of immigrants or the unemployed, children who haven't learned at home how to speak properly.

Can a private school be forced to accept a child of color or one who is culturally backward? If a private school adjusts to the level of these pupils, who are subsidized by the state, how will it maintain its elite status?

But even if we achieve democratic equality, we know perfectly well that there are private schools (I would mention the Leone XIII High School in Milan, or the Jesuits with whom Piero Fassino, the leader of the left-wing DS party, studied evidently without suffering any ideological pressure) that try at all costs to maintain excellence and private schools that specialize in easy diplomas. In my day, the state exercised very strict control over these schools: I remember the ordeals of private school students who had to take state examinations. If we are to have this kind of control, then examinations for a certificate of graduation must become tougher than they are today. Let there be an external examining commission (in addition to the internal teacher) and a full three-year curriculum—complete with the nightmares my generation suffered. Otherwise we end up with a generation of ignoramuses, some from the state schools by now reserved for the lumpenproletariat, others from fraudulent private schools for lazy rich kids.

The problem could be solved by a law protecting the rights of the less wealthy, which would allow a little Italianized Senegalese armed with a state voucher to attend the most exclusive private school. But then, in the interests of the equality of all citizens (and of all beliefs and faiths) before the law, anyone could organize a private school financed with state vouchers. The Scolopians certainly, and the Jesuits, but also the Waldensians, or some lay association might establish high schools in which the students receive a sound rationalist education in which all religions are put on the same level: you read a little from the Koran, a little from the Bible, a little from Buddhist texts, while reviewing Italian history from a secular standpoint. Or Riformazione Communista might establish Feuerbach schools, inspired by criticism of religious prejudices, or the Masons might set up Hiram schools, where pupils are educated in the moral and spiritual principles of that association. The state would be footing the bill, so each of these enterprises (maybe with a little help from sponsors) could make a profit.

Why prohibit (this is a democracy, after all) the Reverend Moon and Monsignor Milingo from setting up their own schools, when we have Steiner schools? And why prohibit a Muslim middle school, or why stop the followers of various South American sects from launching an Oxalà high school, where they transmit the principles of Afro-Brazilian syncretism? Who could protest? The Vatican, by asking the government to reestablish the sovereign authority of the state? But then we would be back to square 1. And, even if we could implement state controls on acceptability, could we exclude a school that teaches complete skepticism with regard to religion, or another that teaches sound Koranic fundamentalist precepts, if both provided the regulation number of hours of Italian, history, and geography?

Whereupon we would have a country of citizens divided by ethnic and ideological groups, each with its own education, incommensurate with the others. Not a healthily multicultural solution. A multicultural society wants its citizens to know, recognize, and accept diversity, not to ignore it.

Some people believe that in other countries freedom of education reigns supreme. But take France, where if you want to become a civil service mandarin, you must attend the ENA, or the École Normale Superieure on rue d'Ulm, and if you want to attend the École Normale, you must first go to one of the great public high schools like Louis le Grand, Descartes, or Henri IV. In these schools the state's concern is to provide its citizens with an education in what they call *la République,* in other words a system of knowledge and values calculated to ensure the equality, in theory at least, of students—whether they are born in Algiers or in Normandy. Perhaps the ideology of *la République* is too rigid, but it can't be corrected by its opposite, Catholics with Catholics, Protestants with Protestants, Muslims with Muslims, atheists with atheists, and Jehovah's Witnesses with Jehovah's Witnesses.

I admit that, if we leave things as they currently stand under the Constitution, we won't be able to eliminate a certain amount of injustice: the rich will continue to send their children where they wish, while the poor are left in the hands of the state school system. But democracy also means accepting a tolerable quantity of injustice to avoid greater injustice.

These are some of the problems that spring from the statement, in itself obvious and painless, that parents should be able to send their children to the school they prefer. If we don't confront these problems, the debate may degenerate into a feud between integralist Catholics and rabidly anticlerical laymen, which would be a bad thing.

Science, Technology, and Magic

We believe we live in a period that Isaiah Berlin identified in its earliest stages as the age of reason. The shadows of the Middle Ages having been dispelled by the critical light of the Renaissance, we now maintain that we live in an age dominated by science.

This vision of the supremacy of the scientific mind, which was heralded naively in Carducci's *Hymn to Satan* and more critically in the *Communist Manifesto* of 1848, is endorsed more by reactionaries, spiritualists, and *laudatores temporis acti* (the praisers of times past) than it is by scientists. It is the former and not the latter who create frescoes smacking almost of science fiction to portray a world that, forgetful of other values, is based solely on faith in the truth of science and the power of technology. The model of an epoch ruled by science is still, in the eyes of the enemies of science, the one proposed triumphantly by Carducci in his *Hymn to Satan*:

A speech given in Rome in November 2002 at an International Scientific Conference (on information in science) chaired by Umberto Veronesi. It later appeared in la Repubblica.

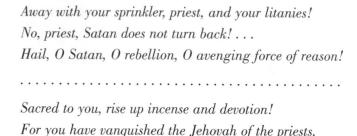

Away with your sprinkler, priest, and your litanies!
No, priest, Satan does not turn back! . . .
Hail, O Satan, O rebellion, O avenging force of reason!

. . . .

Sacred to you, rise up incense and devotion!
For you have vanquished the Jehovah of the priests.

If we take a careful look at this text from 1863 we notice that it describes—as satanic heroes in opposition to the supremacy of religious thought—witches and alchemists, great heretics and reformers from Hus to Savonarola to Luther, but no scientist; not even Galileo, who ought to have made Carducci's anticlerical and republican heart beat faster. As we move on to modern times, the hero, the symbol of reason's victory over faith, is the train:

A monster of awful beauty has been unchained,
It scours the land and scours the seas:
Glittering and belching smoke like a volcano,
It vanquishes the mountains, devours the plains;
It leaps over chasms, then burrows deep
Into hidden caverns along paths unfathomed;
Only to reemerge invincible
From shore to shore.
Like a tornado it howls out its cry.

In other words, even for Carducci, a lover of the classics but a man imbued with passions that were still Romantic, the symbol of the victory of reason is a product of technology, not a scientific idea. So we need to make a first distinction—namely, that between science and technology.

People today not only expect but demand everything from technology and make no distinction between destructive and productive technology. The youngster who plays *Star Wars* games on the computer, uses a cell phone as if it were a natural extension of the eustachian tube, and chats on the Internet lives in technology and cannot conceive of the existence of a different world, one without computers or telephones.

Science is different. The mass media confuse it with technology and transmit this confusion to their users, who think that everything scientific is technological, effectively unaware of the dimension proper to science, I mean to say that science of which technology is an application and a consequence but not the primary substance.

Technology gives you everything instantly; science proceeds slowly.

Virilio talks of our epoch as one dominated, I'd say hypnotized, by speed. We obviously live in the age of speed; the Futurists understood this ahead of their time. Today we are accustomed to travel from Europe to New York in three and a half hours aboard a Concorde, and jet lag and the use of melatonin are a consequence of our high-speed life. We are so accustomed to speed that we get angry if we can't open our e-mail immediately or if our plane is delayed.

This addiction to technology has nothing to do with the practice of science. It has to do, instead, with the eternal resort to magic.

What has magic been over the centuries, and what is it still today, albeit in disguise? The assumption that it is possible to go from cause to effect without taking intermediate steps. I stick a pin in an effigy of an enemy, and he dies. I utter a formula and transform iron into gold. I summon angels and send a message through them. The Benedictine abbot Trithemius of the sixteenth century was one of the forerunners of modern cryptology; he worked out secret codes for rulers and army chiefs—but to make his discoveries and formulas (today easy to create on a computer but brilliant for those days) more appetizing, he demonstrated that his technique was in fact a magical operation thanks to which you could have angels transmit messages in secrecy over a long distance in a single second.

Magic is indifferent to the long chain of causes and effects, and above all it does not trouble itself to establish by constant experiment that there is a replicable relation between a cause and its effect. Hence its appeal, from primitive cultures to the Renaissance to the myriad occult sects to be found all over the Internet.

Faith and hope in magic did not by any means fade away with the advent of experimental science. The desire for simultaneity between cause and effect was transferred to technology, which looks like the natural daughter of science. How much effort did it take to go from the first computers in the Pentagon, or from Olivetti's Elea, which was the size of a whole room (and they say it took the Olivetti programming team months to configure that mammoth machine to emit the notes of *Colonel Bogey,* a feat they were enormously proud of), to our modern PCs in which everything occurs in a split second? Technology does everything possible so that we lose sight of the chain of cause and effect.

The first computer operators compiled their programs in Basic, which was not a machine language but gave us a glimpse of its mystery (early computer users like us did not know machine language but knew that to make chips follow a certain course you had to give extremely complex instructions in binary code). *Windows* has obscured Basic programming: the user can press a button and turn an image upside down, he can link up with a distant correspondent or obtain the results of astronomical calculations, but he no longer knows what lies behind all this (and something does). The user experiences computer technology as if it were magic.

It might seem strange that this magic mentality should persist in our day, but if we look around, it is triumphant and everywhere. We see the revival of satanic sects, of syncretistic rites that social anthropologists used to study in the favelas of Brazil and that Monsignor Milingo now practices, or used to practice, in Rome and not in Salvador de Bahia. Even the traditional religions tremble before such rites and come to terms with them by not talking to the people of the mystery of the Trinity (albeit having different criteria, theological debate is similar to scientific method, for it proceeds by subtle reasoning, step by step), because it's handier to exhibit the lightning-fast action of the miracle.

Theologians talked to us, and still do, of the mystery of the Trinity, but their arguments were and still are aimed at showing how it is either conceivable or unfathomable. The thinking underpinning the miracle is lost; instead, the numinous, the sacred, the divine appears or is revealed by a charismatic voice, and it is this revelation and not the laborious syllogisms of theology that the masses are invited to submit to.

Now, the science that emerges through the mass media is, alas, only its magical aspect. When science does appear, it appears only because it promises a miracle of technology.

There is at times a *pactum sceleris* between the scientist and the mass media, whereby the scientist cannot resist the temptation, or believes it his duty, to communicate ongoing research, sometimes also for fund-raising purposes, but then the research is immediately communicated as a discovery—and then the disappointment when it becomes evident that the result is not forthcoming.

We all know about these episodes, from the announcement of cold fusion to the repeated claims of a cure for cancer. On cancer cures: in Italy, the Di Bella case demonstrated the magical faith in an immediate result.

It's hard to convey to the public that research is a combination of hypotheses, control experiments, and proofs of falsification. Think of the debate between orthodox and alternative medicine: why should the public believe in the remote promises of science when alternative medicine says that it has the answer now?

In a recent number of *Cicap* magazine, Garattini observed that taking a medicine and recovering in a short time is not proof of the efficacy of the medicine. There are other explanations: your cure occurred naturally, the drug acted only as a placebo, or your cure might have been even quicker without the drug. But try getting the public to entertain those possibilities. People will be incredulous, because the magic mentality sees only one process, the ever-victorious short circuit between the cause and effect.

So it is no surprise that the public remains indifferent when big cuts are announced in research funding. People are upset if a hospital is closed or if the price of a drug goes up, but they are insensible to the long and costly time scale of research. Italians may worry that research cuts will persuade some nuclear scientist to emigrate to America (which has the bomb already) but don't stop to think that the same cuts might delay the discovery of more efficient flu drugs or the development of an electric car, and no connection is made between research cuts and children suffering from tetralogy of Fallot or polio, because the chain of cause and effect is long and mediated, not instant as is the action of magic.

You may have seen the episode of *E.R.* in which Dr. Green tells a long line of patients that antibiotics will not be given to flu victims because they are of no use in such cases. His explanation leads to anger and accusations of racial prejudice. The patient sees the magical relation between antibiotics and cure and has been told by the media that antibiotics work. Everything boils down to that short circuit. Antibiotic pills are a technological product; research into influenza causes and remedies is work for a university.

It happens that people in government (who sometimes consult magicians and astrologers, and stories like this have emerged even from the White House) think like the man in the street and not like the man in the laboratory. Which is unfortunate, but I have no solution.

It's pointless to ask the mass media to abandon the magic mentality: they must adopt it because the relationship they draw between cause and effect every day is of a magical nature. True, there have been reliable popularizers of science, and I'd like to mention my friend the late Giovanni Maria Pace, but in these cases too the (inevitably sensationalist) headline approach cannot contain the cautious explanation that research is under way for a vaccine against all forms of influenza. The explanation will inevitably appear as the joyful news that the flu will finally be defeated (by science? no, by a new pill on the market).

How should scientists behave when faced with the pressing questions put to them daily by media thirsting for miraculous promises? With caution, obviously, but we have seen that caution is of little use. Nor can they declare a blackout on all scientific news, because research by nature is public.

I think the classroom can help. It is up to schools, and to all initiatives that can educate, including reliable Internet sites, to ensure that young people gradually acquire a correct understanding of scientific procedure. A most difficult task, because even knowledge transmitted by schools is often deposited in the memory like a sequence of miraculous episodes: Madame Curie who comes home one evening and discovers radioactivity thanks to a mark on a sheet of paper, Dr. Fleming who glances absently at some mold and discovers penicillin, Galileo who sees a lamp swaying and suddenly discovers everything, even that the world rotates—and so we forget, on thinking of his legendary Calvary, that not even he figured out *which curve* it followed. How can we expect schools to provide correct scientific information when to this day many manuals and books—including respectable ones—say that before Christopher Columbus people believed that the Earth was flat, when this is a historic fabrication? The ancient Greeks knew it was round; and the sages of Salamanca who opposed Columbus's voyage had made calculations more accurate than his about the dimensions of the planet.

It is the duty of a man of learning not only to do scrupulous research but also to present his knowledge effectively. Italian scientists

sometimes still feel it's not dignified to take an interest in popular-
ization, although masters in this field include Einstein and Heisen-
berg and the late Stephen Jay Gould. But if we are to teach a
nonmagical view of science, we cannot expect it to come from the
mass media. The scientific community itself must construct it bit by
bit in the collective awareness, starting with the young.

The polemical conclusion to my speech is that the prestige scientists enjoy today is based on false reasoning, and is in any case
contaminated by the two forms of magic, the traditional and the
technological, that still hold the minds of the majority in thrall.

If we do not get out of this spiral of false promises and dashed
hopes, science will have a harder road to follow.

In the centuries of the early Middle Ages, Isidore of Seville, who
has gone down in history as an eminently gullible type and the author of etymologies now considered laughable, such as *lucus* from
non lucendo and *cadaver* from *caro data vermibus*, nonetheless—
albeit on the basis of inaccurate information from Eratosthenes's
day—came up with an almost exact figure for the length of the
equator. But around him wandered unicorns and woodland monsters, and if learned men knew that the Earth was round, artists—
for a variety of reasons—depicted it to the common people and
their masters alike as a flat disk with Jerusalem at the center. In
other words they flattened it for symbolic reasons and for ease of
projection, as some atlases do to this day, but that sufficed to ensure
that most people didn't know what shape the Earth really had.

So, after centuries of enlightenment, we are still like Isidore: the
newspapers will talk of our scientific conferences, but the image of
them that emerges is doomed to be magical.

Should this surprise us? We still massacre one another as we
did in the Dark Ages. Dragged along by uncontrollable fundamentalism and fanaticism, we proclaim crusades while whole continents
are dying of hunger and AIDS and while our televisions portray us
(magically) as a land of plenty, thus attracting to our shores hordes

of desperate people who make a dash for the run-down outskirts of our cities the way the old navigators raced toward the promises of Eldorado. So should we wonder that ordinary people still don't know what science is and confuse it with either Renaissance magic or the fact that somehow (don't ask how) you can send a love letter to Australia at lightning-fast speed for the price of a local phone call?

II

CHRONICLES OF
A REGIME

For Whom the Bell Tolls:
A 2001 Appeal for a Moral Referendum

No one in Italy would like to wake up one morning to discover that the nation's newspapers, *Il Corriere della Sera, la Repubblica, La Stampa, Il Messaggero, il Giornale,* and so on, from *l'Unità* to *Manifesto,* as well as the weeklies and monthlies, from *Espresso* to *Novella 2000,* all belonged to the same man, whose opinions they would inevitably reflect. We would feel less free.

But this is what would happen following a victory for the center-right coalition known as Polo delle Libertà. The same man would run the three TV networks he already owns, while his political power would allow him to control the other three—and, when it comes to shaping public opinion, the six national TV networks count for more than all the newspapers put together. This man already controls important dailies and magazines, but we know what happens in such cases: other papers fall in with the government, either out of tradition or because their owners feel that it is in their interest to appoint editors close to the new majority. In short, we would have a de facto regime.

This article appeared on the Golem –L'indispensabile *Web site and then in* la Repubblica, *May 2001.*

By de facto regime I mean a phenomenon that would occur by itself, even if Berlusconi were a man of absolute probity, his fortune were acquired in an irreproachable manner, and he sincerely wished to serve the state even against his own personal interests. When a man finds himself in a position where he can effectively control all the sources of information in his country, not even a saint could resist the temptation to run things according to the logic of that system. And even if he resisted that temptation, the de facto regime would be created by the people who worked for him. There has never been, in the history of any country, a newspaper or a chain of TV networks that launched a campaign against its owner.

This situation, by now known to the world as the Italian anomaly, makes it clear that a victory for the Polo would not be, as many political scientists say it would, a normal alternation between left and right, which is part of the dialectic of democracy. The establishment of a de facto regime (which, I repeat, occurs over and above the wishes of individuals) is not part of any democratic dialectic.

To explain why this anomaly does not alarm most Italians, we need to look first of all at the Polo's potential electorate. It may be divided into two categories. The first is the Motivated Electorate. This is made up of people who support the Polo out of real conviction: the rabid Northern League supporter, who would like to put non-EU citizens and possibly southern Italians into lead-sealed railroad cars; the moderate Northern Leaguer, who feels that it would be good to safeguard the interests of his own geographic area, because he thinks he can live and prosper there separated and protected from the rest of the world; the ex-Fascist, who, although he accepts (*obtorto collo*, perhaps) the democratic order, will defend his nationalistic cause and undertake a radical revision of the history of the twentieth century; the entrepreneur who maintains (rightly) that any tax exemptions promised by the Polo would favor only the wealthy; anyone who, having had a problem with the law, sees in the Polo an alliance that will curb the independence of public prosecutors; and, finally, anyone who doesn't want his taxes to be spent on depressed areas.

For all these people the anomaly and the de facto regime, if not welcome, are in any case a small price to pay to attain their ends— therefore no counterargument will change their minds.

The second category, which I call the Mesmerized Electorate, the most numerous, has no defined political opinion but has based its values on the creeping form of "culture" imparted for decades by the various television channels, and not only those owned by Berlusconi. What counts for these people are ideals of material well-being and a mythical view of life, not unlike that of people I would call generically the Albanian immigrants. The Albanian immigrant wouldn't have dreamt of coming to Italy if the TV had showed him for years only the Italy of *Open City, Obsession,* or *Paisan*—he would have steered clear of this unhappy country. He comes because he knows Italy as a country where a colorful television hands out easy money to those who know that Garibaldi's given name was Giuseppe: a rich, showbiz Italy.

Now, this electorate (which according to surveys rarely reads the papers and hardly ever books) cares little about the establishment of a de facto regime, which would not diminish but increase the quantity of entertainment to which the electorate has become accustomed. So I smile when stubborn attempts are made to raise public awareness about the conflict of interests. The response I often hear is that nobody cares if Berlusconi looks after his own interests as long as he also defends theirs.

It's no use telling these voters that Berlusconi would modify the Constitution—first, because they have never read the Constitution; second, because they have heard members of the opposition parties (known as the Olive Tree Alliance) talk of changes to the Constitution. So? It doesn't matter to them which article of the Constitution is changed. Let's not forget that after the formation of the Constituent Assembly, Giovannino Guareschi's satirical magazine *Candido* ran some barbed cartoons about the article whose terms stated that the republic must protect the countryside, as if it were some kind of bizarre and irrelevant invitation to take up gardening. This constitutional provision anticipated today's grave concerns about the environment, but it was ignored not only by the general public but also by informed journalists.

With this electorate, it's pointless to raise the cry that Berlusconi would gag the judiciary, because the idea of justice is associated with the threat of intrusion into people's private affairs. The same voters candidly state that at least a wealthy prime minister would not steal, because they conceive of corruption in terms of millions or hundreds of millions of lire, not in astronomical terms of thousands of billions. These voters think (rightly) that Berlusconi could never be bribed by the gift of a three-room apartment with bathroom or a large car, but the difference between ten and twenty thousand billion is meaningless to them (as it is to the rest of us).

The idea that a parliament controlled by the new majority can vote for a law that in some unclear way enriches the head of government by a thousand billion lire does not fit in with their everyday notion of give and take, buying, selling, or bartering. What sense is there in talking to them about offshore tax havens, when all they want from an exotic beach is to spend a package-holiday week lounging on the sand?

Why talk to these voters about *The Economist,* when they don't even know the names of many Italian newspapers or what their political line is? When they take a train, they buy a left-wing or right-wing magazine indiscriminately, as long as there are tits and ass on the cover. This electorate is thus deaf to all warnings, sheltered from all concerns about a de facto regime. It has been produced by our society after years and years of attention only to success and easy money. It has been produced by the non-right-wing press and television; it has been produced by parades of nubile models, by mothers who finally embrace sons emigrated to Australia, by couples who earn the recognition of their neighbors by displaying their conjugal woes in front of a television camera, by the sacred transformed into spectacle, by the idea that all you have to do to win big money is scratch a card; it has been produced by the scant audience appeal of any news item that shows that statistically crime is down, whereas headlines of atrocious crime cases make people think that what happened before could happen again tomorrow and to them.

It is this Mesmerized Electorate that will hand victory to the Polo. The Italy we will have is the Italy they want.

We are faced with the Mesmerized Electorate and the Motivated Electorate of the right wing, but the greatest danger to our country is the Discouraged Electorate of the left (I mean *left* in the broadest sense of the term, from the old secular republicans to kids in Rifondazione Communista, down to Catholic volunteers who no longer have any faith in politics). This electorate is made up of that mass of people who know all the things said here (and don't need to hear them repeated) and are disappointed with the outgoing government. They castrate themselves to punish their wives. They ensure the victory of the de facto regime to punish those who failed to satisfy them.

These people bear an enormous responsibility, and history will criticize not those addicted to the TV soaps, those who will receive the entertainment they wanted, but those who—despite the fact that they read books and newspapers—have yet to realize or are trying desperately to ignore that what awaits us in a few days' time is not a regular election but a Moral Referendum. By rejecting any awareness of this, they are doomed to the circle in hell of the slothful.

To combat sloth, I now call on the undecided and the disappointed to endorse a very simple appeal, which doesn't oblige them to agree with all the opinions expressed in this article, only with this: "Against the establishment of a de facto regime, against the ideology of spectacle, to safeguard the plurality of information in our country, we consider the forthcoming election to be a Moral Referendum that no one has the right to shirk." For many, this will be an appeal to examine their consciences and shoulder their responsibilities.

Because "No man is an island. . . . Never send to know for whom the bell tolls; it tolls for thee."

The 2001 Electoral Campaign
and Veteran Communist Strategy

There is no doubt that the Polo delle Libertà has organized its electoral campaign well, so well that many people are wondering not so
much about its secret but about its key points and model. The first
thing that comes to mind is that the Polo campaign, and notably
Berlusconi (the one and only face driving it), is based on advertising principles. From the model of advertising they have taken the
constant repetition of one symbol plus a few simple slogans, as well
as a shrewd color scheme—a winner, because it looks like the
scheme used by *Microsoft Windows*. The slogans are like those used
to sell products of mass consumption. Another point in common with
advertising is the principle that there is no need for the slogan to be
true. No purchaser actually believes that Scavolini kitchen units are
Italy's most popular (that company's slogan claims they are): the statistics would prove them wrong. And no one really thinks that such
and such a detergent washes whiter than the others: housewives and
househusbands alike know that, above a certain price, brand-name
detergents are all pretty much the same. Yet when buyers make a
purchase, they are more likely to pick a product whose slogan they

This article appeared in la Repubblica, *April 2001.*

recognize. In this sense it is useless (or, at best, amusing) for satirists and politicians to wax ironic about the "worker president" (as Berlusconi once called himself) or about better pensions for everyone: the slogan is not designed to be credible, only to be remembered.

The advertising model works for posters or other types of commercial announcement but not, for example, for parliamentary or media battles, waged with growing intensity as election day gets closer. Some commentators have noted a contradiction between the friendliness of the propaganda and the aggressiveness of political action, and in this they see a tactical error. Which brings us to the interpretation suggested by Indro Montanelli: unable to control some of the heritage of its members and some of the deeper psychological inclinations of its leader, the Polo betrays its authoritarian tendencies and a latent yearning (albeit still symbolic) for the good old cudgel of Fascist memory. This interpretation strikes me as incomplete. It does explain certain excesses, threats, and promises but not the overall conduct of the alliance, which I think follows another, quite coherent model. This model is not Fascist or consumerist but veteran communist, and in some ways it is reminiscent of the 1968 protest movement.

Let us try to remember (at least those of us who are old enough) the propaganda tactics of Italian communism in Palmiro Togliatti's day. Independent of the complexity of the leadership's cultural program, the party's image was conveyed by effective and understandable slogans, which were repeated on every occasion. First and foremost, the attack on capitalist imperialism as the cause of poverty in the world, on NATO as its warmongering right arm, on the government as a lackey of the Americans, and on the police as the armed wing of the government. The party also tried to delegitimize a magistracy that condemned strikers but not their taskmasters, or at least it made a sharp distinction between "good" magistrates, usually tough-minded judges who protected the rights of the masses, and "bad" magistrates, who failed to condemn the wrongdoing of the ruling classes but came down hard on the protests of the working class. As far as the Polo is concerned, all you have to do is replace communism with America and its foolish servants (who can range from the Catholic Scalfaro to the conservative Montanelli), bear in mind the division between "red" judges (who probe Berlusconi's affairs) and "good" judges (brought into play every time it must be proved that an accusation is groundless), and the model seems identical.

In the second place, consider the use of catchy slogans (far simpler than the political strategy they serve): think of Pajetta's speeches in *Tribune politiche,* where despite the dialectical subtlety of the orator, the central idea was "things need changing."

In the third place is the ability to monopolize common values and make them partisan: think of the massive peace campaign, the use of terms like *democratic* (which in the end came to connote only East European regimes), the hijacking of the image of Garibaldi and the struggle for national unity. Just as those today who yell *Forza Italia!* ("Come on, Italy!") in the world of sport (or those who talk of liberal values and liberty) immediately become propagandists of the Polo delle Libertà, so in the past those who wished to talk of peace and pacifism were automatically enrolled among the fellow travelers of the Italian communist party—at least until Pope John XXIII and his *Pacem in terris* recovered the ideal of peace as a noncommunist value.

Another element of veteran communist propaganda and politics (both in parliament and in the streets) was aggressiveness: every opposing point of view was branded as against the people, accompanied by constant complaints about the aggressiveness of others. Later, this attitude was passed on, in a bloodier way, to the South American insurrectionary movements (the Tupamaros, for example) and to European terrorists, whose plan (soon revealed to be utopian) was to commit outrages designed to trigger a repression by the state that the masses would find intolerable. But, without bringing in violence, the aggressive accusation of media conspiracy has become the successful battle cry of the Radical party, which has built enormous visibility on the strength of protests that the media ignore it. A typical feature of Berlusconi's tactics is his use of his own formidable mass media apparatus to accuse the mass media of persecuting him.

Other elements of veteran communist propaganda were the appeal to popular sentiment (now simply "the people"), the use of mass demonstrations with flag waving and singing, the faith in the fundamental appeal of the party color (then red, now blue), and finally (if we must take into account the right-wing analysis) the more or less gradual occupation of the centers of cultural production (then mostly publishing houses and the weeklies). We might even mention the attempts made by the communist Universale del Canguro publishing house to enlist the greats of the past among the ranks of progressive writers: from Diderot to Voltaire, from Giordano Bruno to Bacon and his utopias, and from Erasmus to Campanella. I mention these names only because they are the ones, albeit in expensive, refined editions, that Berlusconi's Publitalia group is currently reexhuming.

A more complex and subtle comparison might be made with regard to Togliatti's "duplicity," but I leave it to the reader to discover interesting analogies.

As I was talking to someone about these analogies, it was pointed out to me that the PCI (Partito Communista Italiano) of the classic period, despite its hostility to the government, backed many of the laws proposed by its opponents (article 7 of the Constitution and other reforms), whereas the Polo typically opposes, often by contemptuous abstention, various government-inspired reforms that it could easily support in part. After Yalta, once Togliatti had accepted the idea that one could not, and perhaps should not, think in terms of revolution, he accepted the idea of a long march through the institutions (whose last chapter, long after his death, was to be consociativism). In this sense the policies of the Polo do not seem veteran communist. But then we see that the Polo's propaganda model and its strategies and tactics for the political struggle are shot through with traces of another model, that of the 1968 extraparliamentary groups.

Many elements of the 1968 model are to be found in the Polo. Just as the people of '68 identified their main adversary as a much more subtle and less visible one than the United States, such as the multinationals, so Berlusconi repeatedly denounces communist plots (although the communist party is no longer of any importance) and attempts to link the magistracy with the communists. The 1968 model also lives on in the tactic of never giving an inch to the adversary, but always demonizing him whatever his proposals are, then refusing dialogue and debate (such as turning down interviews with any journalist seen as a lackey of power). This rejection of compromise was based on the constantly reiterated conviction that revolutionary victory was imminent. And so it was a matter of wearing down the nerves of a complex-ridden bourgeoisie, continually reminding it of the certain victory, after which no prisoners would be taken and the lists of the proscribed that appeared on the tazebao would be considered on the day of reckoning. Extraparliamentary groups used a technique borrowed from wrestling to terrify opponents: ferocious shouts, intimidating slogans such as "Fascists, bourgeois, only a few months left" and "This is only the beginning," or an opponent was dismissed with cries of "Moron, moron!" The march toward power was supported by the image of a charismatic face, be it that of Che or the triad Lenin, Stalin, and Mao.

True, all propaganda activities resemble one another to a certain point, but it's worth remembering here just how many activists both from veteran communism and the 1968 protest movement found their way into the ranks of the Polo. It is not unreasonable to think that Berlusconi listened to these counselors more than he did to the advertising people and the pollsters of the early days.

Moreover, listening to public relations experts is a particularly intelligent move, because in the current political landscape, the true mass party is the Polo, which—after the social breakdown of the masses as conceived by classic Marxism—has identified the new masses, who are characterized no longer by class but by a generic and common membership in the universe of mass media values and hence are no longer receptive to the appeal of ideology but to that of populism. Through the Northern League, the Polo strikes a chord with the Poujadist petit bourgeoisie of northern Italy; through Alleanza Nazionale it can reach the underprivileged masses in the south, who for fifty years voted for monarchists and neo-Fascists; and through Forza Italia it is in touch with what was once the working class, most of whom have ascended to the level of the petit bourgeoisie and share the same worries regarding the threat to their privileges from the new lumpen proletariat. Thus the old working class puts its faith in a party that has taken over the watchwords of all populist movements: the fight against crime, the reduction of the fiscal burden, defense against the excessive power of the state and of capital (the source of all evil and corruption), and severity and scorn for any form of deviant behavior.

Nor should we ignore the populist stamp of some of the arguments with which people, even those of humble origins, used to demonstrate their liking for Berlusconi. The arguments are: (1) being rich, he won't steal (an argument based on the man in the street's slipshod equation of politician with thief); (2) what do I care if he looks after his own interests, the main thing is that he look after mine too; (3) a man who has become enormously rich will be able to distribute wealth among the people he governs (although this didn't happen with either Bokassa or Milošević). This reasoning is typical not only of TV addicts (people who get on quiz shows may become millionaires) but also of those whose roots are sunk deep in primitive, and perhaps even archetypal, beliefs. It suffices to think of the "cargo cults," a religious phenomenon in Oceania from the beginning of colonialism to the end of the Second World War: since the white men arrived on their shores, by ship or plane, unloading food and other marvelous goods (which were obviously for the invaders' requirements), the natives began to wait for the messianic arrival of a ship at first, later an airplane, that would bring the same goods to them.

When you see these deep drives in your own electorate, you have become a mass party, and every classic populist party uses slogans and aggressive tactics. Perhaps one of the original sins of today's left is not having fully accepted the idea that the true electorate of a reformist party is no longer made up of the masses but of the emergent classes, and of professionals in the service sector (who are quite numerous). Left-wing leaders must address these people and not the legendary working class.

So one of the discoveries of this campaign might be that the most communist politician of all is Berlusconi. In reality the tactics of the veteran communists and the leaders of the 1968 protest movement are the same, but they have been put to work for a program that might go down well with many levels of the Italian Confederation of Industry, just as in other times the corporatist program went down well. In any case, as the old communist slogan went, *Avanti, o popolo.*

On Mass Media Populism

Exploiting the People

Many foreign newspapers recently expressed concern that it is the turn of Italy's prime minister to lead the European community for the next six months. There are reasons for this concern, and we all know what they are. It seems to shock the citizens of many countries (afraid that something of the kind might happen to them one day), but it has not—as yet—shocked a significant percentage of Italians. There are other risks connected to the Berlusconi "regime," and it is one of these that I deal with here. But first let's take the sting out of *regime,* because whenever someone comes out with this term, everyone thinks of the Fascists—and then even the harshest critics of the government will admit that Berlusconi is not reorganizing the old party branch offices and corporations, closing down newspapers, or putting the kids into black shirts. *Regime* is a neutral term that means a form of government (we talk of countries with democratic regimes, Christian Democratic regimes, republican or monarchic regimes).

"Exploiting the People" appeared in L'espresso, *July 2003.*

That Berlusconi is setting up a form of government all his own is beyond doubt. Among the characteristics of this government is a dangerous populist tendency. I do not use the term *populism* in its historical sense (Russian populism) but in its current sense, as applicable to Perón and other South American or African leaders.

Let's consider a statement made by Berlusconi when (still not beyond the reach of the law) he attempted to delegitimize the judiciary. He said that, as he had been elected by the people, he would not agree to be judged by those who had attained their position thanks merely to professional qualifications.

If I were to take this statement seriously, I should not agree to be operated on for appendicitis or cancer by a surgeon, I should not send my children to school, and I should resist police arrest, because all these people are authorized to perform their functions by virtue of professional qualifications and not by popular election. But Berlusconi was specifically contrasting his position as a man elected by the people against those (legitimized by qualifications) whose task was to determine his innocence or guilt for common crimes.

In reality, the "people"—understood as an expression of a sole will and identical sentiments, a quasi-natural force that embodies morality and history—do not exist. Who does exist is the citizenry, who have differing ideas, and in a democratic regime (which may not be the best kind, but, as they say, all the others are worse) government is entrusted to those who obtain the vote of the majority of citizens. Not from "the people" but from a *majority,* which is not always decided on the basis of a total number of ballot papers but sometimes on the distribution of votes in a uninominal system. Those elected represent the citizens, proportionally, in Parliament. But the country is not made up of Parliament alone; there are many "intermediate bodies," ranging from industry to the army, from the professions to the press, et cetera—usually these are people who are qualified to do their job, and no one has ever said that their authority is undermined by the fact that they attained their positions through an examination conducted by experts. On the contrary, competitive examinations (if they are not rigged, but elections can be rigged too) are a way for the country to ensure that the representatives of these intermediate bodies know their business. It is on the basis of qualifications that elementary school teachers and history professors have the authority and right to state that when Berlusconi talked about "Romulus and Remulus," he was mistaken, and it is on the basis of an authority sanctioned by examinations that the medical community can warn the population that a certain medicine is harmful. Above all it is the form of qualification known as cooptation that legitimizes (government) ministers, who do not have to be elected parliamentarians but are sometimes chosen on the basis of their professional capacities.

Appealing to the people means constructing a fictitious entity: since the people as such do not exist, populists are those who create a virtual image of the popular will. Mussolini did this by mustering crowds of one or two hundred thousand people who publicly acclaimed him and who, like actors, played the part of the people. Others may create an image of popular consensus by playing with opinion polls, or simply by calling up the phantasm of a "people." A populist identifies his own plan with the will of the people and then, if he can manage it (and he often can), he takes a goodly number of the citizens—who are so fascinated by this virtual image of themselves that they end up identifying with it—and transforms them into the very people he has invented.

These are the risks of populism, which we recognize and fear when they appear in other countries but which, curiously, we do not recognize when they arise at home.

Should Berlusconi Be Demonized?

If I go to the newsstand and buy all the papers on sale, I see that the critical front is at work only in those aligned with the opposition, and also partly in those that, no matter how independent they claim to be, cannot remain silent about certain scandalous events. But readers who buy the other papers remain completely ignorant of these criticisms. The anti-Berlusconi movement has become a club frequented by those who are already in agreement, with the result that exposés (which do occur) have no effect on those among our countrymen whom we would ask to search their consciences about the vote they cast a few years ago. So it's understandable, if not justifiable, when the opposition calls to end the free-for-all against the prime minister because they fear that this might become the stuff of urbane, amused conversation among members of the same club, who, on finding themselves in unanimous agreement regarding their virtuous disapproval, are convinced that at least they have saved their souls.

This leads me to a first conclusion, to which I return later: the front critical of the new regime reaches only the audience that has no need of their criticisms.

Every day in our unfortunate country (and luckily also in other European countries) you hear strong talk about the creeping coup d'état that Berlusconi is trying to bring about. We all realized that the terms of debate about whether he was establishing a regime were poorly expressed, since for us *regime* automatically calls up the Fascist regime.

But a regime is in general a form of government, and Berlusconi was establishing day by day one based on the identification of the party, the country, and the state with a series of business interests. He did this not by ordering police operations or the arrest of members

"Should Berlusconi Be Demonized?" appeared in MicroMega, *September 2003.*

of Parliament but by gradually occupying the most important media (or trying to get his hands on them—with "concert parties" or other financial operations—fortunately not always with success) and those newspapers that were still independent, as well as by creating consensus based on an appeal to populism.

It has been stated, in the following order, that: (1) Berlusconi went into politics with the sole aim of avoiding the trials that could have led him to prison; (2) as a French journalist put it, Berlusconi is establishing *pedegisme* (in French, PDG stands for *président directeur général,* the boss, the manager, the CEO); (3) Berlusconi is carrying out this plan by making use of the effects of an undeniable electoral success, hence he has deprived his opponents of the right to tyrannicide, because they are under an obligation to respect the wishes of the majority, and all they can do is try to persuade people to reconsider; (4) on the basis of this electoral success, Berlusconi has passed laws designed to benefit him and not the country (this is *pedegisme*); (5) Berlusconi does not act like a statesman or even like a traditional politician but employs other techniques, techniques that make him more dangerous than any *caudillo* of the old days, because they seem in line with the principles of a democratic regime; (6) in sum, Berlusconi has gone beyond conflict of interests, and every day, more and more, he is creating an absolute *convergence of interests*—that is, persuading the country to accept the idea that his personal interests coincide with those of the national community.

This is certainly a regime, a form, and a concept of government, and it is taking shape with such efficacy that the European press is concerned, not so much out of compassion and love for Italy as from the fear that Italy may once again become the laboratory for a sinister experiment that might be extended to all of Europe.

The problem is that opposition to Berlusconi, at home as well as abroad, is based on a seventh conviction, which in my view is mistaken. Since Berlusconi is not a statesman but a company executive whose sole aim is to maintain the precarious equilibrium of his coalition, some people argue, he doesn't realize that he says one thing one day and the opposite the next; that, having no political or diplomatic experience, he tends to put his foot in his mouth; that he speaks out when he should keep quiet; that he comes out with statements he must retract the next day; and that he confuses his private life with the public interest to such an extent that—in the company of foreign politicians—he makes jokes in the worst possible taste about his wife, and so on. In this way he lends himself to satire, and his opponents occasionally console themselves by thinking that he has lost all sense of proportion, that he will rush headlong to his ruin without even realizing it.

I disagree. Berlusconi is an entirely new kind of politician, perhaps a postmodern one, and precisely because his actions are baffling he is bringing into play a complex, shrewd, and subtle strategy, one that demonstrates nerve and intelligence—if not a theoretical intelligence, then the unerring instincts of a salesman.

What strikes people about Berlusconi (and also amuses them, unfortunately) is his excess of *sales technique*. It's not necessary to call up the ghost of Vanna Marchi, an Italian telesales operator now in trouble with the law, who was a caricature of this technique—albeit effective with the more backward sectors of the public. Let's consider a car salesman. He'll begin by telling you that the sports car he is suggesting you buy is practically a rocket, all you have to do is touch the accelerator and you'll hit 140 mph in seconds. But when he learns that you have five kids and an invalid mother-in-law, he smoothly proceeds to demonstrate how the car is safe and was built with the family in mind. If you take it, he'll throw in the carpets for free. The salesman doesn't care whether his discourse hangs together; he hopes you will take an interest in some feature. Once you have fixed your mind on that, you will forget everything else. So he uses all arguments, one after another at machine-gun speed, unworried about any contradiction that may result. He makes sure that he talks a lot, with insistence, to prevent you from objecting.

Many Italians will recall a certain Giorgio Mendella, who used to appear on TV (not for a minute, as in a big-company ad, but for hours and hours, on a dedicated channel) to persuade retired people and families in the low- to middle-income bracket to put their money in his hands, guaranteeing them huge profits. (After ruining a few thousand people, he was caught absconding with the gains: he had pushed his luck too far and too fast.) Typically he appeared at ten in the evening, saying that he had no personal interest in collecting other people's money, he was merely the spokesman for a large company; but at eleven there he was energetically declaring that he had put all his own money into this operation, of which he was the sole guarantor, and so his interests coincided with those of his clients. Those who entrusted him with their savings never saw the contradiction, evidently focusing on what made them feel confident. Mendella's strength lay not in the arguments he used but in using lots of them in rapid succession.

Berlusconi's sales technique is of this kind ("I'll increase pensions and reduce taxes") but much more complex. He must create consensus, but he doesn't talk to his clients face to face, like Mendella. Needing to deal with the opposition, with public opinion at home and abroad, and with the media (which aren't yet all his property), he has discovered a way of turning criticism from these sources to his advantage.

He makes promises that—good, bad, or indifferent as they may seem to his supporters—are a provocation to his critics. He comes up with a provocation a day, and if they are bizarre or outrageous, so much the better. This allows him to occupy the front pages of the papers and the breaking news on television, with the result that he is always at the center of attention. The provocation must be calculated to ensure that the opposition cannot avoid picking up the gauntlet and reacting vigorously. By managing on a daily basis to produce an indignant reaction from the opposition (and even from those media that don't belong to the opposition but cannot remain silent about proposals that threaten the Constitution), he can show his electorate that he is a victim of persecution ("You see, whatever I say, they attack me").

Playing the victim of persecution, which seems to contradict the triumphalism that typifies Berlusconi's promises, is a fundamental technique. There have even been entertaining cases of the systematic use of this role: the Radical party leader Marco Pannella managed for decades to occupy prime slots in the media by complaining that the media ignored him. But the persecution role is typical of all forms of populism. With his attack on Ethiopia, Mussolini provoked sanctions, but then used the propaganda machine to play on the idea of an international plot against Italy. He proclaimed the superiority of the Italian race and tried to arouse a new national pride, but did so by saying that other countries held Italy in contempt. Hitler embarked on the conquest of Europe maintaining that other nations were denying the German people vital room for expansion. This is precisely the tactic used by the wolf with the lamb. You justify oppression by the denunciation of an injustice perpetrated against you. Persecution mania is one of the many devices employed by a regime to ensure the cohesion of its internal front by playing on chauvinism: to exalt ourselves, we need to show that there are others who hate us and want to clip our wings. Every form of nationalistic, populist exaltation cultivates a continuous state of frustration.

In addition, by complaining every day about the plot against you, you can appear on the media every day to denounce your opponents. An old technique, known even to children: you shove the classmate sitting in front of you, he tosses a wad of paper at you, and you complain to the teacher.

Part of this strategy is to create provocations, so not only do you speak out, you also give free rein to the lunatic fringe of your supporters. There's no need to give them instructions; if you have chosen them well, they will go into action of their own accord, if for no other reason than to emulate the boss—and the more outrageous their provocations, the better.

It doesn't matter if a provocation defies credibility. If you state, let's say, that you wish to abolish the article of the Constitution that protects the environment (but what else but attacks on this article can we call proposals to raise the speed limit, or various big-industry projects that fly in the face of ecological sense?), the opponent must respond, otherwise he loses his identity and function as protector. You launch a provocation, deny it the next day ("You misunderstood me"), and immediately launch another, in such a way that both the new reaction of the opposition and the renewed interest of public opinion focus on that issue, while everyone forgets that the previous provocation was merely *flatus vocis*.

The unacceptability of the provocation achieves two other goals. The first is that no matter how wild your proposal, it nonetheless serves as a trial balloon. If the public does not react with sufficient energy, then the outrageous path might prove negotiable. This is why the opposition must counter: it knows that the matter is one of provocation pure and simple, but keeping silent will leave the way clear for its renewal. The opposition does what it can to resist the creeping coup d'état, but in the process assists it, because it follows its logic.

The second goal achieved I would call the bomb effect. I have always said that if I were a powerful man embroiled in many shady deals, and learned that in two days the papers would come out with an exposé that would bring them to light, I would have only one solution: I would plant a bomb, or have someone else plant it, in a railroad station, bank, or the square outside the church all ready to explode as the people emerged from mass. In this way I would be sure that for at least two weeks the front pages of the press and the headlines on television would be taken up with the outrage, while the news against me would be confined to the back and go unobserved.

An example of the bomb effect occurred in the European parliament when Berlusconi remarked that a German member would have made a good concentration camp guard. This was followed by supporting fire from a Northern League exponent, who called German tourists a noisy bunch of drunks. A senseless gaffe, given that it sparked off an international incident—and right at the start of Italy's six-month presidency of the EU? Not senseless at all: it aroused the chauvinism of a large section of Italian public opinion at the time the Italian parliament was debating the Gasparri Bill, by which Berlusconi's Mediaset TV channels would definitively sink the state-owned channels while multiplying their own profits. I realized this only as I was driving on the highway listening to Radio Radicale broadcasting live from Parliament. The papers devoted pages and pages to Berlusconi the blunderer, to doubts as to whether German tourists would holiday in Italy all the same, and to the agonizing problem as to whether Berlusconi had actually apologized to Schroeder or not. The bomb effect had worked like a charm.

We would have to reread all the front pages of the dailies over the last two years to calculate the number of bomb effects employed. When faced with preposterous statements—all the judges need to see a psychiatrist, for example—we should ask ourselves what maneuver this bomb is intended to obscure.

By saying such things Berlusconi the CEO controls and directs his opponents' reactions; he uses these reactions to show that his adversaries want to ruin him, and that their every appeal to public opinion is a low blow and an ad hominem attack.

This strategy of irresponsible statement disorients the very media that should criticize it. Let's consider the Telekom-Serbia affair. A historian of the future will see clearly that amid the welter of insinuations and accusations there were six issues in play: (1) whether the Telekom-Serbia deal was good or bad; (2) whether it was politically and morally right to do business with Milošević in the pre-Kosovo period, when the Serbian dictator had yet to be outlawed by the democratic nations; (3) whether public money was used in this deal;

(4) whether the government was supposed to know what was happening; (5) whether the government gave its consent. These five issues, political and economic, could be discussed on the basis of facts (when, how, how much), but the sixth was whether someone took money to permit a deal that was criminal and damaging to Italy. This point is of legal import and can be discussed only on the basis of evidence yet to emerge. So choose a few Italian citizens at random and ask if these distinctions are clear to them and if they know what's going on when there are protests, malicious insinuations, and calls for an inquiry. Only a few editorials have noted the existence not of one but six issues; most of the media has been drawn into a frenetic jumble of daily statements, some of which address points 1 to 5 and others point (6) but without giving readers or viewers enough time to understand or sort out the issues. In order to keep pace with these outbursts, which skillfully muddle and confuse the six points, the media too are confused—which was the whole purpose of the operation.

Until now this strategy has proved successful, and Berlusconi still has the advantage over his adversaries.

How does one counter this strategy? There is a way suggested by McLuhan, who, to check terrorism, which feeds on the publicizing of its actions and of the suffering they cause, proposed a press blackout. But if the media do not become a megaphone for the terrorists, we would have the beginnings of a regime based on censorship. Which is what the terrorists hoped to provoke.

It's easy to say: focus only on the important matters (laws by referendum, false accounting, and so on), and if Berlusconi says he wants to become president of the republic, put that news in a paragraph on page 6, out of the duty to provide information but without playing his game. Who would agree to such a thing? Not the opposition press, which would immediately find itself to the right of the "independent" press. Not the independent press, for the simple reason that such a policy would suggest that it has taken on an agenda. Indeed such a decision would be unacceptable to any medium that takes advantage of even the slightest incident to produce and sell news, and spicy, appetizing news at that. If Berlusconi insults a member of the European parliament, you can't relegate the affair to the back page or a gossip column, because you would lose the revenue from the thousands of extra copies you would sell by playing up the succulent event, with pages and pages of diverging opinions, interpretations, gossip, theories, and biting responses.

True, as long as Berlusconi makes the rules of this game, the opposition must abide by them, but it can take the initiative by adapting those rules—in a *positive* way.

This doesn't mean that the opposition should stop demonizing Berlusconi. As we have seen, if the opposition does not react to his provocations, in a certain sense it endorses them, and in any event it fails in its institutional duty. But this function of critical reaction to provocation ought to be assigned to one wing of the team, on a full-time basis. And its activity should be expressed through alternative channels. If it's true (and it is) that the media still free of Berlusconi's control reach only those who are already opposed to him, while the greater part of public opinion is exposed to media under his sway, then there's nothing else for it but to bypass the media. The *girotondi*, the so-called "ring of roses" street protests, were part of this new strategy, but if one or two *girotondi* make waves, a thousand of them become routine. If I have to say that the TV has suppressed a news item, I can't say so on TV. I have to fall back on tactics such as leaflet or videocassette distribution, street theater, Internet chat rooms, communication via mobile screens placed in various parts of the city, and anything else the new virtual imagination can come up with. If we cannot speak to the misinformed electorate through the traditional media, we need to invent others.

Likewise, on the more traditional party political level of participating in TV interviews (in which one surprises the adversary with unexpected comments), the opposition must launch its *own* provocations.

What do I mean by opposition provocation? Coming up with plans for government on issues about which public opinion is sensitive, proposing ideas about the future organization of the country calculated to make the media devote at least as much attention to them as they do to Berlusconi's provocations.

In a purely Machiavellian spirit (we're talking about politics, after all), I hold that, within the limits of decency, provocation could go beyond the feasible. To give an example, a plan could be proposed that called for a law that a left-wing government would immediately pass: to prohibit any individual from owning more than one TV station (or more than one newspaper and one station). It would explode like a bomb. Berlusconi would be forced to react, this time in defense and not in attack, and by doing so he would give a voice to his opponents. He would be the one to declare the existence of a conflict (or convergence) of interests, and could not blame it on the ill will of his opponents. Nor could he launch accusations of communism against an antimonopoly law tailored to increase access to private ownership of the media.

There's no need to push on into the realm of science fiction. A plan for the control of price increases that result from the introduction of the euro would hit home even with those indifferent to the conflict-of-interests issue.

In short, a series of continuous, positive proposals could give the public a glimpse of another way of governing, could challenge the majority by forcing it to say whether it is in agreement or not. The majority would thus need to discuss and defend its projects and justify its shortcomings—without taking refuge in generic accusations about an aggressive opposition. If you tell people that the government was wrong to do this or that, the people might think that you are wrong. But if you tell the people that *you* would like to do this or that, the idea might strike the imagination and interest of many, thus provoking questions about why the majority hasn't done it.

But to work out a strategy of this kind, the opposition must be united, because you can't come up with acceptable, appealing projects if you spend twelve hours a day on infighting. And here we encounter another obstacle, seemingly insurmountable, an age-old tradition: left-wing movements all over the world have always been taken up by struggles against their own internal heresies, giving these fraternal conflicts priority over the frontal battle against the adversary.

Yet without overcoming this obstacle, we cannot begin to think about a political offensive that will occupy the attention of the media with provocative projects, and beat Berlusconi at his own game. If we don't embrace this logic, which may not please everyone, but is nonetheless the logic of our media-obsessed universe, there's little to do except demonstrate against the flour tax.

Il Duce's Eyes

Last week it was my birthday, and with the close friends who came to celebrate it with me, I thought of the day of my birth. I have an excellent memory but don't recall that moment; I can only reconstruct it through what my parents told me. It seems that, when the gynecologist extracted me from my mother's womb and all the things that needed doing in such cases were done, he presented my mother with the admirable results of her labor and exclaimed: "Look at those eyes, he looks like il Duce!" My family was neither Fascist nor anti-Fascist—like many families of the Italian petit bourgeoisie, it took the dictatorship much like a meteorological event—but when a mother and father heard someone say that their new baby had eyes like il Duce, they must have been pleased.

"Il Duce's Eyes" appeared in la Repubblica, *January 2004.*

Having become a skeptic over the years, I now suspect that the good gynecologist said the same thing to every mother and father, but if I look at myself in the mirror and find myself more like a grizzly bear than il Duce, it doesn't matter. My parents were happy to hear that I looked like il Duce.

I wonder what an ingratiating gynecologist might say to a new mother today. That her baby looks like Berlusconi or the neo-Fascist parliamentarian and Rasputin look-alike Ignazio La Russa? No, a smart gynecologist would say that the newborn has the penetrating gaze of this or that TV host, the dazzling smile of this or that actor . . .

Every epoch has its myths. The one in which I was born had the myth of the Man of State; the one in which today's children are born has the myth of the Man of Television. Thanks to the usual blindness of left-wing culture, Berlusconi's recent statement (that no one reads the papers and everyone watches television) was taken as the latest of his gaffes. It wasn't: it was an act of arrogance, not of stupidity. If we add up the circulation figures of the Italian press, we get a fairly paltry number compared with the number of people who watch television. Moreover, if we observe that only a part of the Italian press is still critical of the present government and that the entire television network, the state-owned channels (RAI) plus Mediaset, has become the mouthpiece of power, Berlusconi was absolutely right. The problem is controlling television, and the press can say what it wants. This is a fact, and facts are facts precisely because they are independent of our wishes.

So in our day, if there is to be a dictatorship, it has to be a media dictatorship and not a political one. For almost fifty years people have been writing that in the modern world, except for some remote Third World countries, you no longer need tanks to bring down a government, just take over the radio and TV stations. The last person to notice this was George W. Bush, a Third World leader who mistakenly ended up governing a highly developed country. Now the theorem has been demonstrated.

It's wrong to say that you can't talk about Berlusconi's regime because *regime* calls up the Fascist regime and the regime in which we are living isn't at all like that. A regime is simply a form of government. Fascism abolished the freedom of the press, but Berlusconi's "media regime" is not so coarse and antiquated. He knows that consensus is managed through control of the most pervasive information media. As for the least pervasive, it costs nothing to allow a few newspapers to dissent (those you can't yet buy—ownership, I mean, not a copy). What's the point of detaining an opposition journalist like Enzo Biagi and thereby risk making him a hero? Just keep him off television, and he will be forgotten.

The difference between the Fascist regime and today's media regime is that, in the former, people knew that the press and radio issued only government-approved news, and that you couldn't listen to Radio London on pain of a prison sentence. It was precisely for this reason that, under Fascism, people mistrusted the press and radio, listened to Radio London with the volume low, and put their trust only in news that reached them by word of mouth. In a media regime where, say, ten percent of the population read the opposition press while the rest get their news through controlled TV channels, people believe that dissent is accepted ("Newspapers speak out against the government, and proof of this lies in the fact that Berlusconi is always complaining about it, therefore we have freedom"), but the reality created by TV news programs (if I hear that a plane has crashed and see the sandals of the dead floating on the water, it doesn't matter if the images shown are stock footage from a previous disaster) ensures that we know and believe only what the television says.

Television under government control doesn't need to censor the news. The minions of power do make attempts at censorship, like the most recent attempt in which it was deemed inadmissible for people to speak badly of the head of government on TV—heedless of the fact that in a democratic society you may speak badly of the head of government, otherwise you're in a dictatorship. But these are only the most visible (and, were they not so serious, laughable) cases. The problem is that you can establish a media regime in a *positive* way, giving the impression that you are saying all there is to say. All you need to know is how to say it.

If no television channel said what a leading opposition figure like Piero Fassino thinks about a certain law, viewers would begin to suspect that the television is concealing something, because they know that there's an opposition out there somewhere. So television in a media regime employs a rhetorical device known as "concession." Let's give an example. With regard to the question of buying a dog, there are fifty pros and fifty cons. The pros are that the dog is man's best friend, that it will bark if burglars try to break in, that the children will love it, and so on. The cons are that you have to walk it every day so that it can see to its bodily needs, that it costs money in food and vet fees, and that it's hard to take it with you when you're traveling . . .

If you wish to speak in favor of buying a dog, the device of concession is: "It's true that a dog is expensive to keep and you can't take it with you when traveling"—and the antidog people will appreciate your honesty—"but you should remember that a dog makes excellent company, is adored by the children, guards against burglars, and so on." This argument is in favor of dogs. Those against would concede that it's true a dog makes excellent company, is adored by the children, and guards against burglars, but—the counterargument follows—a dog is an expense and a problem when traveling. And this argument is against dogs.

Television works this way. If there is a debate about a law, the issue is presented and the opposition is immediately given the chance to put forward all its arguments. This is followed by government supporters, who counter the objections. The result is predictable: he who speaks last is right. If you carefully follow all the TV news programs, you will see this strategy: the project is presented, the opposition speaks first, the government supporters speak last. Never the other way around.

A media regime has no need to imprison its opponents. It doesn't silence them by censorship, it merely has them give their arguments *first*.

How do you oppose a media regime, given that to oppose it you must have the same access to the media that the media regime actually controls?

Until the opposition in Italy finds a solution to this problem and stops its precious infighting, Berlusconi will be the winner.

Killing Little Birds

With regard to the debate about the kind of regime that the Berlusconi government is slowly establishing in Italy, it's worth trying to clarify a few terms—*conservative, reactionary, Fascist, Poujadist, populist,* and so on. Reactionaries maintain that there is an ancient wisdom, a traditional model of the social and moral order, to which we must return at all costs by opposing the so-called achievements of progress, from liberal-democratic ideas to technology and modern science. Reactionaries are not conservatives; if anything, they are backward-looking revolutionaries. History provides us with many examples of great reactionaries who had nothing in common with any twentieth-century Fascist ideology. In fact, Italian Fascism was "revolutionary-modernist" compared to classic reactionary canons. Yet while the Fascists worshiped speed and modern technology (as embodied by the Futurist movement), at the same time—thanks to that rather infantile tendency toward syncretism typical of the movement—they could cheerfully recruit an ideologue like Julius Evola, a reactionary in the historical sense of the term.

Conservatives are not reactionaries, and even less are they fascists. Churchill, for example, held liberal and antitotalitarian views.

"Killing Little Birds" appeared in L'espresso, *March 2004.*

Populism is a form of regime that attempts to bypass parliament in order to establish an immediate plebiscitary relationship between a charismatic leader and the masses. There have been cases both of revolutionary populism, where an appeal to the people was made in order to propose social reforms, and of reactionary populism. Populism is simply a method that plays on the visceral attraction of what are believed to be the most deeply entrenched opinions or prejudices of the masses (sentiments referred to as Poujadism or, in Italy, *qualunquismo*). Italy's Northern League leader, Umberto Bossi, uses populist methods while appealing to Poujadist sentiments, such as xenophobia and mistrust of the state. In this respect there is something definitely Poujadist about Berlusconi's recent appeals to deep, "primitive" feelings—such as the idea that tax evasion is legitimate, that politicians are all thieves, and that the judiciary is not to be trusted because judges put people in prison.

Serious-minded, responsible conservatives would never encourage citizens to avoid paying taxes, because this would jeopardize the very system they want to conserve.

In the light of these various attitudes, many themes of the current political debate are cross-party issues. Take the death penalty. Conservatives may support or oppose it. Reactionaries are usually for it, because they cling to myths like that of sacrifice, reparation, and the purifying qualities of blood (see de Maistre). Populists can turn the death penalty to good account by playing on the apprehensions of the common people in the face of heinous crimes. And communist regimes have never questioned its use.

The attitude toward the environment is different. The preservation of Mother Earth, even at the cost of eliminating the human species, is a singularly reactionary cause. But a responsible conservative (not Bush, who bows to industrial powers interested in uncontrolled development) may fight to defend the environment as much as a left-wing revolutionary extremist. Populists might be in favor of respecting the environment, but only if this is in accord with the will of the people. Over the centuries farmers respected the environment with regard to the agricultural methods within their limited sphere of activity. But they deforested whenever it suited them, not worrying about the consequences on a global scale. If it seems that our countrymen of yore respected the environment more than their modern counterparts do, it's only because forests were so plentiful in those days that their destruction was not considered a problem. "Everyone has the right to build his house wherever he wishes, without being bound by environmental restrictions" might thus be a successful populist battle cry.

In Italy today there is a debate about a bill designed to extend the rights of hunters beyond all measure. Hunting is a popular practice based on atavistic feelings. If society sanctions the raising of chickens, cattle, and pigs to be slaughtered and eaten, why not accept—in special preserves, far from populated areas and in specific seasons—that hunters can kill edible animals that are not endangered species? But within limits. The bill in question, however, would take these limits back to the time before ecological concerns. Why? Because it appeals to an ancestral drive, to the "people" who—mistrustful of any criticism or reform of tradition—form the backbone of all Poujadist-type movements.

This proposed bill emphasizes yet again the populist-Poujadist nature of a creeping regime that appeals to the lower instincts of the less critically oriented segments of the electorate.

Deserting Parliament

On the day when Italian premier Silvio Berlusconi appeared on a major TV talk show to announce the forthcoming withdrawal of the Italian contingent in Iraq, and over the days that followed, I was in Paris for the opening of a book fair. And so I had the chance to talk about Italian affairs with the French, who are specialists in never

---

"Deserting Parliament" appeared in L'espresso, *March 2005.*

understanding exactly what is going on in Italy—often not without reason.

First question: Why did your prime minister announce such a serious decision on a TV show and not in Parliament, where he would have had to ask for opinions or a consensus? I explained that Berlusconi is establishing a regime by mass media populism. The media are used to forge a direct link between the Leader and the people, thus eroding the authority of Parliament. The Leader doesn't need to seek a consensus, because consensus is guaranteed, therefore Parliament becomes a rubber stamp for the agreements made between Berlusconi and talk show host Bruno Vespa.

The questions came thick and fast over the following days, when after severe reprimands from Bush and Blair, Berlusconi stated that he had never said he would withdraw the troops from Iraq. How can he contradict himself like that? people asked me. I replied that this is the good thing about media populism. If you say something in Parliament, it's on the record and you can't say later that you didn't say it. By saying it on TV instead, Berlusconi achieved his goal, which was to gain popularity with the voters. Afterward, when he said he hadn't said it, he reassured Bush—yet without losing the popularity he had gained. Why? Because one of the virtues of the mass media is that the people who follow them (and don't read the papers) forget by the next day what was said the day before, or at most they retain the impression that Berlusconi did something agreeable.

But, my questioners observed, don't the Italians realize that Berlusconi (and Italy with him) will lose credibility not only with Chirac and Schroeder but also with Bush and Blair? No, I replied, the Italians who read the papers may realize this, but they are few compared with those who get their news only from television, and Italian television only gives the news that Berlusconi likes. And this is regime by mass media populism.

Populism Yes, the Masses No

At a meeting in Rimini of the Catholic organization known as Comunione e Liberazione, Marcello Pera, the president of the Senate, warned that politics is made not "in the streets" but in the appointed places, in other words in the two houses of Parliament. In saying this, he gave voice to much irritation within the majority regarding certain expressions of opposition, such as the *girotondi*.

Respectable as this opinion is, it contradicts the spirit of the Western democracies, where it's true that there are three powers—legislative, executive, and judicial—and that the place to hold political debates is parliament, but where it is recognized that the citizens (who elect parliament, after all) also have the right to keep a check on the various powers of the state, to judge their doings, to call for action if need be, and to express any dissatisfaction with the way public business is conducted. In this sense the voice of the electorate, heard not only on election day, is useful to parliament and government alike—to the latter, because it sends a signal, provides a stimulus; to the former, because popular dissatisfaction can be a guide for the next election (note the importance of opinion polls, which would otherwise be a form of unlawful lobbying).

Let it be clear that this voice of the electorate has nothing to do with that "will of the people" to which populism appeals. Populism is a direct appeal to the people (or to a presumptive interpretation of the popular will) made by the leadership; demonstrations in the streets do not represent a generic voice of the people but the free expression of groups, parties, and citizens' associations.

How is the opinion of the electorate expressed? Through newspapers, associations, parties, and opinion leaders, but also through what happens on the streets. Make no mistake, if by action in the streets we mean a disturbance by extremists who smash property,

---

"Populism Yes, the Masses No" appeared in L'espresso, *August 2002.*

then it's called a riot or a revolution, and that's another matter. But democracy has room for many other, peaceful, kinds of demonstrations. They do not have to be huge totalitarian affairs; demonstrations can also be limited to a small group, even just two or three people, who assemble in public to say what they think or want.

Take a look outside Parliament in England, or in any American city, and you will see citizens holding placards, chanting slogans, and trying to involve passersby. In Hyde Park Corner, you will see people on soapboxes haranguing onlookers. But you don't have to go to London; Italian cities also have places where people meet spontaneously to discuss the political events of the day. Demonstrations can be enormous, such as the anti–Vietnam War protest held in Washington in 1969, an event that shook the nation. Such occasions can be sponsored by both the left and right wings, and Italians will remember the forty thousand people who demonstrated in Turin right in the middle of the trade union struggle, to express the position of the so-called white-collar worker, or the demonstrations held by the "silent majorities," the marches organized by the right-wing coalition (Polo), and the pseudo-Celtic celebrations held by the Northern League.

Trade union demonstrations, because of the simple fact that they draw millions and not hundreds of people, and the *girotondi,* because they are picturesque, are somehow considered more antidemocratic than someone like the Radical Party leader Marco Pannella when he has himself put in chains or drinks his own urine in public.

Obviously, when it comes to demonstrations, number is important. It is number that underpins democracy, where the winners are more numerous than the losers. When conducted in a nonviolent fashion, street demonstrations are an expression of civil liberties, and we see as dictatorships those countries where such events are forbidden, or where the leadership organizes simulacra of them, like the immense crowds that thronged Piazza Venezia in Rome during the Fascist period. Such demonstrations were dubious not because of their proportions but because it was impossible to hold counter-demonstrations of different political persuasions.

Now let's ask ourselves what the Rimini meeting is. It isn't a parliamentary session, and it's not a seminar for experts. Like communist party fund-raising operations such as the Feste dell'Unità—indeed more so, because it's held right in the center of the city—the Rimini meeting is a "street" affair, as legitimate as all the others, and it comes with a guaranteed political impact.

And where did the president of the Senate deliver his speech against street demonstrations? In the street, during a rally held outside the houses of Parliament and with a view to expressing the opinions of a part of the citizenry. So this condemnation of street political activity that occurred in the streets seems like the act of a moralist who, wishing to condemn the practice of flashing, shows up in front of the cathedral, opens his raincoat, and displays his organ while yelling, "Don't ever do this!"

The Italy of the Comedians: A Tragic Situation

There are times in which a country is on tenterhooks waiting for an event that could change the course of its history. I imagine that this is how the ancient Romans felt after Caesar's murder and before Mark Anthony's speech, or more modestly how the Italians felt in 1943 when the radio issued the sober announcement that Benito Mussolini had been relieved of his post and the reins of government had been handed to Marshal Badoglio. On the basis of personal experience, and in the numerous pages that all the major Italian newspapers devoted to the event, such suspense occurred regarding Roberto Benigni's appearance at the San Remo Song Festival.

The right-wing journalist (and former communist) Giuliano Ferrara is no fool, and when he didn't do what he promised to do (throw

---

"The Italy of the Comedians" appeared in L'espresso, *March 2002.*

eggs and vegetables at the "comedian of the regime," who opposes
the new regime), he must have had a reason. Although only an ig-
noramus in mass communications (which Ferrara certainly is not) or
an undercover agent of the communist party who infiltrated the
ranks of the Polo (which Ferrara cannot be, since by now the communist party exists only in the prime minister's fervid imagination)
could have hatched a plot that, however it went, would have harmed
the government. To understand the sensational aspect of the affair,
you have to bear in mind that Benigni is an international cult figure.
Some people may not like him, but the fact remains that what he
does is of interest worldwide. Once the threat was made, there were
three possibilities:

The first possibility: Benigni appears at San Remo, and the ex-
communists who have defected to the right interrupt his show by
throwing eggs. The international press announces Italy's new Fascism and protests against this attempt to run roughshod over the
right to freedom of expression.

The second possibility: Benigni appears at San Remo, talks
about "pussy" and other perineal fripperies that characterize this
festival, and doesn't talk politics. Even worse. The international
press bemoans this clear example of psychological terrorism, which
is a form of censorship. In Italy, the press says, no one can express
his opinions now because there are Fascist paramilitary squads.

The third possibility: Benigni appears, talks about the weather,
then begs the presenter not to provoke him, because it's dangerous
to say certain things, we've gone back to the time when we listened
to Radio London in secret. Please don't make me say anything, I
have a family, and so on. Uproar throughout the international press.

Benigni was wiser. I think he did what he would have done even
without Ferrara's provocation. He knew he was appearing not as a
private citizen on an opposition talk show but as an actor on a show
watched by millions of Italians of all political persuasions. Instead
of the usual polemics, he made an appeal for love, stunned the au-

dience by reciting Dante (Benigni is a prodigious reader of Dante, and, as many people are perhaps unaware, he is a highly cultured person). And who would start booing Dante's sublime verses on the Virgin Mary?

No one was expecting the Dante idea (at San Remo of all places!). You have to be a genius to come up with that one. Standing ovation, rapturous applause. Benigni wins, as expected. Never run against someone smarter than you are.

But I think Ferrara considers himself the winner too. He probably thinks that if he hadn't stirred things up, Benigni would have done worse. But in what way, given that all he had to do was allude to the conflict of interests and false accounting, and the audience was in stitches? What Benigni said is common knowledge, and people would have considered it a comical (or more tragically, grotesque) topic even if he hadn't said it.

At the end of the day, we are left with a few melancholy reflections. For some time now everything that happens in Italy, everything that makes waves or creates disquiet, is done by comedians. The rule holds for many cartoonists, and especially for the stories dug up by satirical TV shows. Some Italians will remember when the country's ills were exposed by magazines like *L'espresso* (which during the fifties denounced the corruption of many public institutions), by the opposition, and by the judiciary. No more. No one is interested in what goes on in Parliament (Berlusconi says it's not worth going there to repeat what everyone knows already), political parties are towed along by spontaneous rallies, and the bombshell of the year came not from a politician but from an artist, the film director Nanni Moretti, who accused the opposition of not doing its job. Is a country healthy when comedians and artists are the only ones to inspire argument and debate, obviously without being able to suggest solutions?

On mature reflection, however, this is due not to the fact that comedians are going to Parliament but to the fact that government has fallen into the hands of comedians, or that many people who in the past would have been music hall characters have wound up in government.

How to Make a Contract with the Romans

In 64 BC Marcus Tullius Cicero, already a renowned orator but nonetheless a "new man," unrelated to the nobility, decided to run for consul. His brother Quintus Tullius wrote a little manual for him in which he provided advice on how to succeed in this undertaking. Luca Canali has written an Italian version of this with the original Latin on the facing page. The booklet comes complete with commentary explaining the historical and personal circumstances of that campaign. Furio Colombo wrote the introduction, which includes some polemical reflections on modern Italy's so-called First Republic.

In fact, in its merits (precious few) and demerits, that Roman republic was very similar to our Second Republic. In the course of over two millennia, Rome has had a great influence on successive concepts of the state. As Colombo points out, it was the model of the oldest Roman republic that inspired the authors of the Federalist Papers, who drafted the basic outlines of what was to become the American Constitution, and who saw Rome rather than Athens as an example of popular democracy. With greater realism, the neocons surrounding Bush are inspired by the image of imperial Rome, and much of the current political debate in the United States harks back to both the idea of empire and that of the Pax Americana, with an explicit reference to the Pax Romana.

The image of electoral competition that emerges from Quintus's twenty pages is far less virtuous than the one that inspired the eighteenth-century federalists. Quintus's thinking had nothing to do

---

"How to Make a Contract with the Romans" appeared in L'espresso, *July 2004.*

with politicians who offer their electorate a courageous plan and who are prepared to face opposition in the hope of winning over the voters with a captivating utopia. As Canali points out, Quintus's pages hold no trace of any discussion of ideas; the only idea is that one should never make enemies. For Quintus, the ideal candidate should be charming, do favors, promise things, and never say no to anyone, because it is enough to let people think that something will be done: voters have a short memory and will soon forget about yesterday's promises.

Colombo's interpretation tends to highlight the "incredible affinities, resemblances, and assonances that seem to cross the centuries." The persons referred to in the text as *salutatores*, who go to pay homage to several candidates, are today's "fence sitters," while the *deductores*, whose continual presence attests to the candidate's importance, also serve to enhance his visibility and (mutatis mutandis) carry out the function today performed by television.

The electoral campaign emerges as a spectacle of form, in which what matters is not what the candidate actually stands for but how he appears to others. As Quintus says, the problem—no matter how much importance natural talent has—is to ensure that simulation gets the better of nature.

On the other hand, "flattery is detestable when it makes someone worse, but . . . it is indispensable for a candidate whose attitude, character, and way of expressing himself must change from time to time to adapt themselves to the thoughts and desires of whomever he meets." This must be done in such a way "that your entire electoral campaign is solemn, brilliant, splendid, and popular too. . . . Whenever you can, make sure that your opponents are tainted with some suspicion . . . of iniquity, debauchery, or profligacy." In short, excellent advice, which looks as if it were written today, and one immediately thinks for whose benefit—the reader reads Quintus but thinks Silvio.

When you finish reading, you wonder: Is this really what democracy is all about? A way to gain public favor, based only on orches-
trated appearances and a strategy of deceit? It certainly involves
these things, nor could it be otherwise in a system where power may
be attained solely through consensus and not by force and violence.
But let's not forget that this advice for a wholly "virtual" electoral
campaign was given at a point when Roman democracy was already
in crisis. Shortly afterward, Caesar seized power with the support of
his legions, establishing a de facto principality, while Cicero paid
with his life for the shift from a regime based on consensus to one
based on a coup d'état.

It's hard not to conclude that Roman democracy began to die
when its politicians felt that it wasn't necessary to take policy seriously, only to work out how to be liked by their (how to put it?)
television audience.

Foreigners and Us

Trash and Bananas

As many readers already know, some foreign newspapers have run articles questioning whether the Polo's candidate for prime minister is fit to run the country. That the candidate called those papers trash is understandable. Similarly, when a woman rejects a man's attentions, it is a national custom in Italy for him to call her a lady of easy virtue.

But other voices have been heard complaining about the foreign press's interference in our affairs. That Senator Cossiga said as much is irrelevant because, as the old toothpaste ad goes, with a mouth like that he can say what he wants. That Senator Andreotti also said as much is more complex: the kind of man he is, if he said it, he meant something else. But what struck me was the statement made by Senator Agnelli, who (if the main dailies are not lying) said that the foreign press talks about Italian voters as if Italy were a banana republic.

Senator Agnelli is not only a scrupulous reader of the news, he also has a deeper relationship with the press. So over the years he

---

"Trash and Bananas" appeared in L'espresso, *May 2001.*

must have read in the Italian papers (his own *La Stampa* included) articles about Clinton's conduct, Bush's diplomatic gaffes, the scandals surrounding the Mitterand administration, the Tapies case, the overwhelming power of Bill Gates, the not always irreproachable behavior of certain members of the British royal family, Sharon's policies, not to mention the harshest judgments on Milošević or Haider.

As far as I know, in none of these cases (except perhaps for the last two) did foreigners complain that our articles were an interference in their national affairs. So why do the Italian papers have the right to express opinions about the political situation in other countries, while the foreign press cannot do the same about Italy?

By this reasoning, if a public prosecutor accuses us of a crime, then he is the agent of a plot, and if instead he acquits us, he is virtuous and upright. It's like saying that *The Economist* is trash because it criticizes the Polo candidate, but *The Times* is a model of journalism because it is more indulgent toward him. Where will we end up if we fall into such barbarism?

Literature is not the same thing as politics, but I have never heard of a writer (no matter how touchy) who, upon being panned in the book section of *The New York Times,* called that authoritative publication trash or claimed to be the victim of a demo-pluto-Judaic conspiracy. And if any writer did such a thing, we would think he suffered from severe elephantiasis of the ego.

Yes, there are countries where foreign newspapers are banned if they criticize the government, and the local press censures them. But such countries are known as dictatorships, and some are indeed banana republics.

But why are we so scornful of banana republics? They have governments that must be very easy to deal with, given that many respectable persons do lucrative business with them and transfer their capital to their (off) shores.

Going Against the Flow

Even before the elections, some foreign newspapers expressed the fear that Berlusconi might win, and people complained about this interference, forgetting that the Italian press has frequently criticized (legitimately) electoral candidates in France and the United States, even dwelling caustically on the scandals that occur in friendly nations.

Once the elections were over, various foreign-language papers condemned various initiatives promoted by our prime minister, from imprudent statements about the superiority of Western culture to the various laws that led these barbarians (who speak in strange, unknown tongues) to suspect that the new government might pursue private interests while in public office. The responses showed great irritation, and the line followed by Berlusconi and some of his spokesmen was more or less as follows: these papers are left-wing, influenced by left-wing Italian politicians who persuade them to write defamatory articles about our country.

In this way an image was presented, and persistently circulated, of left-wingers like D'Alema or Fassino or Rutelli who pick up the phone, call the editors of newspapers—maybe even conservative ones—in Spain, France, and Great Britain, asking them to write articles against the Honorable Member Berlusconi. These editors snap to attention, say, "Yes sir," dip their pens in vitriol, and off we go, let's demonize him.

This account portrays the international press as a mafia, and it's only now that we realize how closely it reflects Berlusconi's idea of relations with the media—I say only now, after we have seen the prime minister clearly order the board of directors and the director general of RAI TV to sack journalists who are, let's say, reluctant to adulate him.

"Going Against the Flow" appeared in L'espresso, *May 2002.*

But let's try to be indulgent. Perhaps the conspiracy that Berlusconi complains about really exists and every foreign correspondent in Italy is a slave of the left. In that case, if Rutelli, Fassino, and D'Alema have such power over dailies worldwide, independently of their political position, and if we are to uphold Italy's international prestige, then we ought to hand government back to them without delay.

But worse things have happened. Jospin and Chirac, in the course of their electoral campaign, made Berlusconi and the Italian situation a negative benchmark. In other words, in their search for votes, they promised not to do what Berlusconi is doing. As if to say: "Look, I'm a decent person, I won't do in my country what Berlusconi is doing in Italy."

This is not a first. Many politicians have run for office saying that they wouldn't behave like the Soviet Union, or Haider, that they weren't Nazis or Stalinists, that they harbored no authoritarian ambitions, that they didn't want their country to be reduced to the level of those governed by Idi Amin Dada, François Duvalier, Saddam Hussein, and so on. That Jospin—a socialist, ex-Trotskyite, and a Protestant into the bargain—should choose Berlusconi as a negative example is obvious: Jospin is a member (from the Polo's point of view) of a communist international. But the other player to join that game was Chirac, perhaps (after Margaret Thatcher) the most typical representative of the European right. Chirac says to his supporters, "Vote for the right, because we won't do what Berlusconi is doing."

At this point the idea that D'Alema, Rutelli, and Fassino picked up the phone to tell Chirac to help them is no longer tenable. Such an idea wouldn't enter the head of any satirist or comedian, no matter what his political loyalties. As they say these days, No way.

Which leads me to a question, which I hope will also strike many supporters of the Polo. Could it be that our prime minister always does exactly what a prime minister, of whatever political persuasion, should not do? Every one of us, in his own field, industrialist, businessman, or writer, always does his best to make Italy look good abroad. Of all people, why should the prime minister be the one to go against the flow?

Many a Slip Twixt Cup and Lip

As I write, the debate has just begun about the American announcement that Italy will take part in the Iraqi war, while here in Italy everyone is dumbfounded, including the prime minister (obviously, because decisions of this kind must be made by Parliament). A coup de main on Bush's part to force Italy's hand? Nothing of the kind. It's a question of social anthropology.

It's hard to say who the Americans really are, because they are the descendants of the old British Protestant pioneers, Jews, Italians, Irish, Poles, Puerto Ricans, and God knows how many others. But what makes the United States a nation is the fact that all Americans have absorbed a fundamental principle, one that—when the time is right—also fuels their patriotism. The principle is very simple: This is the country where I make a living and allows me, if I can, to become rich, so I must accept some of its rules for coexistence. Not "must respect the law," because the United States has its share of criminals, gangsters, and thieving financiers, and then there are the dropouts, the outcasts, the tramps, and the homeless who live in basements. But even these people, as they break the law, make an effort to comply with the rules for coexistence.

For example, at the railroad station as in the supermarket, people respect the line. It's inconceivable for someone not to. The line is respected to such a point that if the person in front of us is making difficulties and keeps the cashier or the clerk busy, the others may grumble but won't protest. That person came first and has every right to be there. I recall that once, arriving late at La Guardia

---

"Many a Slip Twixt Cup and Lip" appeared in L'espresso, *February 2003.*

on a flight from the Midwest, I had just enough time to hop into a cab and reach Kennedy Airport for my return flight to Italy. There was an enormous line for cabs, and I realized that I wasn't going to make it. Desperate, I went to the head of the line and said to those who were waiting: "Ladies and gentlemen, I have barely enough time to get to Kennedy Airport in order to fly back to Europe where urgent business awaits me. Would you be so kind as to let me pass to the head of the line?" I never saw so many stunned faces in my life: it was the first time that something like this had happened to them. Bemused, the first ten people gestured at me to go ahead, probably thinking that I had done such a thing only because my house was burning down with my children inside it. I took the first cab and, as I thanked them, understood that I had committed an enormity so great that the people in the line hadn't had the courage to protest. The line is sacred.

Another fundamental rule is that one tells the truth, so you are taken at your word. If people invite you to some occasion and you say you're sorry, but you're busy, they express their regrets and ask no more questions. But it is unthinkable to say yes and then fail to turn up. You also tell the truth to the taxman: Al Capone went to prison not for the St. Valentine's Day massacre but because he had lied to the tax authorities, and Nixon too lost his job because he told a lie.

This trusting nature (naïveté, Europeans might say) of Americans has its grotesque aspects. Once, in America, I lost my credit card and didn't know whom to call. A friend of mine saw to everything and got in touch with the proper office. But at the end of the phone call, the woman at the credit card company asked him if he was Mr. Eco. When he answered no, she said that a new card could be issued only if she spoke to Mr. Eco in person. My friend handed me the phone, and I assured her that I was indeed Mr. Eco. The woman believed me, and I received a new card within twenty-four hours. That it could have been someone else on the phone and I was lying never crossed the clerk's mind. In any case she was covered.

Which explains what happened with Bush. Our prime minister, as usual lavish with promises, must have told him, "Don't worry, I'll see to things, you have our complete support." And Bush believed him. It's not that Bush is incapable of lying when he speaks to his fellow citizens: but that is mass communication, molded on the principles of advertising, and in advertising you may lie. In personal agreements, or when dealing with the authorities, you may not. Bush doesn't know that in Italy people say out of politeness, "Call me, and we'll get together" or "Next time you're in the neighborhood, come for dinner," when they have no intention of seeing that person again. Berlusconi promised him something, and Bush thought he meant it, while our prime minister was just talking, working on the principle that *verba volant*.

That's why I said at the beginning that it's a question of social anthropology. But even in politics you ought to know that outside your own country the rules may not be the same.

That's Texas, Baby!

The press has already run the story about the poll, held in America, about the hundred best (or best remembered) lines from the history of the cinema. Obviously, the poll dealt solely with American cinema. The winner was Gable's "Frankly, my dear, I don't give a damn" remark to Vivien Leigh at the end of *Gone with the Wind*. No objections on my part, just as I find it right that the list contains a few lines from *Casablanca* and one from *Yankee Doodle Dandy*, where Cagney at his all-time best winds up the show by introducing his likable family: "My mother thanks you. My father thanks you. My sister thanks you. And I thank you."

"That's Texas, Baby!" appeared in L'espresso, *July 2005.*

Those who remember this cult classic will warm to the memory. That said, I was struck by the absence of two items. One is from a film whose Italian title, *L'ultima minaccia* ("The Ultimate Threat"), is always hard to recall (probably because it has nothing to do with the plot). The original title was *Deadline USA,* and the story was about the freedom of the press. The finale shows Bogart replying to a caller who is threatening him in a bid to ensure that a certain article does not come out. Bogart lets him hear the sound of the presses, saying: "That's the power of the press, baby. The power of the press. And there's nothing you can do about it." The English is a bit redundant, and perhaps this is why Americans don't remember it very well. For us (the film reached Italy in the early fifties), this line was a good lesson in democracy, and every day I pray that we Italians will be able to go on repeating it for a long time to come.

But, since I have an obvious weakness for both Bogart and *Casablanca,* I feel a burning outrage at the absence of another quotation, and I attribute this lapse to the fact that it wasn't a one-liner but an exchange of dialogue.

In Rick's Café Americain, Bogart is responding to the remonstrations of Yvonne, a girl of not-so-difficult virtue with whom he evidently had a casual erotic interlude: "Where were you last night?—That's so long ago, I don't remember. —Will I see you tonight? —I never make plans that far ahead."

This is sublime dialogue, and I don't need to explain why, because you can't explain it to those who don't get it. But are lines from films the only historic ones? Immediately after the recent Italian referendum on stem cell research, I learned, as I was traveling across the United States, that the Italian politician Rocco Buttiglione said as follows (did he really say it? the *New York Times* says he did; it's the power of the press, baby, and there's nothing you can do about it): "Italy has shown that it is more like Texas than like Massachusetts."

My American friends (even those from Texas) replied that this unknown gentleman must have been joking or else wished to mock their country. No, I said, he was serious. He wanted to say that Italy had improved.

I was reminded of another memorable line. Milan, the fifties, the state university. The event was a conference featuring a confrontation between analytic and Continental philosophers, Marxists and Catholics. The speaker was one of the last supporters of idealism (by then on Sunset Boulevard), and he was delivering a highly rhetorical eulogy of the Spirit ("That Spirit, which, by virtue of its *Aufhebung* unfolds itself as history in the world, etc., etc."). At a certain point, one of the reserve idealists in the audience got to his feet and yelled, "Long live the Spirit!"

The speaker paled and, lips and voice atremble, said: "Sir, if you wish to make game of things to which I have devoted my whole life. . . ." And the other, with a catch in his voice: "No, no, I was serious!" Upon which the speaker (and at this point the whole thing began to look more like something out of a Marx Brothers movie) threw open his arms and exclaimed: "If that's the case, come into my arms!" The pair met and embraced on the podium, while most of the people in the lecture hall gave themselves over to gusts of scornful cackling.

The Buttiglione story strikes me as being of the same stripe. I suppose that there will be someone—maybe someone who bought this book by mistake at the train station—who asks me what's so bad about being more like Texas than Massachusetts. Again, you can't explain it to those who don't get it.

Revisiting History

Some Recollections of My Childhood under Fascism

We are in the middle of a debate about the fact that many distinguished anti-Fascist intellectuals collaborated with the regime. Some have used this as a pretext to say, "So there were no heroes"; others argue more calmly, making distinctions between those who chose exile and those who were guilty of some weakness. But it seems to me that all such discussions assume ethical purity; they do not take certain sociological circumstances into account. As I was born in 1932, I grew up under Fascism until I was thirteen. Not enough to be a leading player, of course, but enough to understand some things: in those days, at about ten years of age, despite family legends, we managed to figure out that babies came from Mummy's belly.

The atmosphere was one of a lethargic but widespread consensus with regard to the regime. Longstanding liberals declared, on the day after the march on Rome, "Maybe this man will finally establish a little order in this country." At school they spoke to me about the "Fascist revolution," but afterward it became clear to me

"Some Recollections of My Childhood under Fascism" appeared in L'espresso, June 2000.

that Fascism hadn't arrived overnight, like the tanks in Budapest or
in Prague, but crept up on the country gradually. Even the Matteotti
case (with the channels of information in those days) was known and
assessed correctly by only a few people.

When a cousin of my father's, an ardent socialist, chanced to
visit on certain summer evenings, my mother would rush to close
the windows for fear that someone might overhear his enormities.
Some family members commented that perhaps "that man" had
good intentions but was surrounded by "bad company," but I believe that if that cousin had had to speed up, say, the red tape regarding a pension request, he would cheerfully have written an
obsequious letter to the authorities, because even dissenters did
such things.

Some chose exile; others went abroad to work as bricklayers.
That there weren't many of them doesn't mean that few could boast
a spotless conscience. In recent times we have read about twenty-
year-olds who, foreseeing imminent arrest, left Rome and headed
for the Val d'Aosta, where they gave a certain sum to a guide to take
them across the border. Now let's ask ourselves why all those anti-
Fascists who submitted to years of internment didn't do the same
thing, despite the fact that they too foresaw their fate. They didn't do
it because in those days Italy was a provincial country: it wasn't
easy to travel from Rome to the Val d'Aosta, that certain sum was
hard to come by, few people spoke a foreign language, they hadn't
traveled before so had had no acquaintances on the other side of the
Alps. They couldn't just drop a few coins in a phone box, call someone in Zurich, and ask to be met at the frontier.

If people accepted internment, it wasn't because they didn't
want to escape but because flight was a huge undertaking. Dissenters saw the dictatorship as their destiny, a world in which they
had no choice but to come to terms with institutions and where a
minimum of duplicity was considered the necessary (and legitimate)
tribute to be paid in order to survive.

It's as if we were to discover today that a person who spent ten years in one of Stalin's gulags had applied to the local soviet for a study grant before his arrest. Of course he would have done this, in Stalin's Russia it would never have occurred to anyone that there might be an alternative. Even ethical conduct should be judged with reference to the environment.

Overt Concealment

That debate has been going on for a long time, but it's clear that with the right in power, it has been tabled again, with greater vigor because as they say, History is rewritten by the winners. Hardly a day goes by without someone's inviting us to rediscover episodes from the last sixty years that have allegedly been carefully covered up by the dominant culture. A historian is always duty bound to reconsider even the battle of Poitiers, perhaps to reveal that it was a less decisive event than the historians of the past would have us believe, but if he were to suggest that the dominant culture had kept us in the dark about that battle, we would say he was exaggerating.

In 1945, at the end of the war, I was thirteen and a half. Old enough to have known the dictatorship, to have thrown myself into a ditch to avoid a fusillade of crossfire between Fascists and partisans, to know about the naval commandos of the Decima Mas, whom people thought of as good lads albeit a little on the idealistic side, and the men of the Brigate Nere (the Black Brigades), whom people tried to avoid, and that there were partisans on Badoglio's side who wore blue neckerchiefs and other partisans, known as Garibaldini, who wore red neckerchiefs.

Other things I learned later: an atomic bomb had been dropped on Hiroshima, German death camps had been discovered, the men of the Republic of Salò had been segregated at the Coltano concentration camp (from which they were released fairly early), Gentile

---

"Overt Concealment" appeared in L'espresso, May 2001.

was murdered, the Cervi brothers were shot by a firing squad, Ezra Pound was arrested for collaborating with the enemy, and at the end of hostilities some ex-partisans became bandits.

Since I was a bright little boy who read the newspapers and weeklies, I learned about the glorious events in Cephalonia, about the mass graves in Istria, and about the repression under Stalin. Reading later some letters written by those members of the resistance who had been condemned to death, I saw that their number included convinced Marxists, monarchists who died for the king, Catholics, and so on. That Marxist historiography heavily stressed the role played by communists in the struggle for liberation struck everyone as obvious. But the transformation of the resistance movement into legend was a very slow process, set in motion (and not only by the Marxists) as a legitimization of the democratic state, because everyone knew instinctively what the historian De Felice was later to rationalize: that, all things considered, the country had accepted the regime.

After the liberation there were purges, but within a few months many thousands of people, who had been Fascists but hadn't killed anyone, were reinstated in their positions, hence the country's bureaucratic backbone was still made up of people nostalgic about the recent past. Many Italians, if in jest, muttered that things were better when things were worse. In 1946, one year after the fall of Fascism, I saw on the walls the first posters put up by the neo-Fascist Movimento Sociale Italiano party. In the years immediately following, a large number of people read not the Communist Party daily *l'Unità* but right-wing publications such as *Il Borghese* and *Candido*. RAI TV began to talk with some intensity about the resistance only when President Saragat (and we are now in the sixties) took to ending his speeches declaring, "Long live Italy, long live the Republic!"—and even that struck many as a provocation.

So if as a young boy I learned about many things that had been covered up, it was because they were widely discussed. Or can it be, at that age, that I was the only Italian in possession of such confidential information?

The Hegemony of the Left

In the early 1960s, Marisa Bonazzi organized in Reggio Emilia a critical exhibition devoted to the textbooks used in Italian primary schools at that time. The exhibition showed duly enlarged pages from the books, complete with commentary. In 1972 the publisher Guaraldi brought out a book by Ms. Bonazzi and me titled *I pàmpini bugiardi* ("Deceitful Embellishments"), in which the comments on the incriminated texts were ironic notes and brief introductions to the various subjects (the poor, work, the homeland, race, civic education, history, science, money, and so on). But the texts really spoke for themselves. What emerged was an image of scholastic publishing that didn't limit itself to repeating the clichés found in readers and Fascist primary school books; it was even more retrograde, bound up with archaic stereotypes, and about as dated as a poor man's version of the style of the poet D'Annunzio and the Vittoriale, the overelaborate, monumental house he built in commemoration of his own oversized ego.

Here I give only two examples. One was a portrait of the World War I hero Nazario Sauro, which owed a debt to the busts of Mussolini: "In that robust body full of quick and ready blood, in that large, powerful head, in that most resolute gaze there has been instilled some of the immortal spirit that hovers over the fields, mountains, and seas of Italy to make it beautiful and strong, *unlike other homelands.*" The second was a chapter about June 2nd, which attempted to explain why the public holiday in honor of the Republic was celebrated with a military parade: "It is a river of iron, of uniforms, of soldiers lined up in perfect order. . . . Enormous tanks

---

"The Hegemony of the Left" appeared in la Repubblica, *November 2000.*

pass by, *the troop carriers that can convey men even through the cloud of an atomic explosion,* the great cannons, the swift, alert storm troops . . ." (the italics are mine).

Clearly, any texts that told children that our troop carriers could gaily drive through the fluffy cloud of an atomic explosion were mendacious texts. That little book of ours enjoyed a certain success, and, in its own small way, together with other critical works, it helped modernize schoolbooks. No authority stepped in; no censorship commission was set up. As happens with cultural matters, free criticism stimulated rethinking and new initiatives.

I think that this is how things should be done in a civilized country. I don't intend to give an opinion of the schoolbooks criticized by modern exponents of the far right like Francesco Storace. In any case I am not familiar with them. They may indeed contain debatable passages, but in a free country debatable passages are open to debate, provided the distinction between debate and censorship remains clear. If there is something scandalous, it will break out all by itself. Those who criticize must have the moral and cultural authority to back up their criticism: but these are medals won in the field.

I am not saying anything that hasn't been said before when I point out that a school textbook, no matter how many shortcomings it may have, interacts with the teacher's authority, and with information that the children receive (especially today) through many other channels. When I was in high school, our philosophy text was the authoritative but unreadable Lamanna, an idealist. Giacomo Marino, my philosophy master, was a Catholic (and a great teacher, who even told us about Freud and, so that we would understand Freud, invited us to read Stefan Zweig's *Mental Healers*). Marino had no love for Lamanna, and he gave us his own version of the history of philosophy. Even though I went on to become a professional philosopher, he taught me many of the things I know about philosophy today.

One day I asked this teacher of mine for the name of a good cultural magazine I might read, apart from *Fiera Letteraria* (run by Catholics in those days, but it dealt with everything). He advised me to try another authoritative Catholic publication, *Humanitas*. Which brings me to the problem of the cultural hegemony of the left.

Today most young people know little about the Italy of the old days, but if they were to read the papers and listen to political speeches (if they ever do such things), they would be convinced that from 1946 up to the Clean Hands Scandal, Italy was governed by the left, which, since it controlled the levers of power, had established its cultural hegemony over the country, the pernicious effects of which are evident to this day. I have to tell these young people that during the period in question Italy was run by the Christian Democratic Party, which had firm control of the Ministry of Education, that there were many flourishing Catholic publishing houses (like Morcelliana, SEI, Studium, Ave, and even a publisher run directly by the Christian Democrats, Cinque Lune), that Rizzoli was then a conservative house, that publishers like Mondadori, Bompiani, and Garzanti were not left-wing, that educational publishers like Le Monnier, Principato, and Vallardi were not run by members of the Communist Party, that the great weeklies like *la Domenica del Corriere, Epoca, Oggi,* and *Tempo* were not Marxist, and that the same certainly held for the national dailies, with the exception of *l'Unità* (bought only by those who voted communist), and that (not counting the houses run by the Communist Party, such as L'Universale del Canguro, whose only outlets were party-organized social or fund-raising events) the *only* left-wing publisher was Einaudi—which in 1948 brought out the first Italian book on Soviet dialectical materialism, and that was written by a Jesuit. Feltrinelli came afterward, and attained success with *The Leopard* and *Doctor Zhivago,* neither of which is a shining example of Marxist hegemony.

What is today referred to cursorily as left-wing culture is really lay, liberal, actionist, even Crocean culture. The universities were run by two large groups that shared the spoils: the Catholics and the secular community. And the lay community included pretty much everyone, even the few Marxist academics of those days.

How did lay culture establish a hegemony? Why didn't the ruling Christian Democratic Party oppose it, and why was it unable to counter the appeal of Bertolt Brecht with that of, say, Diego Fabbri?

It is not enough to say, as some people have recently said, that it was because the government was extremely broad-minded and tolerant. This is true in part, but in the 1950s I remember that some people working for the national broadcasting network (RAI) were refused permanent contracts explicitly because they voted communist, and if we took a look at the papers of those days, we would find polemics, shows of intolerance, and narrow-minded attitudes that are unacceptable today. But it would be fair to say that the party in power made a decision: Leave us the control of the economy, of public bodies, and of the spoils system, and we won't stick our nose overmuch into cultural affairs.

But this too explains little. Why, since the schools didn't make anyone read Gramsci (in fact, he was pointedly ignored), was a student supposed to read him instead of Maritain (or, at least, why did young Catholics of the period read Maritain, but also Gramsci and Gobetti)? When the magazine for committed young Christian Democrats, *Terza generazione*, attempted to bring together Gramsci and Gioberti, the initiative met with failure. Why was this, and why did poor Gioberti (who was no fool) end up abandoned on the shelves of the library? Why did the young Catholics of those days, who cut their teeth on the personalism of Mounier and on the works of Chenu or Congar, also succumb to the appeal of Pannunzio's *Il mondo*?

Because the spirit goes where it will. Catholic philosophy of the 1950s and 1960s was divided, save for a very few exceptions such as the Christian existentialists, between neo-Thomists and spiritualists of the school of Gentile, and there they stayed, while lay philosophy was putting into circulation not so much Marx (as if everyone at the time was devouring the *Grundrisse,* come off it!) as logical neopositivism, existentialism, Heidegger, Sartre, Jaspers, phenomenology, Wittgenstein, and Dewey. Catholics were reading these texts too. I know these are broad generalizations, because the fact that there were many champions of lay thinking was brought to my attention by Catholic teachers like Pareyson and Guzzo and not only by Abbagnano (who was a layman but definitely not a Marxist, and not even a member of the political left), while fundamental works of lay thinking were also published in series directed by scholars with a Catholic background (think of the Armando series). This lay culture, which was then expanding in opposition to Crocean idealism (hence this was no struggle between Catholics and Marxists, many of whom were still firmly in the Crocean camp), established a hegemony and seduced both teachers and students. And when hegemonies of this kind are established, they cannot be demolished by decree.

We can accuse the Christian Democrats of a certain lack of faith in the circulation of ideas, and of having thought that it was more important to control the television news than small-circulation avant-garde magazines—when Italian TV consisted of only two channels and therefore was not as powerful as it is today. And so, after over twenty-five years of political hegemony and control of television, it found itself faced with the generation of 1968.

Left-wing culture became predominant thanks to a policy of insistent ideological blackmail (if you don't see things the way we do, you're behind the times, what a disgrace to deal in art without thinking about the relation between the economic base and the superstructure!). The Italian Communist Party, unlike the Christian Democrats, invested a great deal in the cultural battle. But that you could easily resist the blackmail is proved by Norberto Bobbio's splendid liberal polemics, and when people read magazines like *Rinascita* or *Il contemporaneo* with their diatribes on socialist realism, and their condemnation even of Pratolini's *Metello* and Visconti's *Senso*, they were enthusiastic, but no one, except for card-carrying party members (and maybe not even they) took those *diktats* seriously—and all cultured people thought that Zhdanov was a numbskull.

Above all, if my reconstruction is correct, the famous hegemony of the left was slowly established precisely during the historical period in which, from Hungary to Czechoslovakia, Stalinism, socialist realism, and the *Diamat* itself were all in crisis, even in the minds of militant socialists and communists. So it was not a matter of Marxist hegemony, or not only that, but mainly of the hegemony of a system of critical thought.

By virtue of which plot did those who were influenced by this critical thinking (lay or Catholic, as they might have been) gradually find their way into publishing houses, national television, and the press? Can we justify this hegemony merely by pointing to the politics of consociativism, with which the DC (Christian Democratic Party) successfully tried to compromise the opposition with responsibility for the spoils system? Or by pointing to the opportunism of some intellectuals who moved rapidly to the left when it looked like the consociativist spoils system might create favorable openings, just as they are now embracing the right for the same reason? I don't think so.

The fact is that, during the second half of the last century, this critical culture was more sensitive to the spirit of the times. It played some winning cards and created a national elite (from the grassroots and not from the top; spontaneously and not by alliances between parties).

I understand why Storace is vexed by the authors of history books who don't see things his way. I only wonder why he doesn't feel he has enough instruments of cultural control (and authoritative cadres) to allow him to establish the hegemony of *his* thinking. And to think, in case you haven't noticed, that cultural hegemony is now on his side. The classics of the right enjoy the support of the newspaper cultural pages, contemporary history is revised at every step, and on leafing through publishers' catalogs you see everywhere not only the works of the most important conservative thinkers but even stacks of books inspired by the reactionary occultism that inspired Storace's spiritual forefathers. If I could assess cultural hegemony pound for pound, I would judge that today's dominant culture is mystical, traditionalist, neospiritualist, New Age, and revisionist. It seems to me that television devotes more time to the pope than to Giordano Bruno, to Fatima than to Marzabotto, to Padre Pio than to Rosa Luxemburg. In the mass media of today, there are more Templars than partisans.

How is it that despite right-wing publishers, dailies, cultural pages, and weeklies, Storace still finds so many enemies underfoot? Can it be, orthodox Marxist history having been liquidated, that the last surviving Marxists are all holed up in the middle school system? Were they all employed by left-wing education minister Luigi Berlinguer, in those few months during which he ran a system of public education that had been controlled uninterruptedly by the Christian Democrats for fifty years?

Why does Berlusconi (who has made Storace's concerns his own), with all the media power under his control, succumb to the lures of the hegemony of the left to publish every year, in costly editions published in his name, the *Manifesto of the Communist Party* and protocommunist texts like Campanella's *The City of the Sun* and Bacon's *New Atlantis*? To look good with regard to a lay culture that, despite everything, he admires? Why doesn't he publish his own *Pàmpini bugiardi*? We would all read them and try to draw critical stimuli from them. Because it is through books that you establish cultural hegemony.

The Good Old Bad Old Days

I would prefer to leave satire to the experts, but lately I have been thinking of certain situations that they could exploit rather well.

For example, Joe Blow chews out his twelve-year-old son because he comes home after midnight. Disturbed, the boy hangs himself in the attic. His father is convicted for inciting suicide.

Star striker Don "Cannon" Ball takes a penalty kick and completely fools the goalkeeper, thus demolishing the latter's reputation as an ace defender. Heartbroken, the goalkeeper dies. The Soccer Federation passes a rule stating that anyone shooting at goal must only do so politely, informing the goalkeeper in advance about the kind of shot he has in mind (a bit like the duelist who protested because his opponent kept on dodging about, refusing to let himself be hit).

Doctor Doome tells Mr. Aitken Groane that he has prostate cancer. Groane loses his mind, goes home, kills his wife and seven children, and jumps out the window. The government passes a law forbidding doctors to make diagnoses liable to hurt people's feelings.

The point of all these episodes is that the people involved don't understand that many situations are confrontational by definition. They are governed by certain rules, which establish that you cannot treat your opponent with kid gloves. You can argue, criticize, raise your voice (or foot), and call a spade a spade even if this hurts. A typical example of this is political debate, which is "polemical" in the etymological sense of the term and often couched in metaphors drawn from war or sport (entering the lists, class warfare, attacking the government, and so on). It would be a problem if things were otherwise.

In other words, the absence of political debate spells dictatorship, or imperfect democracy, in which criticism is forbidden and newspapers that don't toe the government line are closed down. In

---

"The Good Old Bad Old Days" appeared in L'espresso, *November 2003.*

an imperfect democracy you don't need to torch the offices of opposition newspapers or banish the editors: simply create the impression that any criticism less than polite might encourage violent fanatics. In a normal dictatorship papers are closed down after a fanatic tries to assassinate the head of government, the opposition having been accused of instigation. In a perfect dictatorship, the government itself organizes the assassination attempt, thus making it easier to wipe out the opposition.

The temptation to play this game sometimes springs from the mourning process. The relatives of a fellow who dies of despair after losing his job may be tempted to say that responsibility for the death lies with the man's boss. When the Italian civil servant Marco Biagi was murdered recently, some recalled that the trade-union leader Sergio Cofferati had severely criticized Biagi's plan for new labor legislation. "See," they said, "Cofferati helped create a climate of hatred toward Biagi." This isn't true. Cofferati spoke out when Biagi was alive, and he had every right to express his dissent. Still, I understand the emotional reaction after the event. What is really worrying, however, is that someone might say: "Don't criticize me, because if I get hurt, it will be your fault!" This is outright blackmail (and, in my view, tempting fate).

It would be disastrous if you couldn't attack a political adversary out of the fear that some maniac might make a paranoid interpretation of your position and react violently.

If you look at the history of Western terrorism over the last few decades, from the Tupamaros to the Red Brigades, you can see that the aim of terrorism was to provoke an authoritarian response in the hope that the masses will finally see how bad things have become and rebel. The fact that this has never worked, that all terrorism has produced is "desaparecidos" and not "revolución," is another kettle of fish.

For these and other reasons the recent clash between the left-wing Italian paper *l'Unità* and the right-wing journalist Giuliano

Ferrara represents an extremely worrying development. *l'Unità* attacked Ferrara because he had dinner with Berlusconi (not a particularly exciting news item), and Ferrara claimed that by so doing the paper had armed the hand of terrorists against him. The message hit home, and some began to say that *l'Unità* should be closed down. I believe that those who opt for such forms of argument must accept a serious political responsibility, which I hope will not become a topic in the history books of the future, in the sense that I still trust that such attitudes are unlikely to lead to deadly consequences.

Between the 1940s and 1960s, *l'Unità* was no parish newsletter. Depicted by the right as the organ of bloodthirsty commie extremists, it fired extremely violent salvos against the ruling Christian Democrats. Despite this, none of the much reviled men of power in those days ever dreamed of demanding that the paper be shut down. As the old Italian adage goes, "We were better off when we were worse off." And there might be some truth in that.

The Revolt Against the Law

These Days We Throw Coins at Judges

The Clean Hands Scandal occurred fifteen years ago, and I'm trying to remember what the atmosphere of those days was like. Great public excitement comes to mind. Without making too many distinctions between right and left, people in general (except those about to go on trial) were glad that the cat had finally been let out of the bag, that it was being said in plain language that thievery had taken place, and that those who were considered untouchable were being hauled into the dock.

Things didn't go exactly as they went on 25 July 1943 (when thousands and thousands of Italians who had always hailed il Duce climbed up on his monuments to decapitate them or pulled them down with ropes) but—and all Italians will remember this—the mob waited for the Powerful to emerge from their erstwhile headquarters and then pelted them with coins, enjoying the proverbial fact that the bigger they are, the harder they fall. Nor should any of this have surprised us: healthy popular indignation added to a ma-

---

"These Days We Throw Coins at Judges" appeared in L'espresso, *February 2002.*

licious pleasure in the humiliation of the powerful man who has lost was within historical norms.

Today, we are witnessing a curious phenomenon. It's not that some people, feeling threatened by judicial inquiry, managed to get into government to keep the magistrates at bay, undermining the court system with the weapon of delegitimization. That this could happen was in the order of things: the dream of every defendant is not only to prove his innocence but also to show that his accusers were prejudiced. What is striking is the widespread opinion, often kept silently, that this magistracy (which fifteen years ago was hailed to the point that there was a surge in student applications to study law, and the prosecutor Antonio Di Pietro was held in such reverence that it's a wonder they didn't distribute holy images of him in front of the churches) has gone too far and should stop being such a nuisance. And while people may not say this openly, they end up voting for those who do.

Such a sentiment is hard to explain, since those who harbor it would still condemn the head of a hospital who gets caught taking a bribe. So what happened? I spoke out against what happened at the time, but I was rebuked by many virtuous colleagues, who wondered why I was so indulgent toward such "rogues." The guilty parties (and even those presumed guilty but later found innocent) were not only tried, as was just, and not only placed in custody for often excessively long periods of time, they were also pilloried on television, in front of the nation, bullied by sarcastic public prosecutors, nailed to their seat in the dock as suspects or proven criminals, sometimes with a touch of foam in the corners of their mouths, sometimes with the nervous hand gestures of those who would love to cover their faces.

The practice began with trials broadcast by various courts throughout the country, where poor wretches who had signed an unsecured promissory note were shamed in front of millions of viewers—and it's no excuse to say that they signed a waiver agreeing to be filmed, because fools must be protected from their own vanity just as suicidal people (though, by definition, they want to die) must be prevented from carrying out their wish. From the magistrates' courts the show moved on to higher courts, the small-time swindler or the loser from the provinces was replaced by the man of power, and, even before his guilt was decided, the masses in front of the TV were gloating over his humiliation and disgrace, as if watching a variety show in which amateurs make fools of themselves. It was bad—bad for those who emerged innocent and bad for the guilty too, because the price they paid was higher than that called for by the law.

I think that, as the years went by, it was the terror (and humiliation) of this ordeal that sent ordinary people off the beaten path of justice. Maybe the judges did right, people thought, but they set up a mechanism that one day, who knows, might trap us, me, you, him . . . This power to pillory people has gradually turned judges into objects of suspicion. We won't be the ones to challenge them, the people perhaps think, but if someone does, let's give him free rein. As if to say: If we buy the police cars that go too fast, tomorrow they might be chasing us.

Some Plans for Revolutionary Reform

Even though, in order not to frighten Berlusconi's mother, the new majority calls itself reformist, it is in fact revolutionary. *Revolution* is defined in Italian dictionaries as "a profound upheaval within the constituted socio-political order, tending to bring about radical change in governments, institutions, and socioeconomic relations," and the process is "violent." We must, however, agree about terms. To be violent you don't need to skin someone and eat his heart; a vi-

---

"Some Plans for Revolutionary Reform" appeared in L'espresso, *March 2002.*

olent person can also be, let's say, someone who gets to my beach umbrella before me, sits down beneath it, and won't go away, saying that if I keep harassing him I'm a dirty communist.

If revolution we must have, let it be done well. All you need to understand is what the country expects—for example, to pay less tax, not necessarily by law but through the encouragement of personal creativity when it comes to tax returns. People will also want not to be prosecuted for false accounting, to be able to drive 100 mph on the highway, leniency about double-parking, and so on. I therefore propose a series of legislative measures in the interests of all citizens, not just for those on one side of the political fence.

PRESUMED BIAS. Why should I be judged by someone I don't like? The law ought to allow a Muslim citizen to recuse a Christian judge, an atheist a judge who is a believer, a gay a heterosexual judge and so on. You ought to be able to recuse a judge who reads a different newspaper from yours or a cross-eyed judge (you never know who he's looking at, which is disconcerting). The defendant must feel calm and not on trial, as if he were standing before Minos. In fact, every citizen should be guaranteed the judge of his choice, just as he has the right to choose his own doctor or lawyer. Such a reform would benefit judges as a profession, because there would be more of them, at least as many as there are doctors, while their fees would be commensurate with the financial status of the client. The poor could have a court-appointed attorney.

THE INTRODUCTION OF DRUGS INTO GOVERNMENT MINISTRIES. If I go into a police station carrying a bag full of cocaine, it's more than likely that I'm turning it in to the officer on duty for the purposes of further investigation. Now, as a ministry is a public institution (even the police depend on a ministry), there should be no suspicion regarding drug delivery. Until someone catches the minister and all his undersecretaries in the conference room completely stoned, coupling with curvaceous prostitutes and uttering blasphemies, we must assume that the substance was turned in for the public good. Every consignment of drugs delivered to a ministerial office, from which it nevermore emerges, means that a harmful substance has been taken out of circulation.

INSULTING THE DECEASED. I believe it is no longer an offense to use words like *shit* to refer to a person who passes us on the wrong side or takes our parking space, because nowadays even children and priests use such language—including many American priests who don't appreciate the inexplicable rebelliousness of certain children. So I don't see why you can't call a deceased person, no matter how his decease came about, a pain in the ass. The wave of prudery that ran through the country on the occasion of a recent gaffe on the part of Minister Scajola as he spoke of a victim of terrorism (the senior civil servant Marco Biagi) was certainly excessive. Since what counts are the ritual norms and their observance, I would suggest the establishment of a liturgical rule whereby, when speaking of the deceased, the ministrant begins with "our dear late lamented pain in the ass," and the matter will be settled.

THE RITUAL SACRIFICE OF THE PRESIDENT. In many primitive societies it was customary, when the monarch had reached a certain age, to lead him into the woods and sacrifice him to the gods. He knew this and put up with it. Plans for constitutional reform ought to include the idea, toward the end of the President of the Republic's term in office and possibly well in advance of it, that the incumbent prime minister announce not only the president's successor but also changes in the presidential functions. It's easy to understand the usefulness of such a law that would keep every President of the Republic on his toes. He would be careful to cultivate the approval of the government, so that his stroll in the woods would not occur before his time was up—thus guaranteeing a fruitful correspondence of interests between the prime minister's office and that of the president.

Against the Guardians

Once upon a time, when a policeman stopped a motorist in order to fine him, the one we shall call the Accused could fall back on three strategies to deal with the Guardian of the Law. One: to admit he was at fault and pay up. Two: to justify himself, trying to prove to the Guardian that he wasn't at fault. Three, if he was an imbecile: to raise his voice and say, "Do you have any idea who I am?"—to which the Guardian would either reply that he didn't give a damn or, quaking, say, "My mistake, please carry on, Sir, Your Lordship, Your Excellency," and so on.

Now it looks as if the Accused has a fourth option at his disposal, the option to say, "Have you any idea who *you* are?"—explaining to the terrified Guardian that he is a dirty communist in the pay of Moscow. Moscow being not the Russian city of today, where they are all good fellows, like Putin (an ex-KGB official and one of Berlusconi's best pals), but the Moscow of before, which still acts as a center of occult power in a cave in Afghanistan, together with bin Laden and maybe even the Jewish International, because, as we know, they are all of the same stripe, even though it's better not to say so out loud.

In short, today the Accused's primary resort is not to prove his innocence and to ask respectfully on what grounds the charge is based but to make an immediate accusation against the Guardian, whether it is a policeman or the Chief Justice of the Supreme Court.

In the light of a few suggestions I previously made for revolutionary reform, the first and foremost being the one whereby every defendant has the right to choose his own judge, I think that all the legislative changes I proposed can be boiled down to one principle: the citizen must have the right to question the integrity not only of his accuser but also of whoever investigates him.

The public prosecutors of the city of Bologna have sent preliminary investigation notices to several public officials, including a

---

"Against the Guardians" appeared in L'espresso, *August 2002.*

police chief, because they may be indicted as accessories to homicide, failing to provide the escort that the murder victim Professor Biagi was entitled to. This is not to say that the recipients of these notices have been formally accused of anything; inquiries are being made, that's all, and possibly the magistrates were overzealous: nobody's perfect. But the first move made by some exponents or supporters of the majority (Cossiga, Giovanardi, Pecorella, and so on) was to attack the magistrates, claiming that they are in the pay of the opposition and acting against the interests of the state.

We've seen this movie before. The best part comes now. It is a substantiated fact that someone was taking cocaine into the offices of a certain ministry, and I suggested earlier that this presumed offense be decriminalized as it should be seen as a meritorious contribution to the struggle to keep drugs out of circulation. But the police have submitted a report to the prosecutor's office in which they say that the cocaine was delivered to the Deputy Minister for the Economy, Gianfranco Micciché. The police can get things wrong too, and a deputy minister who feels he has been unjustly accused might be expected to request evidence to be produced, or he might provide a cast-iron alibi (for example, by proving that he never set foot in the ministry). But what was the Honorable Micciché's reaction? He stated that "within certain units of the police force there are a few 'deviant' agents whose aim is to obtain results different from those that their pact of honor with the force obliges them to respect." A splendid example of delegitimizing the Guardians, who, first, are not men of honor (we know what that expression means when uttered by a Sicilian, and Micciché is a Sicilian) and, second, are clearly in the pay of Moscow. Even the police? Even the police. But wasn't it just the judges? It depends: if the judges accuse you, you delegitimize the judges; if the police accuse you, you delegitimize the police. But weren't we supposed to defend the police after the G8 riots in Genoa? Of course, they weren't against us in

Genoa. But they are against us in Rome—so in Rome they are no longer trustworthy.

You can see that there was nothing airy-fairy about my previous suggestions. Let every citizen have the right to his *fumus persecutionis,* and let *habeas corpus* be replaced with *custos est porcus.* Let us no longer affirm *in dubio pro reo* but *semper contra Custodes.*

From the Riot Cops to the TV Cops

It was in 1952, I think. A student in Turin, I was crossing Piazza San Carlo to go to the university when I came across a demonstration. Not a revolution; there were workers with placards and flags, but it was evidently unauthorized. At first I didn't realize the problem, because I was walking along the arcades, but suddenly I saw the crowd disperse as the green trucks of the riot police of those days began to race wildly across the square. I was twenty and a member of the Catholic youth movement. I was already sensitive to social problems, but there were too many red flags in the square for me to feel involved in the matter. So I quickened my pace along the arcades, to turn into a side street as soon as possible.

But the trucks had also entered the arcades, and it became a problem of personal safety. I began to run, and a truck was hot on my heels. The police were hanging out of the vehicle lashing out furiously with their truncheons. As I hugged one of the columns of the arcade, the passing truck almost grazed it, and a cop aimed a terrific blow at me with his baton. Luckily he hit the edge of the pillar two inches from my head. If I had been sticking out a little more, I would have ended up in the hospital.

I got away from the bedlam, but I will always remember the policeman. Small and badly dressed (they weren't elegant as they are now, and their uniform was in an ugly greenish cloth), with the

"From the Riot Cops to the TV Cops" appeared in L'espresso, *June 2005.*

tanned face of a southern farmhand that spoke of enduring hardship and hunger. He had a nasty look and he didn't care whom he hit. They paid him to hit, and that was enough for him.

Years later I recognized my riot cop in a description given by Pasolini in his memorable tirade against the students (proletarian cops against bourgeois left-wing thugs). Those were the police then. Much like today's American soldiers fighting in Iraq, come to think of it. Poor people who enlisted in order to get away from poverty and did what they had to, not knowing how to do anything else.

At the time I didn't think much about the social problems that underlay police recruitment in the 1950s, and the image of that enraged policeman may have affected my subsequent political choices.

Nowadays I can watch TV police shows every evening (if it isn't an Italian one, it's French, which is the same thing), and I follow with immense pleasure all the shows about police units, sergeants, inspectors, chiefs, whatever comes my way. All in all, the shows are good, the stories as repetitive as they should be in any cop show worthy of the name, and the actors are agreeable. It's fine to spend the time from 9 to 11 in this way (you can always read Homer in bed). I'd love to be arrested by a woman sergeant who looks like the TV star Alessia Marcuzzi.

These TV cops are now amiable, human, obsessed by pathetic family problems, sometimes even gay. In other words, the collective imagination sees them as positive characters—so that when the police do use excessive violence, as during the 2001 G8 conference in Genoa, the country protests, forgetting that back in the days of my old-fashioned riot cop this was the rule.

What do these TV cop shows mean? Do they spring from some perverse plot cooked up by "deviant" parallel intelligence services that are using the right-wing government to extol the virtues of the enemies of the people? Not at all. They have come into being because today law enforcement agencies no longer recruit only poor souls from Italy's poverty-stricken deep south, because the training of candidates is more rigorous and the uniforms smarter. Trainees are taught not to beat up communists but to protect citizens, and so on. The whole social function of the police force has changed—and it should, because now that many workers vote for the center-right, who's left to beat up?

The climate has changed, because, after the tragic years of terrorism, even the left-wing parties are on the side of the state, so they have stopped criminalizing law enforcement agencies. By a wonderful piece of historical irony, it is the center-right that now criminalizes the magistracy and, while still a little overbearing and grouchy, the prosecutors in the various cop shows come out looking as amiable and human as the next man. So television, Berlusconi's channels included, is working against Berlusconi's attack on the judges. It won't be long before TV viewers see the police as a left-wing force—one that, oddly enough, goes on the air under the aegis of a right-wing government.

Unbelievable, how much has changed in less than fifty years.

Pasta Cunegonda

There is nothing unconstitutional in the fact that the coalition now holding a majority in Parliament has proceeded to occupy a variety of public bodies and agencies, RAI TV included. It's known as the spoils system, employed in other countries too. True, the winners could have shown a sense of fair play by considering the minority, which represents about half the electorate, but good manners and democratic sensibility are one thing, the unscrupulous exercise of legally acquired electoral power another. For decades here in Italy, radio and television were wholly controlled by the Christian Democratic Party, which carefully controlled how much female flesh could be exposed, and the country got on perfectly well just the same; indeed, the so-called television of the regime produced the most rebellious generation of the century.

The problem is that the head of government owns the other three national private television channels, so the spoils system has led to an almost total monopoly of the information sector. This is the new factor, new with respect to other democratic countries and to constitutions drafted when phenomena of this kind were unforesee-

"Pasta Cunegonda" appeared in la Repubblica, *April 2002.*

able. It calls for a new response on the part of the nonconsenting electorate. As we have seen, the *girotondi* and demonstrations in the streets are of little use in this case: they may help create a sense of identity for a disoriented opposition, but afterward (if this identity is real) it is necessary to go farther—also because, to put it in technical terms, the government doesn't give a hoot for the *girotondi,* and such things will not persuade those who voted for the current government to change their minds. What effective form of protest is therefore left for that half of the Italian population that doesn't feel represented by the new televisual system?

That is to say a lot of people, of whom several million have already expressed their dissent, but many more would do the same if they could see a truly effective way to do so. Refuse to watch the TV or listen to the radio? Too great a sacrifice. Also, (1) I have a right to watch a good film in the evening, and I don't worry about the views of the owner of the movie house when I go to the movies; (2) it's useful to know the opinions of the ruling party and see how it presents the news—even if there were a program on the wartime resistance conducted solely by die-hard exponents of the right and crypto-Fascists, I should know what these persons think and say; (3) finally, even if that half of the Italians who make up the opposition stopped watching TV, the government and its electorate would not change their minds.

What can be done by those Italians who do not accept the monopoly of television? Use their economic power. Let all those against the monopoly punish Mediaset by refusing to buy any of the products advertised on that network.

Would this be difficult? No, simply keep a sheet of paper by the remote control and note down the products advertised. Do they recommend Aldebaran fish fillets? Good, so at the supermarket you buy only Andromeda fish fillets. Do they advertise a brand medicine with acetylsalicylic acid? When you go to the pharmacy, buy only a generic product that contains the same aspirin and costs less. Since there are many products available, it involves no sacrifice, merely a little care, to purchase Marvel soap powder and pasta Radegonda (not advertised on Mediaset) instead of Wonder soap powder and pasta Cunegonda.

If this course of action were followed by only a few million Italians, within the space of a few months the manufacturers would notice a drop in sales and would act accordingly. You get nothing for nothing, a little effort is necessary, and if you're unhappy with the monopoly on information, then express your unhappiness in an active way.

Set up stalls in the streets to collect signatures: people don't need to attend a single demonstration, just give up eating pasta Cunegonda. With little effort, you express your dissent in a perfectly legal manner and get the attention of those who wouldn't listen to you otherwise. Don't respond to Government Inc. with banners and ideas but by hitting it in its weak spot: money. And if Government Inc. responds to this protest, its electors will see that it is a company-government, one that survives only as long as its boss makes a profit. A new economic situation calls for a new political response. And *that* would be opposition.

Scatological Note

My article on pasta Cunegonda was followed by the birth of a movement, called Pasta Cunegonda (http://web.cheapnet.it/cunegonda), and some newspapers mentioned this. Recently I received a package, and from the envelope, addressed to me at *la Repubblica,* I saw that it came from Caramagna, a charming little town in the south of Italy.

Inside I found a photocopy of a page from a local newspaper that reported my idea, with a handwritten note in the margin: "He who lives by the sword . . . must perish by the sword" (note the erudite use of ellipsis). This was followed by an illegible scrawl of a signature: in short, an anonymous message. He who lives by the sword must perish by the sword? I feared there might be anthrax in the package. Not at all, just a copy of an old book of mine, *La definizione dell'arte,* first published by Mursia and in this particular edition by Garzanti, 1978. On the cover someone had written "shit" in red felt tip, with a double underlining.

Opening the book, I saw that from the first page to the last, for a total of 308 pages, the word "shit" appeared, in red and underlined—but only on the odd-numbered pages, and so the shits weren't 308 but 154, or rather 156, because two had been added on the back cover, recto and verso. This gentleman (out of gallantry I assume it wasn't a lady) must have reasoned as follows: "You've done something that offends me? Well, I'll show you" (in the vein of the words of the Vicomte de Valvert when he challenged Cyrano by alluding to his nose, thinking he was the first to come up with that sublimely sarcastic witticism). But there is some distance between the nose and the anus, and clearly my correspondent wanted to be wittier than the Vicomte de Valvert (who at least exposed himself in person, was prepared to duel, and was wounded at the end of the ballad recited by Cyrano). To show courage by saying "Shit," as Cambronne teaches us, all you have to do is say it once, showing your face. A hundred and fifty times, from the secrecy of a toilet in Caramagna, is not courage but an incomprehensible love of drudgery.

I tried to understand the mind and the walk of life of my correspondent. For the psychology, there's no need of a psychoanalytic session, and I leave it to the reader to draw conclusions. As for the man's social background, I wondered if he already had the book at home, if he bought it specially, or if he stole it. If he already had the book at home, even if it belonged to his children, he must be a person of some status, which makes the business all the more interesting. If he stole it, theft too can be a form of political struggle, but the people who used to steal books were usually on the far left, and I would say that this isn't the case here. Which leaves us with the possibility that he bought it, and if he did, then he spent a certain amount, plus the cost of mailing, in order to give himself this satisfaction. He must have calculated that he wasn't going to contribute to my personal well-being, given the paltry percentage authors receive on paperbacks, but he didn't consider the big check I will receive for this article.

One might guess that the message came from a colleague who disapproved of my thinking. But no, in that case he would have signed his name, otherwise his secretarial labor would have had no value in terms of course credit.

It's not so much the problem of a decline in the means of dissent, because we see worse than this, but of the impotent, infantile rage of which the message was an expression. Not to mention the conclusion one is tempted to draw about the level of certain sectors of the electorate. I imagine my correspondent would have liked to send a similar message to the national football coach Giovanni Trapattoni or to the referee who made Italy lose against South Korea, and I can just see him gnashing his teeth because he couldn't find, say, a collection of poems, a treatise on metaphysics, or a book on nuclear physics written by these other enemies of his.

On a literary level I would ascribe this epistolary rant to a new genre, which isn't trash art and not even turd art, because the late Piero Manzoni filled cans with feces, but he sealed them and addressed them to posterity. Instead, albeit virtually, the gentleman of whom we are speaking wanted me to smell the perfume of his act.

Chronicles of the Late Empire

By the time this article appears, the heat will have gone out of the debate about the statement made by the prime minister, on an official international occasion, regarding his alleged family problems, and I must say that the press—of all political shades—has treated the matter with exemplary discretion, reporting and commenting on the event on the first day but not rubbing salt in the wound. So I return to the issue here, some time later, not out of a lack of taste but because the episode will be discussed in years to come in courses on communication sciences, and the right of scientific reflection is sovereign.

I hope that at a distance of almost two weeks everyone will have forgotten about it, but on welcoming the premier of a foreign government, our prime minister made a few statements concerning a presumed (i.e., rumored) relationship between his wife and another gentleman, describing his wife as a "poor woman."

The episode, as reported in the papers the following day, was susceptible of two interpretations. The first being that, as our prime minister was exasperated, he had given vent in public to a most

---

"Chronicles of the Late Empire" appeared in L'espresso, *October 2002.*

private matter. The second was that the Great Communicator who is our prime minister, on realizing that an embarrassing rumor was making the rounds, decided to cut the Gordian knot and turn the whole thing into a public laughing matter, thus depriving it of any hint of shame.

In the first case, "poor woman" would have been offensive with regard to his wife; in the second case, it would have been offensive with regard to the presumed third party (the lady being a poor soul, that is, if the rumor was true—but obviously it isn't true, since I'm making a joke about it).

If the first interpretation, which I tend to discount, is correct, the case is more a matter for a psychiatrist than a political scientist. Let's accept the second one, which is food for thought not only in seminars on communication science but also in history seminars.

The Great Communicator seems unaware of the principle that a denial is tantamount to giving the same news twice. For example (perhaps because in the last few months I have been traveling a great deal, and in countries not interested in Italian affairs), I heard nothing about this rumor—it was probably circulating among a few politicians and intellectuals, plus a few guests on board luxury yachts on the Costa Smeralda, so at most one or two thousand people. After the prime minister's remarks in public, and considering the existence of the European Union, the matter was communicated to hundreds of millions of people. As far as moves made by great communicators go, it doesn't strike me as brilliant.

We advise our students not to behave like this, because an ad for toothpaste that begins with "despite those who say that toothpaste causes cancer" will raise doubts in the minds of consumers and result in a dramatic drop in sales of this useful product. Perhaps every now and then, like Homer, even Berlusconi nods. It's his age.

But the issue is of historiographic importance. Usually, politicians do their best to keep their domestic problems separate from matters of state. Clinton got caught with his underpants in his hands, but he glossed over the matter and even got his wife to rally around and say on television that it was an insignificant affair. Mussolini was what he was, but he worked out his problems with his wife within the four walls of his home, he didn't discuss them before the crowds in Piazza Venezia. When he sent off a whole lot of men to die in Russia, it was in pursuit of his own dreams of glory, not to please his mistress Clara Petacci.

Where in history do we find such a fusion of political power and personal affairs? In the Roman Empire, where the emperor was the absolute master of the state. No longer controlled by the senate, he needed only the support of his praetorians, and so he could kick his mother, make his horse a senator, and force all those courtiers who didn't appreciate his poetry to slit their wrists . . .

This happens when you have not a conflict of interests but an absolute identity between your private interests and those of the state. Such an identity foreshadows a regime in the imagination of one who dreams of the late Roman Empire. Do you remember how (according to Dumas), at the beginning of the Age of Absolutism, in order to prevent Milady from stealing the queen's jewels, Lord Buckingham (the queen's lover) closed the ports and declared war on France? When there is such an equation of public and private interests, this is the kind of thing that happens.

III

THE RETURN OF
THE GREAT GAME

Between Dr. Watson and Lawrence of Arabia

I've Heard This Story Before

The person I'm going to talk about enrolled as a medical officer with the British expeditionary force in Afghanistan, more precisely in the crack regiment known as the Fifth Northumberland Fusiliers, but then he was seconded to the Royal Berkshires, in whose ranks he found himself up against the ferocious Afghans northwest of Kandahar, fairly close to Mundabad. In that place, an incident occurred involving the intelligence service. The British were informed that the Afghans were less numerous and less well armed than previously thought. The British attacked and got massacred, suffering forty percent fatalities, in the mountain pass called Khushk-i-Nakhud (the Afghan mountain passes are fearsome and, as the journalists tell us, the Afghans are not in the habit of taking prisoners).

Our friend was wounded in the shoulder by a bullet from one of the deadly albeit antiquated Jezail muskets, which shattered the bone and severed the subclavian artery, and he was saved at the eleventh hour by his valiant batman. He went back to London to

"I've Heard This Story Before" appeared in L'espresso, *December 2001.*

convalesce, and an anecdote tells us just how much that tragedy was on everyone's mind.

When he met the person with whom he was to share an apartment, the other man said, "You have been in Afghanistan, I perceive."

"'Here is a gentleman of a medical type, but with the air of a military man. Clearly an army doctor, then. He has just come from the tropics, for his face is dark, and that is not the natural tint of his skin, for his wrists are fair. He has undergone hardship and sickness, as his haggard face says clearly. His left arm has been injured. He holds it in a stiff and unnatural manner. Where in the tropics could an English army doctor have seen much hardship and got his arm wounded? Clearly in Afghanistan.' The whole train of thought did not occupy a second. I then remarked that you came from Afghanistan, and you were astonished."

The conversation took place in Baker Street, and the doctor is Dr. Watson, while the other man is Sherlock Holmes. Watson was wounded at the battle of Maiwand, on July 27, 1880. The London paper the *Graphic* reported the battle on August 7 (in those days the news arrived late). But we know all this from the first chapter of *A Study in Scarlet*.

The episode left its mark on Watson. In *The Boscombe Valley Mystery*, he says that his experience in Afghanistan made him a well-prepared and tireless traveler. But when, in *The Sign of Four*, Holmes offers him some cocaine (in a seven percent solution), Watson declares that after the Afghan campaign his body couldn't take new experiences, and shortly afterward he recalls that he liked to sit down and nurse his injured arm, which gave him pain with every change in the temperature. In *The Musgrave Ritual*, Watson remarks that the Afghan campaign made a deep impression on him.

In fact, Watson would like to talk about that campaign all the time, but people don't usually pay any attention to him. In *The Reigate Puzzle*, he struggles to persuade Holmes to visit an army comrade, Colonel Hayter. In *The Naval Treaty*, he tries in vain to interest a certain Phelps—a querulous, high-strung character—in his Afghan adventures. In *The Sign of Four,* he attempts to tell the story of that war to Miss Morstan, whose curiosity he manages to arouse only once. Veterans, especially when they have been wounded, are boring.

But the memory of Afghanistan persists. In *The Adventure of the Empty House,* in a discussion about Holmes's archenemy Moriarty, we come across the dossier on Colonel Moran, "the second most dangerous man in London," who served in Kabul. Echoes of the Afghan War are heard again in *The Crooked Man.*

Finally, in both *The Adventure of the Cardboard Box* and *The Resident Patient,* Holmes produces a masterpiece of what he erroneously calls deduction (it's *abduction,* as Peirce explains).[1]

While they sit quietly in their apartment, Holmes suddenly says, "You are right, Watson, it does seem a very preposterous way of settling a dispute." Watson agrees, but then he wonders how Holmes had guessed what he was thinking about. By following the movement of Watson's eyes as his gaze shifted to various parts of the room, Holmes managed to reconstruct his chain of thought until he realized that his friend was reflecting on a variety of appalling wartime events. Seeing that he touched his old wound, Holmes inferred that Watson was reflecting sadly on the fact that war is the most preposterous way to solve an international issue.

Elementary, my dear Watson. Why Blair didn't tell Bush about this remains a mystery.

First, Do Your Homework

One of the most fascinating books on Japan is *The Chrysanthemum and the Sword,* by Ruth Benedict. The book was published in 1946,

---

1. See *The Sign of Three,* edited by U. Eco and T. A. Sebeok (Indiana University Press, 1983).

"First, Do Your Homework" appeared in L'espresso, *April 2003.*

after the war therefore, but it was a reworked version of a research project offered to Benedict in 1944, when the war was still going on, by the U.S. military intelligence service. The reason for the timing is obvious: as the author herself says in the introduction to the printed version, the Americans had a war to finish, and then (if all went well) they would have to manage a lengthy occupation faced with a culture that they knew hardly anything about. All the Americans knew was that they were up against a nation that had a well-trained and technologically advanced army but didn't belong to the Western cultural tradition. Who were the Japanese and how should one treat them, paying attention to "how the Japanese would behave and not how we would behave in their place"? Benedict was unable to go to Japan, but by reading anthropological texts, studying Japanese literature and film, and above all availing herself of the cooperation of Japanese Americans, she composed an intriguing picture. Perhaps she didn't get everything right, I don't know, but she certainly helped people understand *sine ira et studio* how the Japanese of those days thought and behaved.

Legend has it that when the military command were deciding where to drop the first atom bomb, they thought of Kyoto—a sign they hadn't read Ruth Benedict, because that would have been like dropping the bomb on the Vatican in order to occupy Rome. But the bomb wasn't dropped on Kyoto, so some members of the high command probably did read this book. I'm not saying that dropping bombs on Hiroshima and Nagasaki was pleasing to the Japanese, but there is no doubt that postwar relations were handled in an intelligent way, as history has proved.

I realize that America under Roosevelt and Truman was a different place from Bush's America, but I wonder if the pressure to go to war in Iraq was preceded by equally accurate and understandable studies in social anthropology. It's enough to go to the Harvard University library or to read some of the excellent essays that are coming out in various American journals to know that the United States has no lack of people with a deep understanding of the Islamic world, but the problem hinges upon how many of their works have been read by Bush and his staff.

For example, considering the White House's irritated, scandalized response every time Saddam shifts the goalposts (first he says he has no missiles, then that he has destroyed them, then that he had only two or three, and so on), I wonder if any members of the high command have read the *Arabian Nights*, which has a great deal to do with Baghdad and its caliphs. It seems pretty clear to me that Saddam's strategy is that of Scheherazade, who tells her lord a different story every night and thus keeps going for two years and ninth months without getting her head cut off.

When faced with delaying tactics that have such deep cultural roots, there are two lines of action. The first is to refuse to play the game, prevent Scheherazade from telling her stories, and chop off her head at once. As I write this, I don't know if Bush has finally chosen this strategy. But even then we should ask if interrupting the tale will not give rise to other forms of delay, resulting in the story's dragging on in another way and for another thousand nights.

The second solution is to oppose Scheherazade's tactic with an opposite one. Perhaps (if Condoleezza Rice has read the stories of Baghdad in the days of the Caliphate) they have decided to do exactly that, countering every tale told by Saddam-Scheherazade with another tale, made up of an escalation of threats, to see whose nerve breaks first.

I fear that a dearth of anthropological studies also underlies the impatience with which Bush reacts to the caution shown by many European countries, not taking into account that they have lived through periods of both peaceful coexistence and armed conflict with the world of Islam for about one thousand five hundred years, and so they have a profound knowledge of it. France, Germany, and

Russia could be the Ruth Benedict of the day; they know more about the Arab world than those who, having been dealt a painful blow by Islamic terrorism, see only one aspect of it.

And don't tell me that when a country is at war, there's no time to listen to social anthropologists. Rome clashed with the Germanic tribes, but she needed a Tacitus to help her understand them. When it comes to clashes between cultures, the conflict can be tackled not only by manufacturing cannons but also by financing scientific research, and this is something that the country that managed to get its hands on the best brains in physics—while Hitler was trying to send them to the concentration camps—ought to know perfectly well.

You Need to Know Culture to Make War

I observed that Bush lacks a Ruth Benedict to help him understand the mentality of a people who first have to be defeated and then helped to make the transition to a democratic regime. The longer the war in Iraq goes on, the more this observation is confirmed.

One of the reasons for the amazement of the British and American high commands (which now admit that what was supposed to be a blitzkrieg is becoming a longer and more costly operation) is that they were convinced, as soon as the attack was launched, that whole divisions would surrender, their generals would throw in their lot with the allied troops, and the Iraqis in the cities would rise up against the tyrant. This didn't happen, and it's no use saying that neither the soldiers nor the people dared rebel because they feared reprisals from their government: by this logic the Italians shouldn't have organized the resistance, because the Germans hanged partisans—it was precisely this repression that prompted many to take to the hills and fight.

What evidently escaped people was the principle that history

"You Need to Know Culture to Make War" appeared in L'espresso, *April 2003.*

should have taught us: dictatorships produce consensus, and that consensus sustains them. Here in Italy many have vainly tried to oppose the opinion of the historian Renzo De Felice, who maintained that Fascism was not the work of a handful of fanatics who ground forty million dissidents under their iron heel but a phenomenon that lasted twenty years because in some way there was widespread consensus. A consensus nourished more by indolence than by enthusiasm, perhaps, but it existed.

The second lesson drawn from history is that in a dictatorship, even when dissent exists, a head-on clash with a foreign enemy triggers identification with one's country. Hitler was a ferocious dictator, not all Germans were Nazis, but the German forces fought to the finish. Stalin was an execrable dictator, not all Soviet citizens felt they were communists, but they resisted the German and Italian troops to the utmost, and in the end they won. And even the Italians, who after 1943 celebrated the Allied landings or fought in the hills, fought with valor at El Alamein.

Was it so hard to understand that the attack of a foreign army would bring about—at least for a while—a certain cohesion on the internal front? There is no need to trouble the professors of Harvard or Columbia University; two or three young social anthropologists at the most remote university in the West could explain such elementary truths.

I don't believe that war produces culture, even though sometimes the cunning ways of reason (as Hegel would put it) are bizarre, as in the case of the Romans who waged war on Greece, perhaps thinking to Latinize it, and instead it was vanquished Greece that culturally conquered the proud victors. More often war increases barbarism. But while it doesn't produce culture, it must at least start from cultural thinking.

Cultural thinking certainly lay behind the deeds of Julius Caesar, and, at least until the Empire, Napoleon acted in Europe knowing that there were different expectations in the various countries to which he led the armies of the revolution. I imagine that Garibaldi had some idea about the weaknesses of the Bourbon troops and the possible support he might find in some strata of Sicilian society, although, at the end of the day, neither he nor Cavour foresaw that the invasion of southern Italy would produce a robust loyalist resistance and a popular opposition that took the form of brigandage.

The Italian revolutionary Pisacane made an error in his calculations, and he was massacred by those from whom he expected an enthusiastic welcome. And probably, given that there is once more talk about the Seventh Cavalry, a certain lack of information about Indian psychology was responsible for the tragedy of General Custer.

It would be interesting to see which wars were waged without scorn for or knowledge of the opponent's culture, and which were undermined from the start by ignorance. (It has no doubt been done, but I'm simply not an expert in this field.)

The war in Iraq seems to be a conflict begun without consulting the universities, due to the American right's ancestral mistrust of "eggheads" or, as Spiro Agnew called them, "effete snobs."

It's a pity that the most powerful country in the world spends so much money on enabling its finest minds to study, and then doesn't listen to them.

Winning Doesn't Make You Right

War makes people Manichaean; it makes them lose the gift of reason. An old story. The war in Iraq has resulted in certain statements that, beyond the collective nastiness that a war produces, we must put down to bad faith.

At first, some said that those against the war were therefore pro-Saddam, which is like saying that questioning the advisability of giving a sick person a certain medicine means that you are on the side

"Winning Doesn't Make You Right" appeared in L'espresso, *April 2003.*

of the disease. No one has ever denied that Saddam was a bloody dictator. The question was whether, by ousting him in that violent fashion, we weren't throwing the baby out with the bathwater.

Then some said that anyone against Bush's policy was un-American, which is like saying that anyone who is against Berlusconi hates Italy. Quite the reverse, if anything.

Finally, though not everyone had the gall to say so outright, it was insinuated that the peace marchers were supporting dictatorships, terrorism, and maybe even white slavery. But never mind.

However, the most interesting syndrome emerged after the war in Iraq was won—formally at least. They began to crow triumphantly on our TV screens that the peace party had been wrong. Great argument. Who says that the winners of a war had good reasons for fighting it? Hannibal beat the Romans at Cannae because he had elephants, the smart missiles of his day, but was he right to cross the Alps and invade the peninsula?

Then the Romans beat Hannibal at Zama, but it doesn't follow that they were right to wipe out Carthage altogether instead of trying to seek a balance of power in the Mediterranean. And were they right to hunt him across Syria (Syria's always in there somewhere) and Bythinia and then to force him to take poison? You just can't say. Maybe yes, maybe no.

What's more, where's the sense in repeating the refrain "See who won?" As if the people who criticized this war had any doubt that the Anglo-Americans would win it. Did anyone really think that the Iraqis would hurl them into the waters of the Gulf? Not even Saddam believed that; he said what he said to hearten his people, unless of course he had gone completely soft in the head. If anything, the question was whether the Western forces would win in two days or two months. Given that for every additional day of war many get killed, better twenty days than sixty. What the TV scoffers ought to say is, "Look, you said that the war would not eliminate the terrorist threat, but it has." Which is the one thing they cannot say, because the truth of this has yet to be proved. Critics of the war, over and above all moral and civil considerations about the concept of preventive war, maintained that a conflict in Iraq would increase and not diminish tension in the world, because it would push a large number of Arabs, who until then had espoused a moderate line, into hating the West. Therefore the war would produce greater support for the jihad. Well, the only tangible results of the war so far are the volunteer brigades of kamikazes headed from Egypt, Syria, and Saudi Arabia toward the trenches around Baghdad. An alarming sign.

Even if we allow that those who saw grave danger in the conflict were wrong, what happened and what is still happening has yet to prove this. On the contrary, it looks as if there has been an outbreak of ethnic and religious hatreds down there that are not only hard to handle but also constitute a serious threat to the equilibrium of the Middle East.

In the last piece I wrote, which was handed in before the Americans entered Baghdad and the collapse of the Iraqi army, I mentioned that the Iraqi army had not yet collapsed because, regrettably, dictatorships produce consensus and this consensus is strengthened when the people are faced by a foreign invader. Then the army fell apart, and the crowds (but how many people were there, really?) turned out to welcome the Westerners. And so some people wrote me, saying, "See?" See what? I pointed out that before 8 September [1943], Italian Fascism was able to count on the consensus of the poor souls who had fought at El Alamein or in Russia. Then came defeat, and the statues of il Duce were pulled down from their pedestals, and everyone was suddenly an anti-Fascist. In Italy this process took over three years, in Iraq a lot less, but the dynamic is the same. In view of what is happening now between the various factions that want to run the country without the Westerners in the way, it seems to me that the consensus formerly enjoyed by Saddam has dissolved but—unlike in wartime Italy—not the feelings of diffidence and intolerance toward the foreigner.

Chronicles of the Great Game

One of the most compelling books I read this summer was *The Great Game*, by Peter Hopkirk. Don't be put off by the fact that it's 624 pages long. I can't say it's unputdownable, but it's better to savor it evening after evening as if it were a great adventure story, filled with characters who really existed and about whom we knew nothing. The story is about the tangle of espionage activities, sieges, wars, and guerrilla wars that unfolded between the Russian and British armies over the ridge that separates India from Afghanistan. All this in addition to the doings of Uzbek and Circassian potentates, with the action ranging from the Caucasus to Tibet and Chinese Turkestan. If you get the impression that you are looking at those maps frequently featured on the front pages of newspapers in recent years, you are right.

Note also that Rudyard Kipling invented nothing when he wrote *Kim,* all he did was provide a brilliant synthesis of a history that began in the Napoleonic period to end (end?) in the early twentieth century. It is a story of ambitious officers and hard-nosed adventurers who disguised themselves as Armenian merchants or pilgrims and crossed mountains and deserts never before seen by Europeans. The Russians wanted to study ways and means of expanding into India, the English to safeguard their colonial empire and protect the frontier with a series of buffer states ruled by puppet emirs, khans, and kinglets. It is a history of ambushes, decapitations, and assassins in royal palaces.

The most striking thing is that, at a time when people thought the whole world had been mapped, Europeans knew little or nothing about the geography of these areas, the mountain passes, the navigability of the rivers. Consequently they had to put their faith in the work of itinerant spies and geographers, who would then give an oral account of what they had managed to see or dash off a few notes on the subject.

"Chronicles of the Great Game" appeared in L'espresso, *September 2004.*

We also discover that the monarchs and petty sultans of fabulous realms (places like Bukhara, Samarkand, Chiva, and Chitral) were locked in an occasionally deadly game with Britain and Russia, while they had only the vaguest notions about those countries. Sometimes they even thought of them as neighboring tribes, so much so that one of the kinglets once asked the British envoy if Queen Victoria possessed twenty cannons as he did.

Then there are stories of horrific massacres, like the sixteen thousand British soldiers, civilians, women, and children slaughtered in the mountains of Afghanistan (which the British thought they had pacified), because an inept or ambitious general had made a poor assessment of the difficulties of the terrain, tribal divisions, and the subtle oriental arts of deceit. All these emirs emerge as untrustworthy and treacherous (and they were), but there's no doubt that the Russians and the British were no better and didn't hesitate to make friends with them in order to dupe them later.

The immediate impression is that Bush and Putin ought to read this book in order to understand that there are places in the world where the most powerful and well-organized army can do nothing against tribesmen who know the terrain; and it's enough to read Italian writers like Beppe Fenoglio to see that the local resistance fighters knew their countryside far better than the occupying German forces did.

Some might object that things have changed a lot since those days: Great Games are no longer played undercover, and to dispel the mists of ignorance all you need do is go off to war with a *National Geographic* atlas under your arm. Not true. Reading this book, you learn that this globalized world (I mean to say the world of the End of History) still contains immense pockets of reciprocal ignorance.

The Iraqi bands that kidnap journalists today know that Britain has more than twenty cannons, but the demands they make show that they have only a vague idea of what Europe really is. They are capable of capturing a left-wing journalist with the goal of blackmailing a right-wing government. They don't realize that by threatening France they may draw into Iraq a country that so far has kept out of it. They show Italian hostages on television and demand that Italians demonstrate for peace without knowing that this has already happened. They take two pacifists and thus create enormous problems for all those who have been urging the West to get out. In short, they try to influence Western policies without any clear understanding of the fault lines within Western society.

And what about us? Try asking someone, not the super of your apartment building but a university professor (provided that s/he is not an Islamist, obviously), the difference between Shi'ites and Sunnis, and you'll discover that s/he knows less than the emir of Bukhara did a century ago about the dimensions of the British Empire. And don't ask where the Hidden Imam is, because you'll probably be told to contact one of those TV shows that specializes in finding missing persons. With globalization fully under way there are still enough confused ideas around to give you gooseflesh. To see just how little we know, it is truly spine-chilling to follow Hopkirk as he discovers how little Asia and Europe knew of each other in the days of the Great Game.

Words Are Stones

The War of Words

As many people have said, the tragedy of the Twin Towers had a symbolic effect. If the hijacked aircraft had crashed into two skyscrapers in Oklahoma, killing the same number of people if not more, the world would not have felt the same shock. Hence symbols have their importance, and so do the words we use to define (or cause) events.

First, it's not clear what we mean by *war*. The word has nineteenth-century connotations. We think that certain events were anticipated by recent "disaster movies," but instead they appeared in old films featuring British officers in pith helmets and elusive Afghans taking potshots at them from the heights of a ridge.

Now, was it an act of war or an act of terrorism? Some have pointed out that the Twin Towers were insured for billions of dollars against acts of terrorism, but not against acts of war. So the language used by Bush could help either the insurance companies or the companies that had suffered losses. Perhaps this is why Bush talks

---

"The War of Words" appeared in L'espresso, *October 2001.*

sometimes of war and other times of terrorism—maybe he's not sure whom to favor.

But if this is war, must it be perceived as a "crusade"? When Bush let that word slip out, there was pandemonium. He was one of the few who did not know that the Crusades were waged by Christians against the world of Islam (which in the end succeeded in driving the invaders out).

Bush retracted his gaffe, then spoke of Infinite Justice, and that was worse. We don't need a world governed by philosophers (Plato's idea in this regard was disastrous). Government should be in the hands of people with a better grasp of history and geography.

The word *Arab* also deserves some reflection. Many Muslims are not Arabs, and some Arabs are not Muslims but Christians, while there are Muslims who are not fundamentalists, far less terrorists. And plenty of non-EU citizens are neither Arabs nor Muslims but criminals, though they are professing Catholics and have white skin. But symbols count, and in airplanes the passengers tremble if a gentleman with a mustache and a swarthy face boards. In America they murdered a few men wearing turbans (held to be a sure sign of Islam), though the victims believed in Brahma, Shiva, and Vishnu, or were Sikhs (neither Arabs nor Muslims). We really should reread Kipling.

The list of ambiguous words doesn't end here, and we are well aware of the dangerous words used by bin Laden. Put them all together, and they spell more innocent victims.

The People Who "Understand" Bin Laden

We live in murky times. Not just because of the tragic things that are happening but also because, if we are to understand what's happening, we need to be very subtle, and yet this doesn't seem to be a

---

"The People Who 'Understand' Bin Laden" appeared in L'espresso, *November 2001.*

time for subtleties. All around us people are wielding the saber, not the rapier. In his last message bin Laden gave up on the distinction he started with (the wicked West made up of Americans and Israelis, and the others, which for the moment he didn't mention) and moved on to talk of a clash with "Christians" in general (who in his view include Jews, the secular community, the former Soviet materialists, and maybe the Chinese).

But, in words at least, things aren't much better at home. If you happen to say that bin Laden is a villain, they tell you that you want to kill the children of Kabul, and if you express the hope that the children of Kabul will not die, they call you a supporter of bin Laden. The only way not to play bin Laden's game is to reject black-and-white crusades and cultivate that profound wisdom transmitted to us by our culture, the capacity to make distinctions.

Some weeks ago a poll came out according to which a large majority of the left "understood" bin Laden's arguments. Good God! Did those who answered this way approve of the destruction of the Twin Towers? I don't think so. I think rather, that when the question was put, no clear distinction was made between *explain, understand, justify,* and *sympathize with.*

Here in Italy a girl called Erika was recently accused of stabbing her mother and little brother to death. Can we *explain* this event? Of course, and this is a task for psychiatrists and psychologists. Can we *understand* Erika? If they tell me she was seized by a fit of madness, I can understand her, because there's no reasoning with insanity. Can we *justify* her act? Certainly not: what she did must be condemned in court, and she must be put in a place where she can do no further harm. Can we *sympathize with* what she did, in the sense that we would do the same? I really hope not, unless we are one of those maniacs who send her messages of solidarity.

Again in Italy, there is an ongoing polemic about understanding those who adhered to the Republic of Salò. Can we *explain* historically why they made this decision? Of course, and this has been done. Can we *understand* why many people did this? We can understand this perfectly well, and we can understand not only those who did so in good faith but also those who acted out of desperation or self-interest. Can we *justify,* historically, that decision? No, at least not from the standpoint of democratic values. You can understand the person, but you can't justify the decision. Can we *sympathize* with it? In 1943 I was only eleven, and I often wonder what I would have done had I been twenty, but at least in hindsight I hope I wouldn't have sympathized with it.

Can we *explain* the St. Bartholomew's Night massacre, when the French Huguenots were slaughtered by the Catholics? Certainly, there are stacks of books that explain why it happened. Can we *understand* why the perpetrators did what they did, perhaps thinking they would go to heaven? If you study the psychology of the people who lived five centuries ago, the bloody climate of the religious wars, and many other things, then yes. Can we *justify* that massacre? From our point of view as modern men and women, obviously not, and far less can we *sympathize* with it, in that any person of good sense would think it criminal to do such a thing today.

It all seems so simple. You can explain the actions of bin Laden much as he explained them himself in his first message; the frustration of the Muslim world after the fall of the Ottoman Empire. You can also take into account his political and economic interests (bin Laden's actions can be explained by the fact that he wants to get his hands on Saudi oil). Can we understand his followers? Certainly, given the education they have received, the frustration mentioned earlier, and many other reasons. Can we justify his actions? We cannot; they have been condemned, and the hope is that bin Laden will be put in a place where he can do no further harm.

And if you can't explain the actions of bin Laden or understand why hundreds or thousands of volunteers are leaving Pakistan to join forces with him, you're going to have a problem when you want to act against him, in other words, a problem understanding what must be done to neutralize the danger he represents. To sum up, precisely because you cannot *justify* and *sympathize* with Muslim fundamentalism, you have to *explain* and *understand* the motives, arguments, and drives that make it what it is.

What does a person mean when he says he "understands" bin Laden's actions? That he can explain them, understand them, justify them, or sympathize with them?

Until we return to a state of mind that permits and encourages distinctions, we'll be like bin Laden, and we'll be exactly the way he wants us.

Fundamentalism, Integralism, and Racism

In recent weeks there has been much talk about Muslim fundamentalism. To the extent that we've forgotten that Christian fundamentalism also exists, especially in America. But, people will say, Christian fundamentalists hold TV shows on Sundays while Muslim fundamentalists bring down the Twin Towers, and so they are the ones we're worried about.

But do they do what they do because they are fundamentalists? Or because they are integralists? Or because they are terrorists? And, just as there are non-Arab Muslims and non-Muslim Arabs, are there not fundamentalists who are not terrorists? Or integralists? Usually we consider fundamentalism and integralism as closely connected, and as two forms of intolerance. Which prompts us to think that all forms of fundamentalism are integralist and hence intolerant, and hence terrorist. Even if this were true, it cannot lead to the conclusion that all intolerant people are fundamentalists and integralists, or that all terrorists are fundamentalists (the Red Brigades weren't and neither are the Basque terrorists).

"Fundamentalism, Integralism, and Racism" appeared in L'espresso, *October 2001.*

In historical terms, fundamentalism is bound up with the interpretation of a holy book. Protestant fundamentalism in the United States of the nineteenth century (which survives to this day) is characterized by the decision to interpret Scripture literally, especially regarding notions of cosmology. Any form of education that undermines faith in the biblical texts, like Darwinism, is rejected. Muslim fundamentalism is also based on the literal interpretation of a holy book.

Is fundamentalism necessarily intolerant? It's possible to imagine a fundamentalist sect that assumes that its members are privileged to possess the correct interpretation of the holy book but does not carry out any form of proselytism or force others to share their beliefs, and does not fight to establish a society based on them.

By integralism, we mean a stance whereby one's religious principles must become the model of political life and the basis of the laws of the state.

While fundamentalism is in principle conservative, there are progressive and revolutionary forms of integralism. There are integralist Catholic movements that aren't fundamentalist; they struggle for a society wholly inspired by religious principles but without imposing a literal interpretation of the Scriptures—they might even be open to a theology like that of Teilhard de Chardin. But extreme forms of integralism can become theocratic regimes, perhaps grafted onto a form of fundamentalism. This strikes me as being much like the Taliban and their madrassas.

Every form of integralism contains a certain amount of intolerance for those who don't share its ideas, but this amount reaches its peak in theocratic forms of fundamentalism and integralism. A theocratic regime is destined to be totalitarian, but not all totalitarian regimes are theocratic (apart from the sense that they replace a religion with a dominant philosophy, like Nazism and Soviet communism).

And racism? It may seem odd, but a great part of Muslim integralism, although it is anti-occidental and anti-Semitic, cannot be described as racist in the way Nazism was, because while Muslim integralists hate a single race (the Jews) or a state that doesn't represent a single race (the USA), they don't see themselves as a chosen people but accept as members all those who practice Islam, even those who are of a different race.

Nazi racism was totalitarian, but there was nothing fundamentalist about the doctrine of race (which replaced the holy book with Aryan pseudo-science).

And intolerance? Can it be boiled down to these differences and affinities among fundamentalism, integralism, theocracy, and totalitarianism? There have been nonracist forms of intolerance (such as the persecution of heretics or the intolerance of dictatorships toward their opponents); there are nonintolerant forms of racism ("I've nothing against blacks; as long as they work and know their place they can stay with us, but I wouldn't want my daughter to marry one"); and there are forms of intolerance and racism among people we would deem to be nontheocratic, nonfundamentalist, and nonintegralist—as is the case with many democratic countries.

Fundamentalism, integralism, and pseudo-scientific racism are theoretical positions that presume a doctrine. Intolerance and popular racism come before any doctrine. They have biological roots, manifested in the animal kingdom as the territorial instinct, and are based on emotional reactions (we can't stand those who are different from us).

It could be said that with these few notes I have not helped clarify ideas so much as confuse them. But I'm not the one who confuses ideas; we have merely discussed ideas that are confused, and it's a good thing if we understand that they are—because that way we can reason better about them.

Civil War, Resistance, and Terrorism

In the last issue of *Espresso* magazine, one of the doyens of Italian journalism, Eugenio Scalfari, ended his article by writing: "You can't talk about the Iraqi resistance without appearing to be a partisan or an imbecile." On that same day in the *Corriere della Sera* leader-writer Angelo Panebianco wrote: ". . . the Iraqi 'resistance fighters,' as certain thoughtless Westerners call them. . . ." An observer from Mars would say that, while all around people are slicing off heads and blowing up trains and hotels, in Italy they're playing word games.

Our Martian would say that words count for little, given that he has read in Shakespeare that a rose by any other name would smell as sweet. Yet using one word in place of another often counts for a lot. It's clear that—in Italy at any rate—some of those who talk about the Iraqi resistance intend to support what they believe to be a people's war; others, on the opposing side, seem to imply that giving the name of resistance fighters to these cutthroats is tantamount to tarnishing Italy's own resistance movement during World War II. The curious thing is that most of those who think it is scandalous to use the term *resistance* in Iraq are the same ones who have been trying to delegitimize the Italian resistance, describing the partisans themselves as a bunch of cutthroats. Not to worry. People tend to forget that *resistance* is a technical term that does not imply a moral judgment.

First and foremost, there is the problem of civil war, which happens when people who share the same language start shooting one another. The Vendean revolt was a civil war, as was the war in Spain and the resistance movement in wartime Italy, because there were Italians on both sides. But the Italian struggle was also a resistance movement, given that this is the term used when some of the citizens of a country rise up against an occupying power. If by chance,

"Civil War, Resistance, and Terrorism" appeared in L'espresso, *October 2004.*

after the Allied landings in Sicily or at Anzio, bands of Italians formed to fight the Anglo-Americans, this would have been called resistance—even among those who maintained that the Allies were the good guys. Banditry in eighteenth-century southern Italy was a form of resistance in favor of the Bourbon royal family, but the Piedmontese (the good guys) beat the bad guys, who are now remembered as mere brigands. During World War II, the Germans called the Italian partisans "bandits."

Civil wars rarely involve pitched battles and are more commonly a matter of encounters between armed bands. War between armed bands is also a resistance war, employing hit-and-run tactics. Sometimes, in such wars between rival bands, "warlords" also appear with their private armies, and there are also groups with no ideology who take advantage of the confusion. Today the war in Iraq has aspects of a civil war (Iraqis are killing Iraqis) and of a resistance movement, with the addition of all sorts of bands. These bands take action against foreigners, and it doesn't matter whether these foreigners are in the right or in the wrong—even when they have been called in and welcomed by fellow citizens. If the locals are fighting against foreign occupying forces, we're looking at resistance, and that's that.

Finally there is terrorism, which is of another nature, and has other ends, and other strategies. There has been and there still is, terrorism in Italy, without either resistance or civil war, and there is terrorism in Iraq, between bands of resistance fighters and civil-war formations. In civil wars and in resistance movements we know who and (more or less) where the enemy is, but not in the case of terrorism. The terrorist may be the person sitting beside you on the train. Civil wars and resistance actions are fought through direct engagements; terrorism is fought with espionage. Civil wars and resistance struggles are fought *in loco*; terrorism is often fought elsewhere, where the terrorists have their sanctuaries and refuges.

Iraq's tragedy is that the Iraqis have a bit of everything. Resistance groups may have recourse to terrorist tactics—while the terrorists, for whom it is not enough merely to drive out the foreigners, may claim to be resistance fighters. This complicates matters, but refusing to employ technical terms complicates them even more. Let's suppose that, while saying that *Armed Robbery* is a good film, in which even the bad guys are likable, someone refuses to describe a bank job as armed robbery and prefers to talk in terms of petty theft. But petty theft is dealt with by a few plainclothes police officers who patrol railroad stations and tourist resorts. The officers usually already know the small-time local pros, while defense against bank robberies requires expensive electronic surveillance systems and rapid-response units, against enemies who are still unknown. Therefore choosing the wrong name leads to the choice of the wrong remedy. The belief that you can defeat a terrorist enemy through the roundups normally used against resistance groups is an illusion, but the belief that you can defeat hit-and-run fighters with the methods that should be used for terrorists is equally mistaken. We ought to use the technical terms when necessary, without yielding to passions or blackmail.

Back to the Seventies

One feels a certain embarrassment on thinking about (and even more on writing about) the return of terrorism. As if one were writing verbatim copies of articles written in the seventies. This tells us that, although changes have occurred since then, there has been no change in the logic of terrorism. However, the new situation in which terrorism has reappeared leads us to reinterpret it in a slightly different way.

Terrorist acts are said to aim at destabilization, but this is a vague expression, because right-wing terrorism, terrorism sponsored by "deviant" parallel secret services, and left-wing terrorism aim at different forms of destabilization. I assume, until proved wrong, that the assassination of Marco Biagi was the work, if not of the Red Brigades, of an organization with similar principles and methods, and this is the sense in which I'll use the word *terrorism* from now on.[1]

---

1. Professor Marco Biagi was a senior civil servant and an expert on labor law. In 2002 he was murdered in Bologna by left-wing extremists. This caused a scandal because he had received death threats and had the right to a police escort. But, mysteriously, this escort was called off and he was shot to death in the street.

"Back to the Seventies" appeared in la Repubblica, *March 2002.*

What is a terrorist act usually intended to accomplish? Since a terrorist organization pursues an insurrectionary utopia, its primary aim is to prevent the establishment of any kind of agreement between the opposition and government—be it obtained, as in Aldo Moro's time, through patient parliamentary negotiation, or a head-on clash, strike action, or any other demonstration intended to persuade the government to review some of its decisions. In the second place, terrorism aims to goad the government in power into hysterical repression, which the citizens will then find antidemocratic and unbearably dictatorial, and hence to spark an insurrection among the vast pool of "desperate proletarians or lumpenproletarians" who were only waiting for the last straw.

Sometimes terrorist plans are successful, and the most recent case is that of the attack on the Twin Towers. Bin Laden knew that there were millions of fundamentalist Muslims in the world who, before rising up, were waiting only for proof that the Western enemy could be dealt a lethal blow. And that is what happened, in Pakistan, Palestine, and elsewhere too. The American response in Afghanistan did not reduce but increased that pool. But if the plan is to come to anything, this "desperate" and potentially violent pool must actually exist, I mean to say that it must *exist as a social reality*. The failure not only of the Red Brigades in Italy but of many movements in Latin America was due to the fact that they laid all their plans on the assumption that this pool existed and that it numbered not in hundreds of people but in millions. Most of the Latin American movements managed to goad some governments into ferocious repression, but they did not bring about a revolt: the pool was evidently much smaller than the terrorists had bargained for. In Italy, the world of the working classes and of the political powers reacted in a balanced way, and, no matter how much some people criticize some measures of prevention and repression, the dictatorship that the Red Brigades were expecting did not come about. That is why they lost the first round (and we were all convinced that they had given up).

The defeat of the Red Brigades convinced everyone that, all things considered, they had failed to destabilize anything. However, we didn't reflect enough on the fact that actually they did a great deal to stabilize things, because a country in which all the political forces commit themselves to defending the state against terrorism has persuaded the opposition to be less aggressive and to try the path of so-called consociativism. Hence the Red Brigades acted as a stabilizing or, if you will, conservative movement. It matters little if they did so by blundering politically or because they were manipulated by a party that had an interest in attaining that result. When terrorism loses, it doesn't only fail to bring about revolution, it promotes conservation—in other words, it slows down the processes of change.

The remarkable thing about the Biagi killing is that terrorists usually kill to prevent an agreement (as in the Moro case), whereas this time they seem to have acted to prevent a disagreement. After the Biagi case, many thought that the opposition should have toned down, refined, and tamed its dissent, and the trade unions should have put off the general strike.

If we were to follow the ingenuous logic of *cui prodest,* we might think it was a government assassin who put on his helmet, got on his moped, and went off to shoot Marco Biagi. Which would seem extreme even to the most frenetic demonizers of the government—and suggest that the new Red Brigades don't even exist and are therefore not a problem.

The new terrorism trusts in the support of millions in a potentially violent revolutionary action, but above all it sees the disorientation and the breaking up of the left as an excellent source of discontent among the people. But the *girotondi* (made up of distinguished fifty-year-olds who are peace-loving and democratic by vocation), the response of the opposition parties, and the regrouping of the trade unions were reestablishing equilibrium between government and opposition in Italy. A general strike is not armed revolt; it's merely a very vigorous way to modify an agreement. Whereas the

Biagi killing was apparently calculated to prevent disagreement, it was actually meant to prevent agreement: if trade union opposition had modified the government line, it was intended to weaken the real enemy of terrorism—that is, democratic reform.

This time too, therefore, if terrorism succeeded in its primary goal (attenuating union protest), it would achieve what it has always achieved: the stabilization and the preservation of the status quo.

If this is how things stand, the opposition and the trade unions should not give in to terrorist blackmail. The democratic confrontation should proceed, in the most aggressive forms permitted under the law, such as strikes and demonstrations in the streets, because those who give in are doing exactly what the terrorists want.

Likewise, the government (if I may give the government advice) should resist the temptation raised by terrorist action: to implement unacceptable forms of repression. Antidemocratic repression can have subtle reincarnations, and nowadays it doesn't necessarily mean stationing tanks in the main squares of the city. When you hear on television members of the government who in different ways (some with discretion and vague allusion, others explicitly) suggest that people who made accusations against the government, who signed petitions in favor of the trade unions, who criticized Berlusconi for conflict of interest or the passing of questionable laws—a subject of debate outside Italy as well—armed terrorists (morally, *morally,* they specify), then you are hearing the expression of a dangerous political principle.

The principle can be put like this: Because terrorists exist, anyone who attacks the government is encouraging them. The corollary: It is criminal to attack the government. The corollary of the corollary is the negation of every democratic principle, blackmail of the press, denial of the freedom to criticize, denial of every act of opposition and every expression of dissent. This is not the abolition of Parliament or of the press (I'm not one of those who talk about the new Fascism) but something worse. It is using moral blackmail, holding up to civic disapproval all who express (nonviolent) disagreement with the government, equating verbal violence—common to many forms of heated but legitimate debate—with armed violence.

If things finally came to that, democracy risks being emptied of all significance. We would have a new form of censorship, silence out of fear of being lynched in the media. The government must resist this diabolical temptation.

And the opposition must carry on, in all the ways permitted by the Constitution. If not, then really (and for the first time!), the terrorists will have won.

Kamikazes and Assassins

Some time ago, well before the fateful September 11, a question was going around on the Internet as to why the Japanese kamikaze pilots wore helmets. Why would men about to crash into aircraft carriers protect their heads? Maybe they didn't really wear a helmet, just a ritual headband? Some replies, suggested by common sense, were that a helmet might help you avoid being deafened by the noise of the engine, and might defend you against attack before you went into your death dive. Also, kamikaze pilots were the type who observed rituals and rules, and if the book said to put on a helmet before getting into the plane, you did.

Joking aside, the question betrays the unease each of us feels with regard to those who coldly sacrifice their lives to kill others.

After September 11 we think (rightly) of the new kamikaze as a product of the Muslim world. This leads many to make the equation fundamentalism = Islam, and allows Northern League cabinet minister Roberto Calderoli (whom I'm always glad to see on television, because he looks like a stooge in an old comedy film) to say that this

"Kamikazes and Assassins" appeared in L'espresso, *August 2005.*

is not a clash between civilizations because "that lot" are not civilized.

Historians tell us that in the Middle Ages a heretical variant of Islam practiced political murder using killers sent off on missions from which they knew they wouldn't return alive. Legend has it that, to ensure that they remained the slaves of their masters, the kamikaze of those days were dosed with hashish (whence the Sect of the Assassins). True, Western sources, from Marco Polo on, exaggerated this business a bit, but the phenomenon of the assassins of El Alamut is the subject of many authoritative books, which may be worth reading again.

Recently I found on the Internet a debate about a book by Robert Pape, *Dying to Win: The Strategic Logic of Suicide Terrorism,* which, on the basis of a wealth of statistical evidence, offers two fundamental theses. The first is that suicide terrorism arises only in occupied territories and as a reaction to occupation (Pape shows how suicide terrorism ceased in Lebanon as soon as the occupation was over). The second is that it is not only a Muslim phenomenon: Pape cites the Tamil Tigers of Sri Lanka, and twenty-seven suicide terrorists in Lebanon, all non-Muslims and either members of the lay community, communists, or socialists.

There haven't been only Japanese and Muslim kamikaze. The Italo-American anarchists who paid Bresci's fare so that he could go shoot King Umberto I did not buy him a return ticket. Bresci knew he would not survive his mission. In the first centuries of Christianity there were the circumcellions, people who attacked wayfarers in order to win martyrdom, and later the Cathars practiced a form of ritual suicide known as *endura.* Finally we come to the various sects of modern times (all in the Western world), who occasionally choose mass suicide (and I would ask the anthropologists to tell us about other forms of "preemptive" suicide practiced by other ethnic groups over the centuries).

In short, history and the world have always been and still are full of people who for religious, ideological, or other motives (and helped by a suitable mind-set, or subjected to some sophisticated form of brainwashing) have been and are prepared to die in order to kill others.

We therefore should ask ourselves whether the problem that deserves attention and study on the part of those responsible for our security is not only the phenomenon of Muslim fundamentalism but the psychological aspects of suicide attacks in general. It isn't easy to persuade a person to sacrifice his life, and all people have the instinct of self-preservation, be they Muslims, Buddhists, Christians, communists, or idolaters. Hatred of the enemy is not enough to overcome this instinct. We need to know more about the personality of the potential kamikaze. That is, to become a kamikaze, it's not enough to frequent a mosque where a firebrand imam preaches holy war. And perhaps closing down that mosque will not allay the death drive that exists in some people—who remain in circulation.

How to identify such people? What methods of investigation and surveillance can we use that won't become a nightmare for our citizenry? Perhaps we also need to ask ourselves if this death wish is not beginning to become a disease of the contemporary world (like AIDS or obesity) that can occur in groups that aren't necessarily Muslim.

IV

THE RETURN
OF THE CRUSADES

Holy Wars, Passion, and Religion

That Prime Minister Berlusconi recently made inappropriate remarks about the superiority of Western culture is of secondary importance. It is secondary when someone says something he feels is right but says it at the wrong time, and it is secondary when someone believes in something unjust or erroneous, because the world is full of people who believe in unjust and erroneous things, even a gentleman called bin Laden, who is perhaps richer than our prime minister and better educated.

What is not secondary and should worry everyone—politicians, religious leaders, and educators—is that certain expressions, and all those fervent articles that legitimized them, may become a subject of general debate, may preoccupy the young, and lead them to conclusions dictated by the momentary emotion. I worry about young people, because, as we know, it's hard to get old people to change their minds.

All the wars of religion that spilled blood in the world for centuries sprang from emotional loyalties and simplistic antagonisms, such as Us versus Them, good guys versus bad guys, black versus white. If Western culture has shown itself to be fertile (not only since the

---

"Holy Wars, Passion, and Religion" appeared in la Repubblica, *October 2001.*

Enlightenment but even before, when the Franciscan Roger Bacon called for people to learn languages because there is something to be learned even from unbelievers), it is because it made an effort—in the spirit of inquiry and critical thinking—to undo harmful simplifications.

This wasn't always the case, because the history of Western culture also includes Hitler, who burned books, condemned "degenerate" art, and murdered members of so-called inferior races. And it includes fascism, which taught me at school to say, "May God damn the English" because they were the "five-meals-a-day-people" and hence gluttons who were inferior to the frugal, spartan Italians.

But it is the finer aspects of our culture that we should discuss with young people, of whatever stripe, if we wish to avoid the collapse of new towers in the future, when we have passed away.

One element of confusion is that we often fail to grasp the difference between identifying with our roots, understanding those who have other roots, and judging what is bad or good. As for roots, if I was asked whether I would prefer to spend my retirement in a little town in Monferrato, amid the magnificent setting of the national park in the Abruzzo, or in the rolling hills around Siena, I would choose Monferrato. Which doesn't mean that I think other regions of Italy are inferior to Piedmont.

So if by his words (spoken for Westerners but deleted for the Arabs) the prime minister wanted to say that he prefers to live in Arcore (where he actually lives) rather than in Kabul, and to be treated in a Milanese hospital rather than one in Baghdad, I would second his opinion (apart from Arcore, that is). And I'd do that even if they told me that in Baghdad they have opened the best-equipped hospital in the world: I'd feel more at home in Milan, and that would improve my capacity to recover.

Roots can also go beyond regional or national boundaries. I'd rather live in Limoges than in Moscow. Why is that, isn't Moscow a beautiful city? Of course it is, but in Limoges I would understand what people were saying.

To sum up, everyone identifies with the culture in which he grew up. Cases of radical transplanting exist but are in the minority. Lawrence of Arabia dressed like an Arab, but at the end of the day he returned home.

Let's move on to the clash between cultures, because this is the point. The West, albeit often only for economic expansion, has shown curiosity about other civilizations. On many occasions it dismissed them with scorn: the Greeks labeled those who did not speak their tongue barbarians, literally stammerers, as if those peoples didn't speak at all. The more mature Greeks, such as the Stoics (perhaps because some of them were Phoenician in origin), realized that while the barbarians used words different from Greek words, they nonetheless referred to the same thoughts. With profound respect, Marco Polo tried to describe Chinese customs and habits; the great masters of medieval Christian theology tried to get hold of translations of Arab philosophers, doctors, and astrologers; the men of the Renaissance did their utmost to recover lost oriental wisdom, from the Chaldees to the Egyptians; Montesquieu tried to understand how a Persian might see the French; and modern anthropologists based their first studies on the reports of the Salesian monks, who sought out the Bororo tribe to convert them, if possible, but also to find out how they thought and lived—perhaps mindful of the fact that the missionaries of earlier centuries, having failed to understand Amerindian cultures, encouraged their extermination.

I mention anthropologists. I say nothing new by pointing out that, from the mid-nineteenth century on, social anthropology developed as an attempt to assuage the remorse of the West with regard to Others, especially those Others who had been defined as savages, societies without a history, primitive peoples. The West had behaved harshly with the "savages": it "discovered" them, tried to convert them, exploited them, enslaved many of them—and with the help of the Arabs at that, because while the slave ships were unloaded at New Orleans by refined gentlemen of French origin, they were loaded off the African coast by Muslim slave traders.

Social anthropology (which flourished thanks to colonial expansion) tried to make amends for the sins of colonialism by showing that the cultures of those Others were indeed cultures, with their own beliefs, rites, customs, all eminently reasonable within the context in which they developed, and absolutely organic: in other words, they were based on their own internal logic. The task facing social anthropology was to show that there existed forms of logic unlike Western models, and that they were to be taken seriously, not despised and repressed.

Which didn't mean that, once anthropologists had explained the logic of the Others, they decided to live like them; on the contrary, except for a few cases, when their many years abroad were over, they went back to spend a tranquil old age in Devonshire or Picardy. Yet reading their books, someone might think that social anthropology espoused a relativist position—that one culture was as good as another. I don't believe this. At best, anthropologists told us that, as long as the Others stayed in their own place, we should respect their way of life.

The real lesson to be drawn from social anthropology is that, to determine whether one culture is superior to another, we need to fix some parameters. It's one thing to say what a culture is, another to choose the parameters we judge it by. A culture can be described in a passably objective manner: these people behave in such and such a way, they believe in spirits or in a single divinity whose essence pervades all nature, they unite in kinship groups according to rules, they think that nose rings are beautiful (as many Western youths now do), they believe that pork is unclean, they circumcise their children, they raise dogs to be put in the pot and eaten on feast days.

Anthropologists know that objectivity can be badly shaken by many factors. Last year I was in the land of the Dogon and asked a little boy if he was a Muslim. He answered me in French, saying,

"No, I'm an animist." Now, believe me, an animist doesn't describe himself as such unless he has a diploma from the École des Hautes Études in Paris. That boy was talking about his culture as it had been defined by anthropologists.

The African anthropologists told me that when a European anthropologist arrives, the Dogon—who are by now streetwise—tell him the things written many years ago by an anthropologist called Griaule. According to my cultivated African friends, the natives gave Griaule a fairly disconnected account of things, which he later assembled into a system that was fascinating but dubious. Nonetheless, allowing for all the possible misunderstandings about the culture of Others, you can still make a pretty "neutral" description.

Parameters of judgment are another matter. They depend on our roots, preferences, habits, passions, and system of values. Let's take an example. Do we feel that prolonging the average life span from forty to eighty is good? Personally, I think so, but many mystics might tell me that, between a trencherman who lives to eighty and Saint Aloysius Gonzaga, who lived to twenty-three, the saint had the fuller life. But if we value the prolongation of life, then Western science and medicine are clearly superior to many other forms of science and medical practice.

Do we think that technological development, the expansion of trade, and rapid transportation are good? A great many people do, and so they consider our technological culture superior. But in the Western world, some feel that a life in harmony with an unpolluted environment is of primary importance, therefore they are willing to give up airplanes, cars, and refrigerators. Weaving baskets and walking from one village to the next, they say, is better than having a hole in the ozone layer. So you see, to define one culture as better than another, it's not enough to describe them; we need to refer to a system of values we feel we cannot do without. Only then can we say that our culture is better, *for us.*

Recently I have seen cultures defended on the basis of debatable parameters. Only the other day I read a letter published in a major newspaper in which the writer asked sarcastically why Nobel prizes go only to Westerners and not to Asians. Apart from the fact that we are talking about a person unaware that many Nobel prizes for literature have been awarded to authors with dark skins and to great Muslim writers, apart from the fact that the 1979 Nobel prize for physics went to a Pakistani called Abdus Salam, to state that science prizes go to people working within the framework of Western science is to state the obvious, because no one has ever doubted that modern Western science and technology are in the vanguard. In the vanguard of what? Of science and technology.

How absolute is the parameter of technological development? Pakistan has the atom bomb, and Italy doesn't. So are we an inferior culture? Is it better to live in Islamabad than in Arcore?

Proponents of dialogue call upon us to respect the Muslim world, pointing out that it has given us men like Avicenna (born in Bukhara, not far from Afghanistan) and Averroës—and it's a shame that they always mention those two, as if they were the only ones, and don't mention Al Kindi, Avenpace, Avicebron, Ibn Tufayl, or that great historian of the fourteenth century, Ibn Khaldun, whom the West considers the father of the social sciences. They remind us that the Arabs in Spain were cultivating geography, astronomy, mathematics, and medicine when the Christian world was lagging far behind. All very true, but if we follow this reasoning, we would have to say that the noble Tuscan township of Vinci is superior to New York, because Leonardo was born in Vinci when in Manhattan a handful of Indians sat around for 150 years waiting for the Dutch to arrive and buy the entire island from them for twenty-four dollars. But it isn't like that: I don't wish to offend anyone, but today the center of the world is New York, not Vinci. Things change. There's no sense in pointing out that the Arabs in Spain were tolerant toward Christians and Jews while elsewhere in Europe people were attacking the ghettos, or that when Saladin reconquered Jerusalem, he was more merciful with the Christians than the Christians had been with the Saracens when they first took the city. Again, all very true, but in the Muslim world today there are fundamentalist and theocratic regimes that do not tolerate Christians, and bin Laden was not merciful with New York. The Bactrian Way was once a crossroads of great civilizations, but today the Taliban destroy statues of the Buddha with cannon fire. Conversely, the French were responsible for the massacre of St. Bartholomew's Night, but today no one would say that they are barbarians.

Let's not bring history into this, because it's a two-edged sword. The Turks impaled people (and that's bad) but the Orthodox Byzantines gouged out the eyes of dangerous relatives and the Catholics burned Giordano Bruno. The Barbary pirates did many nasty things, but the corsairs of His Britannic Majesty, with letters patent and all, burned the Spanish colonies in the Caribbean. Bin Laden and Saddam are ferocious enemies of Western civilization, but Western civilization also produced gentlemen called Hitler and Stalin (Stalin was so wicked, he was called Oriental, though he had studied in a seminary and had read Marx).

No, the problem of parameters should be posed not from a historical viewpoint but from a contemporary one. One laudable thing about Western cultures (which are free and pluralistic, values that we consider inalienable) is that they have realized for a long time that advantages and disadvantages go together. The prolongation of life is a plus and air pollution a minus, but to have the great laboratories in which medical advances are made, you need an energy supply that, in turn, produces pollution. Western culture has developed the ability to confront its own contradictions. Maybe it doesn't solve them, but it knows they exist and says as much. This sums up the entire proglobalization-antiglobalization debate, no matter what the vandals of the so-called Black Bloc say: how can we attain a tolerable degree of positive globalization while avoiding the risks and injustices of negative globalization, how can we prolong life for the millions of Africans dying of AIDS (while prolonging our own at the same time) without accepting a planetary economy that has AIDS victims die of starvation and has us eat polluted foods?

This very critique of parameters, which the West pursues and encourages, shows us just how tricky the question of parameters is. Is it right and civilized to protect confidential bank information? Many people think so. But what if this secrecy permits terrorists to keep their money in the City of London? Is the defense of privacy a genuine or dubious value? We continually question our parameters. The Western world does this to such an extent that it allows its own citizens to see technological development as negative and become Buddhists or go and live in communities where the buggies are horse-drawn and don't even use tires. Schools should teach young people to analyze and discuss the parameters on which our emotive statements are based.

The problem that social anthropology has not solved is what we do when a member of a culture whose principles we have perhaps learned to respect comes to live in our country. In reality racism in the West is largely due not to the fact that some of the people of Mali are animists (as long as they stay there, as the Northern League would say) but to the fact that they might come to live here. Never mind the animists, or those who wish to pray in the direction of Mecca, but what if they want to wear a chador or to infibulate their little girls, what if (as occurs in certain Western sects) they refuse to let their sick children receive blood transfusions, or what if the last cannibal in New Guinea (if there are any left) wants to emigrate here so he can roast a young fellow once a week for Sunday lunch?

As far as our cannibal goes, we are all in agreement: you can put him in prison (especially because there aren't a billion cannibals around). But I see no reason to raise a fuss if girls go to school wearing a chador if that's what they want to do. As for infibulation, the debate is open (some people are so tolerant as to suggest that this operation be carried out in local medical centers, for the sake of hygiene), but what should we do with the request that Muslim women have their passport photos taken while wearing a burka? We have laws, the same for everyone, that establish the criteria for the identification of citizens, and I don't think we can deviate from them. When I visited a mosque, I took off my shoes, because I respect the laws and customs of the host country. So what do we do about veiled passport photos? We can negotiate. At bottom, passport photos are always unfaithful, useful only to a limited extent, so why not invent smart cards that react to a fingerprint and make those who want this privileged treatment pay a surcharge? And if these women attend our universities, they may also learn about rights they didn't know they had, just as many Westerners have attended madrassas and then decided to become Muslims.

Thinking about our parameters also means deciding that we won't tolerate everything, that certain things are intolerable for us.

The West has devoted funds and energy to studying the ways and customs of the Others, but no one has really allowed the Others to study the ways and customs of the West, apart from schools run overseas by whites, or the wealthiest Others who study in Oxford or Paris—and then look what happens, they return home to organize fundamentalist movements, because they feel a bond with their compatriots who cannot afford such studies (an old story: the struggle for Indian independence was led by intellectuals who had studied in England).

Ancient Arab and Chinese travelers studied the lands where the sun sets, but we know little about this. How many African or Chinese anthropologists have come to study the West to describe it not only to their fellow countrymen but also to us—I mean to say, to tell us how they see us?

For some years now an international organization called Transcultura has been fighting for an "alternative anthropology." It invited African scholars who had never visited the West to describe the French provinces and life in Bologna, and I can assure you that when we Europeans read about their amazement on discovering that Europeans take their dogs for walks and remove all their clothes when they go to the beach—well, this exchange was stimulating on both sides, and interesting discussions came out of it. As I write, in preparation for a conference that will be held in Brussels next November, three Chinese scholars (a philosopher, an anthropologist, and an artist) are completing Marco Polo's travels in reverse, except that they won't just be writing their version of Polo's *Il milione* but also recording and filming it. I don't know what their observations will mean to the Chinese, but we will find them significant.

Imagine if Muslim fundamentalists were invited to carry out research on Christian fundamentalism (I'm thinking of certain American Protestants, more fanatical than any ayatollah, who would expunge all reference to Darwin from the schoolbooks). Studying the fundamentalism of others helps us understand our own fundamentalism better. Let them come and study our concept of holy war (I could suggest a very interesting reading list, with some recent works), and perhaps they will view the concept in their own countries with a more critical eye. We Westerners have reflected on the limitations of our own way of thinking by describing *la pensée sauvage*.

One of the topics most discussed in Western civilization is the acceptance of diversity. Theoretically we all agree, it's politically correct to say in public that someone is gay, but then at home we snigger and call him a fairy. How can we teach the acceptance of diversity? The Académie Universelle des Cultures has set up a Web site where the elaboration of various themes is under way (color, religion, customs, and so on) for the educators of any country where people want children to learn how to accept those who are different from them. It was decided, first, not to tell the children that we are all equal. They can see that some neighbors and classmates are not the same: they have a different skin color, almond-shaped eyes, curlier or straighter hair, they eat strange food, and don't take First Communion. Nor is it enough to say that we are all God's children, because animals are God's children too, but the kids won't see a goat standing at the blackboard teaching them spelling.

Instead, we should tell children that human beings are different, and explain what those differences are, to show that they can be a source of richness. A teacher in an Italian city should help her Italian pupils understand why other youngsters pray to a different god or play music that doesn't sound like rock. A Chinese teacher should do the same thing with Chinese pupils who live near a Christian community. The next step is to show that there is something in common between our music and theirs, and that their religion too has some good rules.

A possible objection: We may do this in Florence, but will they do the same in Kabul? We are a pluralistic civilization because we allow people to build mosques in our country, and we can't stop being pluralistic because in Kabul they put Christian propagandists in prison. Or we too would become Taliban. The parameter of tolerance is one of the strongest and least debatable. We think of our culture as mature because it tolerates diversity, and we consider barbarians those members of our culture who do not. And that's that. Otherwise, it would be as if we decided, if there were still cannibals in some corner of the world, that we should go off and eat them, because that would teach them a lesson.

We hope, since we permit the presence of mosques in our country, that in other countries one day there will be Christian churches and that the locals won't bomb statues of the Buddha. We hope this, trusting in the goodness of our parameters.

There is much confusion in the world, and some very odd things are happening these days. It seems as if the defense of Western values has become a banner of the right, while the left is as usual pro-Islamic. Now, apart from the fact that there is a decidedly Third-Worldist, pro-Arab Catholicism and a political right with the same views, a historical phenomenon that is right under everyone's nose is not being taken into account.

The defense of the values of science, of technological development, and of modern Western culture has always been a characteristic of the secular and progressive left. Moreover, an ideology of technological and scientific progress can be traced back to all communist regimes. The Manifesto of 1848 opens with a dispassionate eulogy of bourgeois expansion; Marx doesn't say that it's necessary to change course and shift to Asian production methods; all he says is that the proletariat should learn from these values and successes.

Conversely, at least after the rejection of the French Revolution, reactionary thought (in the noblest sense of the term) has always been opposed to the secular idea of progress, affirming instead that we ought to return to traditional values. Only a few groups of neo-Nazis identify with a mythical idea of the West and would be prepared to slit the throat of every last Muslim at Stonehenge. The most serious thinkers within the Tradition (including many Italians who vote for the right-wing party Alleanza Nazionale) have always turned not only to the rites and myths of primitive peoples but also to Buddhist teachings, and to Islam itself, as still-modern sources of alternative spirituality. These sources have always been there to remind us that we are not superior, that we have been made barren by the ideology of progress, and that we should go seek the truth among Sufi mystics and whirling dervishes. And I'm not the one who says these things—just go to a bookshop and look on the right shelves.

In this sense a curious split is now forming in the ranks of the right. But maybe it's only a sign that in times of great disorientation (and we are living through such a time) no one knows where he stands anymore.

It is precisely in such moments of disorientation that we need to apply the tools of analysis and criticism—analysis of our own superstitions as well as those of others. I hope that these things will be discussed in the schools and not only at press conferences.

Negotiating in a Multiethnic Society

The fundamental principle that governs—or ought to govern—human affairs, if we wish to avoid misunderstandings, conflicts, or pointless utopias, is negotiation. The model of negotiation is an oriental bazaar: the seller asks for ten, you offer three, he says nine, you four, he goes down to eight, you go up to five, and finally you both agree on six. You feel you've won because you went up only three and he came down four, but the seller is equally satisfied because he knows the item is worth five. But, in the end, if you are interested in those goods and he is interested in selling them, you are both pleased.

The principle of negotiation governs not only the market economy, trade union struggles, and (when things are going well) international affairs, it also lies at the very base of cultural life. Negotiation occurs in a good translation (in translation you inevitably lose some of the original text, but you can work out ways to compensate for this) and even in how we use words: you and I assign different meanings to a certain term, but to communicate, we agree on a common core of meaning that allows us to understand each other. For some people

"Negotiating in a Multiethnic Society" appeared in la Repubblica, *July 2004.*

it's raining only when it comes down in buckets; for others, a few drops on the hand is rain. But when the problem is whether to go to the beach or not, we are able to agree on the quantity of "rain" that makes the difference between going and not going. A principle of negotiation also operates in the interpretation of a text (be it a poem or an ancient document), because, no matter how much we may have to say about it, we are faced with that specific text and not another one, and a text is a fact too. Just as we can't change the fact that it is raining today, we can't change the fact that Manzoni's *The Betrothed* begins with "That branch of Lake Como," and if we write (or understand) Lake Garda instead of Como, we are changing the novel.

If, as some say, there are no facts in the world but only interpretations, negotiation would be impossible, because there would be no criterion that would enable us to decide whether my interpretation is better than yours or not. We can compare and discuss interpretations precisely because we can weigh them against the facts they are intended to interpret.

According to the newspapers, a misinformed clergyman recently numbered me among the doctrinaire ideologues or so-called *cattivi maestri* ("bad teachers") because I maintain there are no facts, only interpretations. I have no problem with the bad-teacher label (my devilish side says I would like to be one, but as I grow in age and wisdom, I find myself at best an appalling pupil), but the thing is that in many of my works I have said the exact opposite, that our interpretations continually beat their heads against the hard core of facts, and the facts (even though often difficult to interpret) are there, solid and aggressive, to challenge untenable interpretations.

We negotiate because, if everyone stuck to his own interpretation of the facts, we would go on ad infinitum. We negotiate to bring our diverging interpretations to a point of convergence, if only a partial one, that enables us to deal with a Fact—a thing that is there and is difficult to get rid of.

This entire discourse (pointing to our need to come reasonably to terms with the inevitable) springs from a decision made by a Milanese high school, after a request from immigrant parents, to establish a class solely for Muslim students. The case seems strange, because it wouldn't take much, in the best of possible worlds, to put some of the Muslim students in one class and some in another, thus encouraging them to mix with schoolmates from another culture while enabling their Italian schoolmates to understand and accept their Muslim companions. It is nonetheless a Fact that this world is not the best, even though some theologians and philosophers think God himself couldn't do better, so we must content ourselves with this one.

I am always one hundred percent in agreement with my friend Claudio Magris (well, let's say ninety-nine point nine percent), but I'd like to put forward a few objections to a recent article of his published in *Corriere della Sera*. In terms of "what ought to be," his reasoning is impeccable. Pointing out that the high school decision was determined by the fact that the parents of the students had effectively imposed an ultimatum (Do things our way, or we won't send our children to school), Magris wrote:

> This request to be closed up in a ghetto, which might have been made by a rabidly anti-Muslim racist, is an insult to everyone, and to Islam in the first place, which yet again risks being identified with its basest forms of degeneration. . . . Why must it be terrible, scandalous, or repugnant for them to have a schoolmate who is Catholic, Waldensian, Jewish, or one who is neither baptized nor circumcised? . . . Pluralism—the salt of life, democracy, and culture—does not consist of a series of worlds closed in on themselves, each one unaware of the other, but in coming together, in dialogue and comparison. . . .

I am naturally disposed to endorse these observations, and in fact for a few years now I have been trying to set up, with some friends and colleagues, a Web site where advice is provided for teachers of all races and in all countries about how to lead their pupils to mutual understanding and an acceptance of diversity (the site is hosted by the Académie Universelle des Cultures and Kataweb). Obviously, in order to understand and accept one another, we have to live together. This should be explained to the parents who demanded that their children be segregated, but, uninformed about the specific situation, I don't know to what extent these people would be open to Magris's arguments, which I make my own.

The only point in Magris's article that I disagree with is the statement that this request was "inadmissible," that "it shouldn't have even been taken into consideration but tossed in the wastebasket." Can we consider a request that offends our convictions? These convictions of ours concern Oughtness (a state of being that, since it doesn't exist yet, is always beyond, therefore the source of endless debate and infinite interpretations). But the Oughtness, in the case in point, clashes with a Fact, which, like all Facts, is not a matter of discussion. Faced with a fact like a volcanic eruption or an avalanche, we don't make judgments on its merits, we seek a solution.

The Fact here is that a group of parents (Egyptian apparently) were ready to take their children out of school. I don't know what their options were: send the children to school in Egypt, not let them study at all, or give them an exclusively Muslim education in some private school. If we exclude the first possibility (which might please the Northern League: We'll get rid of these brats by sending them home—a watered-down version of "better to kill them young"), the second would be deplorable, because it would deprive these young immigrants of the right to a complete education (even though this would be the fault of the parents and not of the state).

This leaves us with the third option, which has three disadvantages: it would segregate these youngsters completely, prevent them from learning about the host culture, and probably lead to a sort of fundamentalist isolation. What's more, we are talking not about el-

ementary education, which could be provided by a group of volunteer parents, but about high school education, which is rather more
complex. Unless we were to establish Koranic schools on a par with
state schools—a possibility, given that there are Catholic private
schools. But this, to my mind, would be another form of segregation.

If these are the facts and the alternatives, we can understand the
decision made by the Milanese school, the result of reasonable negotiation. Since refusal means sending the children elsewhere, or
nowhere, we grant the request—even though we don't agree with it in
principle—and so choose the lesser of two evils, in the hope that the
decision will prove a temporary one. The children will stay in a separate (which is a loss for them as well) class but in compensation receive the same education as their Italian peers, and they will also
learn more about our language and history. Since they are not infants
but high school students, they might think for themselves and make
the necessary comparisons, and even try to make contact on their own
initiative with their Italian (or Chinese or Filipino) schoolmates.
There is as yet no evidence that they agree entirely with their parents.

Moreover, we are dealing with a school where many subjects
and doctrines are taught, so if the teachers are skilled and tactful,
the students will learn that in Italy certain beliefs, customs, and
opinions are shared by the majority, but it wouldn't be a bad thing
if someone suggested that the Italians read a few pages of the
Koran—for example, this passage:

> We believe in God, and in what He has revealed to us, and in
> what He revealed to Abraham, to Ishmael, to Isaac, to Jacob,
> and to the Tribes, and in what was said to Moses and Jesus,
> and in what was given to the prophets of the Lord: we make no
> distinction between them. . . . Those who practice Judaism,
> Christians, Sabeans, whoever believes in God and in the last
> day and does good works, will be rewarded before God. . . . Vie
> among yourselves in good works. All shall return to God, who

will then tell you about the things that divide you. . . . And dispute not with the people of the Book unless you do so courteously, except with those of them who act unjustly, and say: "We believe in that which has been handed down to us and in that which has been handed to you: your God and our God are one."

How and what these young people might think after a few years spent living, albeit separated, within the framework of the host culture, we don't know, for the obvious reason that the future is in the hands of Allah. But the result would probably be more interesting than if they had spent the time in the double segregation of a private school.

We all aspire to the best, but we have all learned that sometimes the best is the enemy of good, that by negotiating we must choose the lesser of two evils. Heaven knows how often we will have to negotiate this way to avoid bloodshed in a multiethnic society. But accepting the lesser of two evils, hoping that the lesser evil won't become a habit, doesn't mean we shouldn't strive for the best—though, as the best is not a fact but an end, it remains subject to many interpretations.

The Taking of Jerusalem:
An Eyewitness Report

July 14, morning. Hello? Can you hear me there in the studio? Right, you're coming through perfectly, okay. Jerusalem here, live from Mount Zion, just outside the walls. The attack on the city was launched at first light. From where I stand, I overlook the rough square of the city walls; toward the east stands the Temple Mount, where the Dome of the Rock now stands; to the northeast is Herod's Gate; outside the walls to the northeast lies the Mount of Olives; and the Tower of David is to the southeast. Formidable walls, and to the east they plunge into the vale of Cedron, and over another valley to the west. So the troops of the Christian alliance can attack only from the southeast and the north.

Now that the sun is up, I can see the big wooden towers, the mangonels, and the catapults trying to cross the ditch that separates them from the walls. You will all remember how crucial the problem of the siege engines is. The city has been surrounded since the 7th of June, and on the 12th, after listening to the words of a fanatical hermit who prophesied that victory was at hand, the Christian

---

This piece appeared in la Repubblica, *July 1999, to mark the thousandth anniversary of the taking of Jerusalem.*

armies attempted a first attack. A disaster: they clearly lacked the means to scale the walls. The commanders knew this well, but in this war various pressures are in play. Noblemen and knights know that you can also make war through truces and agreements, and above all you take your time. But in its train the army has brought an immense horde of pilgrims, poverty-stricken outcasts driven by mystical urges and the lust for plunder. They are the same ones who put the ghettos of the Jews to fire and sword as they made their way down the Danube. Dangerous people, and hard to control.

I think that this was the main reason for the stalemate of June 12, which ushered in a month of starvation and thirst. Real thirst, because the governor of Jerusalem, Iftikhar ad-Dawla, had the outer wells poisoned (while the city has an excellent system of reservoirs), and the Christians—especially those burdened by heavy armor—couldn't stand the infernal heat and drank even foul water. The only fresh water was in the south, too close to the enemy walls. And there was a shortage of timber then, and of the equipment needed to construct siege engines. The hills around here are barren, and the nearest supplies of wood are far away. As for the equipment, it took until mid-June before two Genoan galleys and four English ships arrived in the port of Jaffa with nails, bolts, and everything else you need for military carpentry work. So only now are we able to attack with high-tech armaments.

Right now I can see three enormous towers, three stories tall, moving toward the walls. Teeming with men-at-arms, each can drop a drawbridge on top of the walls. The problem will be crossing the ditch to get at those walls without cover, exposed to enemy fire. A dirty job that will mean many losses. That's war for you.

How many men do we have? You won't believe this, but I can't come up with a figure. The Christian alliance is made up of various armies, whose leaders often squabble over positions of prestige, and they are capable of cooking the books. Then there's the crowd of pilgrims. Some speak of fifty thousand people overall. I think that's too high a number. The most generous estimate is twelve thousand men-at-arms, one thousand three hundred knights; the most cautious, five thousand men-at-arms, one thousand knights. As far as trained troops go, the Moors have only a few thousand Arabs and Sudanese, but then there are the inhabitants, all prepared to fight. What's more, Iftikhar has had a brilliant idea. He sent all the Christians out of the city, and now they will have to be fed by our forces; so he has rid himself not only of extra mouths to feed but also of possible saboteurs. He let the Jews stay, perhaps in exchange for money. If he had sent them out, our pilgrims would have torn them to pieces.

By now, many of our listeners will have accepted that this expedition was undertaken to restore the holy places to the Church, and they will be amazed to learn that Christians can live in peace in Jerusalem, with their churches and everything. But remember that the Christian alliance recently occupied Bethlehem at the request of the local Christian community, a clear sign that such a community existed. And in fact, we are gradually learning that Christians and their religion are more or less tolerated in Saracen lands—like the Jews, for that matter. So we are besieging a city of infidels so that Christians may visit it, and the first result is that all the Christians who lived there have been kicked out. Not the only paradox of this war, which some think is based on a principle (the holy places should be reserved for the Christians), others see as a chance for conquest, and others again see as God knows what, a sort of huge, cruel party . . .

My informants tell me that the attack is more interesting on the northwestern front, at Herod's Gate. I will hop on a mule and try to get to the other side of the walls. And now, back to the studio.

July 14, evening. Hello? Can you hear me there in the studio? Right, good. It took me several hours to get near Herod's Gate: I had to keep a fair distance from the walls, because rocks are raining down all over. I went through the smoke from many fires. Flames in the

night. Fascinating and terrible. The Moors know the Byzantine technique of Greek fire, and their fireballs fall nonstop on the wooden
towers. Look out, I have to move back, the Moors are making a sor-
tie to set fire to our engines . . . One tower has caught fire, and our
men are leaping off, but the enemy archers are hitting them. The
upper part of a tower just crashed to the ground, sending out a
shower of sparks, but luckily it smashed some of the Moors who
were heading back to the safety of the walls, and it also set fire to
the doors of the gate. Why don't our men shift all the battering rams
in that direction? Greek fire hit the other engines, I'm told, so things
have gone badly for us today. We'll need to work through the night
to repair the siege engines. And now, back to the studio.

July 15, morning. I can't hear you very well . . . no, okay, you're
coming through now. It seems that we have managed to repair most
of our engines, and the attack is under way once more. A hail of
rocks is falling on the walls, and our battering rams have made it
across the ditch. The old testudo formation is good but not infallible,
many of our brave lads have fallen under enemy fire from above, but
they are instantly replaced. Our siege engines are making Jerusalem tremble to its foundations . . .

From my new position I have a clear view of Godfrey of Bouillon directing the final assault from the top of a tower. The first Christians are on the top of the walls. They are Luthold and Engelbert of
Tournai, I'm told, Godfrey and the others follow them, the Moors are
falling under their blows, others are leaping from the walls. Herod's
Gate is down—unless it was opened by our men already inside. The
men of the Christian Alliance have entered the city on foot and
horseback!

They tell me the battle is still raging at the Zion Gate . . . hold
on, here is some breaking news, it seems that the Provençal troops
of Raymond de Saint-Gilles have broken through at the Zion Gate.
Raymond has stormed the Tower of David and captured Iftikhar

with his garrison, granting him his life in exchange for a ransom. Saint-Gilles immediately had him escorted to Ascalon, which is still in Saracen hands. The enemy is routed, victory is ours! This is a historic moment and, amazingly, it is three in the afternoon, the hour of the Passion of Our Lord!! What a coincidence!! Now I'll try to join the mass of our men rushing into the city, it won't be easy, I risk being trampled by the horses . . . Can you hear me? I can't hear you, but I'll go on . . .

Now I am inside the walls of Jerusalem. I have to climb over piles of swarthy corpses, yet resistance ought to have ceased by now. I interviewed a sergeant on his way back to the Christian camp, covered with blood, his hands full of precious fabrics. "Resistance? Not at all; as soon as we got in, those devils ran for it and holed up in the Mosque of the Rock. But the great Tancred of Altavilla surprised them before they could organize themselves, and they surrendered. Tancred raised his standard over the mosque, to put them under his protection." So I asked him why all these corpses: "Sir, are you joking? We conquered a city here, and an infidel one at that. So we kill them all, young and old, men, women, and children. It's the rule, isn't it?" What about the people under Tancred's protection? I asked. He made a gesture: "You know, noblemen will say anything."

I am now blocked by a crowd of Moors fleeing in all directions, pursued by our troops . . . Forgive me, but my voice trembles at what I am seeing. The men of the Christian Alliance are mercilessly cutting all their throats. Oh God, some are even smashing the children's heads against the walls . . . And they're not only soldiers venting the stress of the battle, I also see bands of pilgrims falling savagely on the wounded . . . One moment . . . News is coming in about the synagogue, where the Jews left in the city took refuge. It has been put to the torch, and the entire Jewish community of Jerusalem has perished. I see an old friar weeping: "True, they were only despicable Jews, but why give them to the flames now when the fires of hell awaited them? Our Christians have become maddened beasts who don't obey their captains anymore."

Hello? Can't you hear me? No wonder, all the buildings are crackling in the blaze, collapsing everywhere, and the screams of those put to the sword. Jesus Christ Our Lord, I can't take any more of this. I'll be in touch tomorrow, and now back to the studio.

July 16. Can you hear me in the studio? Not much more to add. There are times when you feel ashamed to be a reporter . . . Tancred promised the Moors in the mosque that their lives would be spared, but a group of madmen (Flemings, they say, but I don't know) today disregarded his orders, and there was another bloodbath. Some of the knights are even accusing Raymond de Saint-Gilles of treason because he saved Iftikhar's life. Everyone seems to have gone mad here; the blood has gone to their heads. I am talking to Raymond de Aguilers: "Around the mosque the blood is knee-deep. Tancred is beside himself, feels dishonored because he wasn't as good as his word, but it's not his fault. I don't think there's a single Moor or Jew left alive in Jerusalem." I ask him for a body count, how many victims in all? He talks of seventy thousand dead, but I think he's exaggerating—he's in shock. To the best of my knowledge, after the expulsion of the Christians there were a few thousand men of the garrison, plus fifty thousand inhabitants. Some may have fled through breaches in the wall. I'd say that about forty thousand people overall were killed these past two days. It seems impossible to slaughter so many in such a short time. But all around me is a sea of corpses and, in the hot sun, the stench is terrible.

A monk I spoke to this morning pointed out that this massacre amounts to a defeat. If we are to establish a Christian realm in these lands, we ought to be able to count on the acceptance of the Muslim inhabitants and on the tolerance of the neighboring kingdoms. But the slaughter has raised a wall of hatred between Moors and Christians that will endure for years, perhaps centuries. The conquest of Jerusalem is not the end but the beginning—of a very long war.

Stop. I just learned that yesterday, while the massacre was at its peak, Tancred of Altavilla, Robert of Flanders, Gaston of Béarn, Raymond of Toulouse, Robert of Normandy, and all the other captains went in procession to hang up their weapons in the Holy Sepulcher and to worship there, thus releasing themselves from their vows—to use the words attributed to Godfrey of Bouillon. It was a most moving ceremony, in which all concerned felt a little better.

Apologies for missing this, but in the middle of that carnage I lost my bearings. From liberated Jerusalem, I hand the line back to the studio.

Beauty Queens, Fundamentalists, and Lepers

By the time you read this, most of you will have forgotten what happened during the recent Miss World contest in Nigeria, when over two hundred people were murdered. Which is a good reason not to let the matter drop.

Perhaps the situation deteriorated, even after the contest was moved to London, because it was clear to everyone that the arrival of the beauty queens in Nigeria was merely a pretext to create tension or foment far more serious subversion, though it's hard to understand why a protest against a beauty contest should make it necessary to murder Christians and burn down their churches, since the bishops can hardly be accused of organizing the event. What led to this appalling fundamentalist reaction?

Wole Soyinka, the Nobel Prize winner who has seen the inside of Nigerian prisons for defending the basic freedoms of his hapless country, wrote an article in *la Repubblica* in which, together with some enlightening reflections on Nigerian conflicts, he said (to sum up his remarks) that he had no liking for the various national and

"Beauty Queens, Fundamentalists, and Lepers" appeared in L'espresso, *December 2002.*

international beauty contests, but, faced with the anger of the Muslim fundamentalists, he felt obliged to defend the rights of the body and beauty. I think that if I were Nigerian, I would agree with him, but as I'm not, I'd like to try to look at the business from an Italian standpoint.

There's no doubt—even if you are a bigot who wishes to protest against an event where girls parade in bathing suits—that you cannot justify the killing of more than two hundred people who had nothing to do with it. In that respect, we are all on the side of the girls. But, in deciding to hold the event in Nigeria, the Miss World organizers played a dirty trick. Not so much because they could have or should have foreseen the reaction as because holding this vanity fair (whose cost would be enough to feed several tribes for a month) in a depressed country like Nigeria, where children die of hunger and where adulterers are sentenced to be stoned to death, is like selling pornographic videotapes and comedy movies in a home for the blind or handing out beauty products in a leprosarium complete with publicity photos of Naomi Campbell.

And there's no point in saying that a beauty contest is a way to change ancestral customs, because such things work only in small doses and not as a result of large-scale, blatantly provocative events. Although this episode was no more than an indecorous, absolutely cynical affair clearly organized for publicity purposes, it pertains to matters that interest us directly these days—that cluster of problems known as globalization. I am one of those who think that out of every ten phenomena of globalization, at least five may have a positive outcome but if globalization does have a negative aspect, it is that violent imposition of Western models on underdeveloped countries to induce consumption and raise hopes that such countries cannot fulfill. If I show you beauty queens in swimsuits, it's because I want to promote the sale of Western beach wear, maybe sewn by hungry children in Hong Kong. The clothing will be bought in Nigeria by those who aren't dying of hunger (if these people have money to spend, they are making it at the expense of those dying of hunger) and who actively help Westerners exploit the poor and keep them in a precolonial condition.

So I wouldn't have minded if the most combative members of the antiglobalization movement had gathered in Nigeria during the contest, both the peace-loving adherents who dress in white and the violent Black Bloc. The "whites" could have given the contest organizers a good, peaceful (but energetic) kick in the pants, stripped them down to their briefs (like their beauty queens), smeared them with honey, covered them with ostrich feathers—or those of any other winged creature available—and paraded them through the streets while mistreating them as they deserve. The "blacks" could have taken on the local fundamentalists—those accomplices of Western colonialists who are perfectly happy for the country to remain underdeveloped—bringing to bear all their aggression to prevent the fundamentalists from carrying out their massacres. And perhaps we would all have applauded (just this once) the warriors of peace. If you are violent, you should have the courage to tackle violent adversaries.

What of the aspiring beauty queens? Perhaps the milder wings of the antiglobalization movement could have persuaded them to go and wiggle their pretty little asses around the villages distributing cans of meat and bars of soap, plus antibiotics and powdered milk. Then we would have found them beautiful indeed.

What Are We to Do with the Pre-Adamites?

Ever since I started writing this column, eighteen years ago, I said that I wouldn't necessarily be dealing with topical matters—in other words, if one evening I chanced to read a passage from the *Iliad*, I might find a connection to current events. Now, as the winds of war are shaking the world, I have found in an antique book dealer's catalog a little book I had been seeking for a long time, one that I had come to think was lost: the work in question was condemned to be burned at the stake, a fate its author risked sharing, so I imagine that both he and the publisher hastened to get rid of any copies in their possession. I bought it for a negligible sum, not because the dealer didn't know it was rare but because it is small, has no particular graphic or typographic appeal, and no one (excepting a few scholars) was dying to have it on his or her shelf.

It comprises two small treatises, *Prae Adamitae* and *Systhema theologicum ex praeadamitarum hypothesi,* published in 1655 by a Protestant called Isaac de la Peyrère. What did the author say that was so extraordinary as to make him become a Catholic and submit to the pope in order to save his skin?

"What Are We to Do with the Pre-Adamites" appeared in L'espresso, *April 2003.*

Peyrère's period was marked by a boom in studies regarding a mother tongue thought to underlie all civilizations, usually identified as the Hebrew spoken by Adam. At the same time, 150 years after the discovery of America, more and more information was coming in about remote peoples, the result of new exploration and increasingly frequent journeys to exotic countries, China included. In "freethinking" circles there was talk about a hypothesis attributed to Epicurus (a letter to Herodotus) and later picked up by Lucretius, according to which names had not been fixed in a privileged tongue once and for all at the beginning of the world but depended on the diverse ways in which human groups responded to their environments. Hence in different ways and periods, these groups produced different families of languages (and different cultures).

Which brings us to the proposal put forward by Isaac de la Peyrère, a Calvinist who through debatable interpretations of certain biblical texts (he had to find orthodox support for his decidedly heterodox thesis) suggested the polygenesis of peoples and races. Peyrère realized that the biblical chronologies, with their six thousand or so years since the beginning of the world, were too short with respect to the chronologies of the Chaldeans, the Aztecs, the Incas, and the Chinese, especially regarding their accounts of the origin of the world. Hence there must have been pre-Adamic humans. But if so, then that civilization (which he identified as the Gentiles, but it could have been identified with other races) could not have been touched by original sin, because both the sin and the Flood affected only Adam and his descendants in the land of the Jews.

This hypothesis had already appeared in Muslim circles. In the tenth century, working on the basis of the Koran, Al Maqdisi mentioned the existence of other beings in the world before Adam.

It's easy to see how heretical Peyrère's idea must have seemed. It cast doubt on the Flood: If only Noah's family was saved in the ark, then the Flood should have destroyed all the other races, but new ethnological evidence showed that these people had continued to flourish. It also cast doubt on the centrality of the Passion of Christ in human history: only a small part of humanity had therefore committed original sin and required redemption in order to be saved. In short, six thousand years of sacred history reduced to a minor incident in the Mediterranean. Being burned at the stake was the least of his worries.

Note that some might see Peyrère's theory in a racist light, thinking that his pre-Adamites were populations superior to the Jews. But his position was quite different; he was interested in the Jewish tradition and favored an open, ecumenical approach to them. He was merely carrying out a singularly antiethnocentric operation, trying to show that the whole world (and civilization) is not made up solely of "us" but also of others whose history was longer than that of Judeo-Christian civilization.

This is where the chance nature of my discovery shows itself to be, if not less casual, then at least more providential than I first thought, now that we have once more let ourselves be blinded by the idea of a crusade against those who (we think) have less history and a lesser claim to nobility.

As for his hypothesis, Peyrère got almost everything wrong. But, as far as the broad-mindedness of his approach to different cultures is concerned, this poor victim of persecution and his ill-used book can still provide us with food for thought.

V

THE *SUMMA* AND THE REST

The Roots of Europe

The news this summer has been enlivened by a debate as to whether it would be appropriate to include a clause in the European Constitution mentioning the continent's Christian roots. Those who demand this base their arguments on the fact—an obvious one—that Europe sprang from Christian culture, even before the fall of the Roman Empire, at least since the Edict of Constantine. Just as we can't conceive of the oriental world without Buddhism, we can't conceive of Europe without taking into account the role of the Church, the various most Christian majesties, scholastic theology, or the deeds and examples of its great saints.

Those who oppose mentioning Europe's Christian roots appeal to the secular principles that underpin modern democracy. Those who want the clause remind us that secularism is a recent European acquisition, a legacy of the French Revolution: nothing to do with roots sunk deep in monasticism or Franciscanism. Those who oppose the clause are thinking above all of the Europe of tomorrow, destined to become a multiethnic continent and one where explicit mention of Christian roots might block both the assimilation of

---

"The Roots of Europe" appeared in L'espresso, *September 2003.*

newcomers and reduce other cultures and religions (which might become quite large) to the status of merely tolerated minority cultures and religions.

So, as we can see, this is not only a war of religion, because it involves a political plan, an anthropological standpoint, and the decision whether to depict the physical features of European peoples on the basis of their past or their future.

Let's look at the past. Did Europe develop solely on the basis of Christian culture? I'm not thinking about the enrichment that European culture drew over the centuries from Indian mathematics, Arab medicine, or contact with the Far East—not only in Marco Polo's day but also in that of Alexander the Great. Every culture assimilates elements from other cultures near and far, but then characterizes itself by how it makes them its own. It's not enough to say that we owe the zero to the Indians or the Arabs, when Europeans were the first to state that nature is written in mathematical characters. But we are forgetting Greco-Roman culture.

Europe has assimilated Greco-Roman culture in law, philosophy, and popular beliefs. Often with a certain nonchalance, Christianity absorbed pagan myths and rituals and forms of polytheism that linger on in popular devotion. It wasn't only the Renaissance that stocked up on Venuses and Apollos as it embarked on the discovery of the ancient world with its ruins and its manuscripts. The Christian Middle Ages built its theology on Aristotle's thinking, rediscovered via the Arabs, and while it knew almost nothing of Plato, it knew a lot about Neoplatonism, which had a huge influence on the Fathers of the Church. Nor could we conceive of Augustine, the greatest Christian thinker, without the absorption of Platonic ideas. The very notion of empire, which lies at the roots of a thousand years of struggle among European states, and between states and the Church, is Roman in origin. Christian Europe elected Latin as the language of holy ritual, of religious thinking, of law, and of university debate.

On the other hand, a Christian tradition without Jewish monotheism is inconceivable. The text on which European culture is based, the text whose translation (by Luther) virtually founded the German language, the principal text of the Protestant world, is the Bible. Christian Europe was born and raised singing the psalms, reciting the works of the prophets, and meditating on Job and Abraham. Jewish monotheism was in fact the sole bond that enabled a dialogue between Christian monotheism and Muslim monotheism.

That's not all. Greek culture, at least from Pythagoras's day on, would have been unthinkable without Egyptian culture, and the teachings of the Egyptians and the Chaldeans inspired that most typically European phenomenon, the Renaissance, while from the first men to decipher the obelisks down to Champollion himself, from the Empire style to the ultramodern and very Western whimsies of the New Age, the European collective imagination has fed on Nefertiti, the mysteries of the pyramids, the pharaoh's curse, and golden scarab beetles.

I don't think there would be anything inappropriate about a constitution that referred to the Greco-Roman and Judeo-Christian roots of our continent, allied to the affirmation—precisely by virtue of those roots, and just as Rome opened its pantheon to gods of all races and put dark-skinned men on its imperial throne (nor should we forget that St. Augustine was an African)—that the continent is open to the integration of all other cultural and ethnic contributions, and considers this broad-minded approach to be one of its deepest cultural characteristics.

The Crucifix, Its Uses and Customs

Some years ago, discussing the wave of immigration that is transforming our continent (a mass migration, not merely intermittent immigration), I wrote that in thirty years Europe would become a colored continent, with all the changes, adaptations, agreements, and clashes that this would involve, and I warned that the transition would not be painless. The row that has flared up about the presence of crucifixes in Italian classrooms is one episode in this transition full of confrontations, as is the debate in France over the chador.

The painful thing about this transition is that it will not only lead to political, legal, and religious problems; it will also bring into play emotional drives, which are immune to both legislation and argument. The case of the crucifix in classrooms is one such issue, and reactions to it unite people who think differently, believers and nonbelievers alike.

There no reasoning with emotional issues: it would be like trying to explain to an abandoned lover on the verge of suicide that life is beautiful, that there are plenty of other fish in the sea, and that the unfaithful partner didn't really possess all the virtues attributed

---

"The Crucifix, Its Uses and Customs" appeared in la Repubblica, *October 2003.*

to him or her by the bereft one. A waste of breath, for that person will suffer, and there's little to be done about it.

Judicial questions are irrelevant. Whatever royal decree required the presence of the crucifix in Italian classrooms also required the presence of a portrait of the king. So if we were to comply with royal decrees, we would have to hang up in classrooms a portrait of Vittorio Emanuele III (Umberto was never formally crowned). Any new decree by the Republic that eliminated the crucifix to underline the secular nature of the state would likely meet with the disapproval of most of the public.

The French republic prohibits the display of religious symbols in state schools, both the crucifix and the chador, if the chador can be seen as a religious symbol. It is a rational position, and juridically acceptable. But modern France springs from a secular revolution. Not Andorra, however, and curiously enough that state is cogoverned by the French president and the bishop of Urgel. In Italy, the communist leader Palmiro Togliatti had his party vote for article 7 of the Constitution, which recognized the Lateran Pacts previously signed by Mussolini and which granted the Roman Catholic Church various privileges. The French education system is strictly secular, and yet some of the great currents of modern Catholicism flourished in republican France, on both sides of the political spectrum, from Charles Péguy and Leon Bloy to Maritain and Mounier, right down to the worker priests, and if Fatima is in Portugal, Lourdes is in France. We can see that, even if religious symbols are banned from schools, this does not affect the vitality of religious sentiment.

In Italian universities there are no crucifixes in the lecture halls, but many students are members of Catholic groups like Comunione e Liberazione. However, at least two generations of Italians spent their youth in classrooms where the crucifix was hung between portraits of the king and Mussolini, and out of every thirty students in every class some became atheists, others fought with the resistance, and others again—the majority, I believe—voted for the

Republic. All anecdotal evidence, if you will, but of historical importance, and this tells us that the presence of religious symbols in schools does not affect the spiritual development of the students.

Some might say that the question is irrelevant even from a religious point of view. Clearly not irrelevant in principle, because the crucifix in class reminds us that we are in a country with a Catholic tradition, and so the reaction in ecclesiastical circles is understandable. But principles don't necessarily jibe with observations I would call sociological. From being a classic emblem of European civilization, the crucifix has unfortunately been secularized, and for some time now. Crucifixes outrageously studded with precious stones have adorned the décolletages of sinners and courtesans, and some will remember how Cardinal Lambertini, on seeing a cross on the voluptuous bosom of a beautiful woman, remarked salaciously on the sweetness of such a Calvary. Girls who go around with their navels exposed and wearing microminis carry crucifixes on chains around their necks. Our society has dealt shabbily with the cross over time, but no one has ever been really scandalized by that. Over the centuries, crosses have sprung up in Italian cities like mushrooms, and not only on bell towers, and we accept them as part of the urban landscape. Nor do I think that the gradual replacement of crossroads with roundabouts has anything to do with the secularization of society.

Just as the crescent moon (a Muslim symbol) appears on the flags of Algeria, Libya, the Maldives, Malaysia, Mauritania, Pakistan, Singapore, Turkey, and Tunisia (there is discussion about the entry into the EU of a formally secular Turkey that nevertheless has a religious symbol on its flag), crosses and cruciform structures are to be found on the flags of such decidedly secular nations as Sweden, Norway, Switzerland, New Zealand, Malta, Iceland, Greece, Finland, Denmark, Australia, the United Kingdom, and so on. Many Italian cities, perhaps with left-wing town councils, have a cross on their crests, and no one has ever protested. These would all be good reasons to make crucifixes in schools acceptable, but as we can see they have nothing to do with religious sentiment. It may be awful to say so to a believer, but the cross has become a secular and universal symbol.

To avoid any overly explicit reference to a specific religion, we might suggest putting unadorned crosses in the schools, the kind you could find in an archbishop's study, but I think that such a thing would today be seen as yielding to pressure.

The problem lies elsewhere, which brings me back to emotional considerations. In this world some customs and traditions are more deeply rooted than any faith or the revolt against any faith, and customs and traditions should be respected. This is why a female atheist visiting a church should not wear provocative clothing. I am the least superstitious person in the world and I love walking under ladders, but I know some completely secular and even anticlerical people who are horrified if someone spills salt at the table. As I see it, it's a problem for their psychologist (or personal exorcist), but if I invite people to dinner and I see that there are thirteen of us, I try to bring the number to fourteen, or I put eleven at one table and two at a side table. This kind of thing makes me laugh, but I respect the sensibilities, and the customs and traditions, of others.

The pained and indignant reactions we have been hearing recently, even from agnostics, tell us that the cross is a socio-anthropological phenomenon rooted in the common sensibility. Muslim fundamentalists like Italy's Adel Smith ought to realize this: if a Muslim wants to live in Italy—apart from religious principles, and so that his religion will be respected—he should accept the customs and traditions of the host country. If I visit a Muslim country, I drink alcohol only in designated areas (such as hotels for Europeans) and don't provoke the locals by swigging whiskey out of a hip flask in front of a mosque. If a monsignor is invited to hold a conference in a Muslim community, he agrees to do so in a room decorated with verses from the Koran.

The integration of a Europe ever more crowded with non-EU immigrants must take place on the basis of mutual tolerance. I take this opportunity to disagree with my friend Elisabeth Rasy, who recently observed in *Corriere della Sera* that "tolerance" struck her as a racist expression. I would point out that Locke wrote an epistle on tolerance, and Voltaire a treatise. It may be that today some people use "tolerate" in a disparaging way (I tolerate you even though I think you are inferior to me, precisely because I am superior), but the concept of tolerance has history and philosophical dignity and refers to mutual understanding between people who are different.

School curricula of the future must be based not on the concealment of diversity but on teaching techniques that lead youngsters to understand and accept it. For some time now people have been saying it would be nice, along with religious instruction (and not as an alternative for those who aren't Catholics), if schools devoted at least one hour a week to the history of all religions, so that Catholic kids might understand what the Koran says or what Buddhists think, and so that Jews, Muslims, and Buddhists (and even Catholics) might understand how the Bible came into being and what it says.

An invitation to Adel Smith, therefore, and to all intolerant fundamentalists: Try to understand and accept the customs and traditions of the host country. And an invitation to the hosts: Make sure that your customs and traditions don't turn into the imposition of your faith.

But we also have to respect the gray areas, welcome and comfortable to many, that elude the spotlight of reason.

On the Soul of the Embryo

Recently, the argument about the dignity of the embryo has seen a clash among a number of diverging opinions. But no one ever mentions a centuries-old debate that involved some of the greatest figures in Christian theology. This ancient debate began with Origen, who held that God had created the human soul right from the start. This opinion was immediately confuted, in the light of the passage from Genesis (2.7) that says, "And the LORD God formed man of the dust of the ground, and breathed into his nostrils the breath of life; and man became a living soul." So according to the Bible, God created the body first, then breathed a soul into it. But this solution posed problems about the transmission of original sin. Then Tertullian maintained that the soul of the parent was "translated" from father to son via the semen—a position that was instantly deemed heretical, because it presumed a material origin of the soul.

At this point St. Augustine found himself in difficulty. He had to deal with the Pelagians, who denied the transmission of original sin. So on the one hand he upheld the creationist doctrine (against

"On the Soul of the Embryo" appeared in L'espresso, *September 2000 and March 2005.*

corporeal translation) while admitting a kind of spiritual "translationism" on the other. But all commentators consider this to be a fairly contorted position. Thomas Aquinas, definitely a creationist, solved the problem of original sin in a most elegant manner: original sin is translated through the semen like a natural infection (*Summa Theologiae* 1–2.81.1), but this has nothing to do with the translation of the rational soul.

Aquinas believed that vegetables had a vegetative soul, which in animals was absorbed by the sensitive soul, while in human beings these two functions were absorbed by the rational soul. The rational soul gave man the gift of intelligence—and I would add made him a person, insofar as by ancient tradition a person was an "individual substance of a rational nature."

Aquinas had a very biological notion of the formation of the fetus: God introduces the soul only when the fetus gradually acquires first a vegetative and then a sensitive soul. Only at that point, in a body already formed, is the rational soul created (*Summa Theologiae* 1.90). The embryo has only the sensitive soul (*Summa* 1.76.2 and 1.118.2). In his *Summa contra gentiles* (2.89), Aquinas says that there is an order, various stages of generation "on account of the intermediate forms of the fetus from the beginning through to the final form."

At what point in the formation of the fetus is the rational soul infused, the element that makes a person human for all intents and purposes? Traditional doctrine has always been cautious about this. In Pietro Caramello's commentary on an Italian edition of the works of Aquinas, it is acknowledged that, according to Thomist doctrine, the soul enters the fertilized egg when the egg "possesses sufficient organization," but "according to recent authors" there is already in play "a principle of organic life in the fertilized egg." A most prudent note, because a principle of organic life can also refer to the vegetative and sensitive souls.

Finally, in the Supplement to the *Summa Theologiae* (80.4) it says that embryos will not take part in the resurrection of the flesh before a rational soul has been infused in them. In other words, after the Day of Judgment, when the bodies of the dead rise again so that the flesh may participate in celestial glory (when, according to St. Augustine, not only those born dead but also freaks of nature, the mutilated, and those born without arms or eyes will live again in the fullness of a beautiful and complete adult form), embryos will not be included. The rational soul has not yet been infused in them, and they are not human beings.

The Church, albeit in a slow, subterranean way, has shifted its ground many times in the course of its history, and it could have done so in this case too. But here we are faced with the tacit disavowal not just of any authority but of the Authority par excellence, the fundamental pillar of Catholic theology.

Which leads to some curious conclusions. We know that the Catholic Church resisted the theory of evolution for a long time. Not so much because it seemed to clash with the biblical account of the Creation in seven days as because it negated the radical leap, the miraculous difference between prehuman life forms and the appearance of Man; it erased the difference between brute beasts, such as monkeys, and Man, who had received a rational soul.

Now, the decidedly neofundamentalist battle for the alleged defense of life, according to which the embryo is already a human being because in the future it might become one, seems to be leading the most rigorous believers to take up the position once adopted by the materialist-evolutionists of the past: there is no dividing line (like the one defined by Aquinas) in the course of evolution from plants to animals to humankind. Life always has the same value. As Giovanni Sartori recently wrote in *Corriere della Sera*, one wonders whether there might not be a certain confusion between the defense of life and the defense of human life, because defending life at all costs wherever it manifests itself, and in whatever form it manifests itself, would lead us to define as homicide not only the spilling of one's seed for nonprocreational purposes but also the consumption of chicken or swatting mosquitoes. Not to mention the respect due to vegetables.

Conclusion: not only is the current neofundamentalist Catholic stance of Protestant origin (the least of our concerns), but it also leads Christianity into conformity with notions that are at once materialist and pantheist, positions akin to those forms of oriental panpsychism that make certain gurus walk around with gauze over their mouths so as not to kill microorganisms by breathing.

I have no desire to pronounce judgment on this most delicate question. I am merely pointing out a historic/cultural curiosity, an odd reversal of positions. It must be the influence of the New Age.

Chance and Intelligent Design

It seemed a dead issue (or a matter limited to the American Bible Belt, the most backward part of the States, cut off from the rest of the world, where people cling to an intense form of fundamentalism, a place that only Bush seems to take seriously, probably for electoral reasons), but now the polemic about Darwinism has once more raised its head—and they have even flirted with the idea of reforming the schools here in Italy, Catholic or lay state schools as they may be.

I emphasize "Catholic," because Christian fundamentalism springs from Protestant circles and is characterized by the decision to interpret the Scriptures to the letter. But if the Scriptures are to be interpreted that way, believers must be able to interpret them freely, and this is typical of Protestantism. Catholic fundamentalism cannot exist—and this was what the Counter-Reformation was all about—because for Catholics the interpretation of the Scriptures is mediated by the Church.

Now, even before the Fathers of the Church, even before Philo of Alexandria, a less rigid hermeneutics had been developed, like

"Chance and Intelligent Design" appeared in L'espresso, *November 2005.*

that of St. Augustine, who was willing to admit that the Bible often speaks in metaphors and allegories, and therefore it's perfectly possible that the seven days of the Creation were seven millennia. The Church had fundamentally accepted this hermeneutical position.

Note that, once you say that the seven days of Creation are an expression of poetic license and can be taken figuratively, Genesis seems to allow Darwin everything: first there is a Big Bang with an explosion of light, then the planets are formed and enormous geological upheavals take place on Earth (the land is separated from the waters), then the plants appear, the fruits and the seeds, and finally the sea begins to teem with living creatures (life arises first in the water), birds take flight, and only later do mammals appear (the genealogical position of the reptiles is hazy, but you cannot ask too much of Genesis).

Only at the culmination of this process (even after the great apes, I imagine) does man appear. Man who—lest it be forgotten—was created not out of nothingness but out of clay, that is, previously existing matter. Apart from the high epic tone, it would be hard to be more evolutionist than this.

What has Catholic theology always said in order to avoid identifying with materialist evolutionism? Not only that this was all the work of God but also that evolution took a remarkable leap forward when God breathed a rational immortal soul into a living organism. It is on this point only that the battle between materialism and spiritualism is based.

One interesting aspect of the campaign under way in the United States for the reintroduction of creationist doctrine in the schools, together with the Darwinian "hypothesis" (let us not forget that Galileo, during his trial, wriggled out of trouble by saying that his idea was not a discovery but a hypothesis), is that—to prevent the issue from seeming like a clash between religious belief and scientific theory—the talk is not of divine creation but of "intelligent design."

In other words: We don't want to present you with the embarrassing presence of a bearded, anthropomorphous Yahweh, we merely want you to accept that, if there was evolutionary development, it didn't happen by chance but in accordance with a plan, a project, and that this project depends on some form of Mind. The idea of intelligent design could even admit a pantheist God in place of a transcendent God.

Curiously, this notion of intelligent design does not rule out a chance process like the Darwinian one, which operates by trial and error and by which the only individuals who survive are those who adapt best to the environment in the struggle for life.

Let's think about the noblest idea we have of intelligent design: artistic creation. It was Michelangelo who wrote, in a celebrated sonnet, that when the artist finds himself faced with the block of marble, he has no idea of the statue that will emerge from it, but proceeds tentatively, testing the resistance of the material and trying to eliminate the "excess" in order to coax the statue gradually out of the stone that holds it prisoner. But if the statue is really inside, and if it is a Moses or a prisoner, this is something the artist discovers only at the end of this continuous process of trial and error.

So intelligent design can also manifest itself through a series of acceptances and rejections of those elements offered by chance. You have to decide which comes first: the design, which accepts or rejects; or chance, which by accepting or rejecting manifests itself as the only form of intelligence—and that is like saying that chance has become God.

This is no small problem, and we can't solve it here. The issue is philosophically and theologically a bit more complex than the fundamentalists would have us believe.

Hands off My Son!

Well, fearing a series of questions and in order to make up my mind once and for all, I went to see Mel Gibson's *The Passion of the Christ*. I even saw it abroad (in a country where they had at least given it a Restricted rating), before it came out in Italy. The characters speak in Aramaic, so at best you can understand the Roman soldiers yelling "I!" to mean "Push off, you!" I must say right away that this film, technically very well made, is neither an expression of anti-Semitism nor of a Christian fundamentalism obsessed by a mystique of bloody sacrifice.

It is a splatter film, calculated to make a lot of money by offering spectators enough blood and violence to make *Pulp Fiction* look like a cartoon for the kindergarten market. It borrows a device from Tom and Jerry cartoons in which characters are flattened into CDs by steamrollers, fall from skyscrapers, and are smashed to smithereens or get squashed behind doors. Plus blood, gallons of it, presumably collected by setting all the vampires in Transylvania to work and then sending the results to the set by the truckload.

"Hands off My Son!" appeared in L'espresso, *April 2004.*

It is not a religious film. Of Jesus's message it offers merely an ill-digested interpretation of the things you learn for First Communion. Jesus's relations with the Father are hysterical and totally secular. They might as well be those between Charlie Manson and Satan, but Satan appears obliquely here and there, dressed up like a queer, and faced with all that waste of red corpuscles even he feels bad in the end. But the least convincing image is the final one, of the Resurrection: more like *The Night of the Living Dead* than any Renaissance painting. There is no trace in this film of the sublime reticence of the Gospels. It shows everything that they, leaving the faithful to silent contemplation of the greatest sacrifice in history, do not say. Where the Gospels limit themselves to the statement that Jesus was scourged (three words in Matthew, Mark, and John, none in Luke), Gibson has him first beaten with rods, then with belts studded with nails, and finally with mallets, until he has reduced him to what looks like a badly cooked hamburger.

Gibson's hatred of the Nazarene is indescribable. Who knows what atavistic repressions he was venting on this ever-bloodier body. And it's a good thing that history stopped him there, otherwise he would have had them attaching electrodes to Jesus's testicles while administering a petroleum enema. This is how, according to some, we experience a salutary shudder at the mysteries of Redemption. Ridiculous.

An anti-Semitic film? If the idea was to make a "splatter western" (rather, an "eastern"), the roles should have been clear-cut: good guys against bad guys, and the bad guys must be as bad as possible. The priests of the temple are very bad, but the Romans are even worse, like Pegleg Pete guffawing as he ties Mickey Mouse to the torture chair. Gibson must have thought that portraying the Romans as bad guys (which has already been done in *Asterix* anyway) involved no risk of someone torching the Capitol, but—these days—it might have been prudent to tread more carefully in the case of the Jews.

But you can't ask too much of someone who only wants to serve up a steak tartare with plenty of pepper and ketchup. Gibson does show an occasional qualm: three Jews and three Romans, who are almost good, are suddenly seized by doubt (they look at the public as if to ask, "We're not going too far here, are we?"), but that only enhances the impression that everything in this film is awful, if you haven't already thrown up on seeing what squirts out of the victim's side.

Gibson is fixated on the idea that Jesus suffered, and like Poe who thought that the most moving thing was the death of a beautiful woman, he concludes that the most profitable form of splatter is one in which you put the Son of God through a meat grinder. He manages this very well, and I must say that, when Jesus finally dies and has stopped making us suffer (or enjoy his suffering) and the storm breaks, the earth shakes, and the veil of the temple is rent asunder, one feels a certain emotion. In that moment, albeit in a meteorological sense, we catch a fleeting glimpse of the transcendence that is appallingly lacking in this film. Yes, at that point the Father makes his voice heard. But the spectator of good sense (and, I hope, the believer) knows that the Almighty is pissed off with Mel Gibson.

Codicil

This article triggered a lively debate on the *L'espresso* Web site. Obviously, some were for and some against. But among the vast number of those against (I skip the ones who went so far as to accuse me of being the *longa manus* of the Jewish lobby), most felt that I had been making fun of the Passion of Christ (the historic event) and not of the *Passion* according to Gibson.

In other words, these people were unable to distinguish between the Christ of the Gospels and the one of the film. They saw not an actor portraying Christ but Christ himself in the flesh.

To see a representation as the Thing Itself is one of the modern forms of idolatry.

In any case, I am grateful to the reader who wrote, "Dear Umberto, I'll never forgive you for giving away the end of the film."

Those Who Don't Believe in God Believe in Everything

Believing in the Year Zero

The end of the year 2000 AD is drawing near, and in the papers and even in everyday conversation, it has been taken for granted that the third millennium begins one second after midnight on 31 December 2000.

Nothing is shorter than the memory of the mass media, and so perhaps many readers will have forgotten the furious diatribes of last year. An immense commercial operation, ranging from travel agencies to restaurants to champagne producers, decreed that the second millennium ended on 31 December 1999 and that the year 2000 was the beginning of the third. No one paid attention to the mathematicians, who pointed out that, if you start counting from one, the numbers ending in zero complete (and don't begin) the tens, hundreds, and so on. Writing in *Corriere della Sera*, Armando Torno recently reviewed the whole story but acknowledged that the

---

The quotation "Those who don't believe in God believe in everything" is attributed to Chesterton, but the American Chesterton Society (see the Internet), which has various versions of it, holds that it is a synthesis of various, more detailed quotations. "Believing in the Year Zero" appeared in L'espresso, January 2000.

double zero has always been alluring. It persuaded a great many
people to celebrate the beginning of the twentieth century on the
first second of 1900—thus flying in the face of common sense and
arithmetic.

So the power of the double zero gets the better of common
sense, and the consumer society decided that everyone would be
happy to celebrate the beginning of the new millennium at the end
of 1999. So people now await the next new year with the usual,
moderate excitement.

People are like that. Yet I remember that last year, when I mentioned in an article that we were not yet entering the third millennium, I was snowed under by letters containing complicated
calculations to demonstrate that the millennium began one year ago,
dragging in Dionysius Exiguus, and assuming (without realizing it)
a strange universal calendar containing a year zero. (As a logical
consequence, twelve months after his birth, Jesus would have been
zero years old.) Those who wrote me were not just gullible or future
devotees of "Big Brother" but also first-rate scholars, philosophers,
linguists, experts in hermeneutics, aphorists, romance philologists,
entomologists, and archaeologists.

How did it happen that such wise people, despite all the evidence, wanted with all their hearts for the millennium to begin in
2000, even though they weren't leaving for the South Seas or for the
Aleutian Islands to celebrate a double new year in the space of
twenty-four hours?

I tried to understand this by remembering that when I was
small, daydreaming over the pages of adventure books about the
marvels of the future, I would wonder: "Will I make it to the year
2000?" I did my sums and discovered that I would have to live to
68, and I said to myself, "I'll never get that far, no one gets that old."
But then I recalled that I had met seventy-year-olds and so I concluded that maybe, if all went well, I might make it after all. And I
confess that last year, around autumn, I began to fear that a sudden

car accident, a heart attack, or manslaughter, premeditated or involuntary, would halt my victorious march toward the third millennium with only a few weeks to go.

I harbored some small fears until 11:45 of last New Year's Eve, then sat down with my back to the wall, avoiding the window from which you could see a menacing fireworks display. I waited patiently for the last chime, and only then did I get down to some serious drinking, because, even if I died immediately afterward, I had made it.

That's the explanation. For numerological reasons, at least for the most ancient among us, surviving to the year 2000 was like winning a race against death. So it was obvious that people were prepared to do anything to bring the finishing line forward. A cunning move (albeit an unconscious one), but to cheat death some are prepared to do this and more, as in the desperate chess game in *The Seventh Seal*.

Believing in Alchemy

What's irritating about the New Age spirit? Not so much that some people believe in astrology, because lots of people have always believed in that. Nor that some consider Stonehenge to be a prodigy of astral magic. People had already invented the sundial, so it wasn't altogether incredible to have stones oriented according to the rising and setting of the sun, but it is impressive to realize that those builders watched the sun better than we do. No, what's irritating about the New Age is syncretism. Syncretism consists in believing not in some things but in all things, even when they contradict one another.

The risk of syncretism is always lying in wait, and I found a good example in *Corriere della Sera* of February 23, which ran two articles by Cesare Medail on the same page, side by side. Note that,

---

"Believing in Alchemy" appeared in L'espresso, *March 2001.*

taken individually, both articles are correct. One starts off with a book called *Newton,* by Michael White. The book is heavily sensationalistic and presents as original information material already known to experts, misquotes the titles of famous books, has us believe that Cornelius Agrippa and Johannes Valentin Andreae wrote in English, and accepts without question the legend that Thomas Aquinas dabbled in alchemy, but it also gives a compelling account of how the father of modern science, Newton, was not only deeply interested in what we would now call esoteric studies but made his great physico-mathematical discoveries precisely because he believed that the world was governed by occult powers. Exactly.

In the other article, Medail talks of the renewed interest in ancient alchemical texts and cites as an example some volumes published by Edizioni Mediterranee, which for years has been producing books that satisfy the expectations of those who still believe in alchemy (proof of which is that they recently reprinted works by that old lunatic Fulcanelli). Sometimes they also publish the works of reliable scholars, but the effect of syncretism is that even the reliable books—once they have been placed in the pile—seem to confirm what the unreliable ones say.

What is suggested by placing these two articles side by side? Since occultists inspired Newton's scientific research, they must have said something that can still seriously interest us today. This shortcut can seduce the unsophisticated reader.

The discovery of America came about because it was believed that by sailing west you could get to the Indies. A good discovery made for the wrong reasons is a case of serendipity. That Columbus arrived in America is not proof that you can go east by going west. On the contrary, Columbus's discovery teaches us that you can get to the Indies quicker by going the other way. The Portuguese exploration of Africa was inspired by the idea that Ethiopia was the home of the fabled realm of the all-powerful Prester John. Some had identified this kingdom as Abyssinia, but as soon as this happened, we learned that there was no Prester John (and what was found in Ethiopia was so weak, it was later conquered by Marshal Badoglio). The same goes for the legend of Terra Australis. It led to the discovery of Australia, but at the same time showed people that the land that should have covered the entire southern cap of the world did not exist.

Two things are not always true at the same time. Thanks to the alchemists, Newton showed us that the alchemists were wrong. This doesn't mean that they will not continue to fascinate me as much as they do Medail, and many others. But I'm also fascinated by Superman, Mickey Mouse, and Mandrake the Magician, and yet I know perfectly well that they don't exist.

Believing in Father Amorth

I wrote an article on Harry Potter almost two years ago, when the first three books had already come out and the English-speaking world was locked in debate as to whether it was bad to tell kids stories that might induce them to take seriously the nonsense to be found in certain occult writings. Now that, thanks to Hollywood, the Harry Potter phenomenon has become truly global, I happened to see an Italian TV show whose guests included a self-styled wizard known as Mago Otelmo, overjoyed about this advertising for gentlemen like himself (he was dressed in an outfit so over-the-top wizardly that not even Ed Wood would have cast him in one of his films) and an eminent exorcist named Father Amorth (*nomen omen*), for whom the Harry Potter stories are a vehicle for diabolical ideas.

Most of the people on the show considered both black and white magic to be nonsense, but the exorcist took all forms of magic (black, white, even polka dot) seriously, as works of the devil.

I think I ought to put in a good word for Harry Potter. These are stories about magicians and wizards, and it's obvious that they are

"*Believing in Father Amorth*" appeared in L'espresso, December 2001.

popular, because children have always liked fairies, dwarfs, drag-
ons, and necromancers. And yet no one ever thought that Snow
White was part of a Satanic plot. The stories have enjoyed and still
enjoy success, because the author (whether by highly cultured cal-
culation or by prodigious instinct) has come up with situations that
are true narrative archetypes.

Harry Potter is the son of two good magicians killed by the
forces of evil, but he doesn't know this at first and lives as an orphan
barely tolerated by a tyrannical, wicked uncle and aunt. Then his
nature and vocation are revealed to him, and he goes off to a college
for young magicians of both sexes, where he has astonishing adventures. The first classic situation: take an innocent youngster, put him
through the mill, then tell him that he is of pedigree stock and destined for a bright future, and you have not only the Ugly Duckling
and Cinderella but also Oliver Twist. Hogwarts, where Harry studies how to make magic potions, resembles many other English col-
leges in which games are played that fascinate the English because
they intuitively understand the rules and fascinate foreigners because they know they will never understand them.

Another archetypal situation: a group of young students meet to
plot against eccentric (and sometimes depraved) teachers. Harry and
his schoolmates ride flying broomsticks, so we have Mary Poppins
and Peter Pan. Finally, Hogwarts looks like one of those mysterious
castles we used to read about in the *Children's Library* published by
Salani (the same house that published the Italian versions of Harry
Potter), where a close-knit group of boys in short trousers and girls
with long golden hair unmask the schemes of a dishonest superinten-
dent, a corrupt uncle, or a gang of criminals and go on to find a treasure, a lost document, or a crypt full of secrets.

Although in Harry Potter there are gruesome spells and frighten-
ing beasts (after all, the stories are aimed at kids who grew up with
the celluloid monsters of Sergio Rambaldi and Japanese animated
cartoons), Harry and his friends nonetheless fight for good causes

like the heroes of *Boys' Own Paper* and heed the counsels of virtuous teachers so carefully that we are on the verge of the sentimentalism of a Charles Kingsley.

Do we really think that children, by reading stories about magic, will believe in witches when they're grown up (that's what both Otelma and Father Amorth think, albeit from opposite sides of the fence)? We have all enjoyed a healthy shudder at ogres and werewolves, but as adults we have learned to be more afraid of the hole in the ozone layer than in poisoned apples. When we were small, we believed that children were brought by the stork, but as adults this didn't stop us from employing a more suitable (and pleasurable) way to produce them.

The real problem isn't the children, who grow up believing in Pinocchio and that nefarious duo, the Cat and the Fox, but in later life learn to worry about completely different, less fantastic villains. The problem is the adults, perhaps those who didn't read stories about magic as children, the same ones who now consult people who read tea leaves, fiddle with tarot cards, or hold black masses, the clairvoyants, faith healers, table rappers, tricksters who produce ectoplasm, and those who claim to know the mystery of Tutankhamen. By believing in magicians, they go back to believing in the Cat and the Fox.

Believing in Psychics

If you are not satisfied with your financial situation and want to change your job, being a clairvoyant is one of the most profitable and (contrary to what people think) easiest jobs around. All you need is a pleasant personality, a little ability to understand others, and a thick skin. Even without these gifts, statistics are on your side.

You might try this experiment. Go up to anyone, a person chosen at random (it helps if he or she is open to the possibility of your paranormal powers). Look her in the eye and say: "I sense that

---

"Believing in Psychics" appeared in L'espresso, *January 2002.*

someone is thinking intensely about you, it's someone you haven't seen for many years, but whom you loved very much, and you suffered because your love was not returned . . . Now this person realizes how much he made you suffer, and he's sorry, even though he knows it's too late . . ." Is there anyone in the world, anyone not a child, who has not had an unhappy love affair? Your "client" will meet you more than halfway, and tell you that she knows the one whose thoughts you have so clearly read.

You can also tell someone that "there is someone who speaks badly of you, but he does so out of envy." It's unlikely that this person will say that he is admired by all and has absolutely no idea who the backstabber might be. Chances are, he will identify the party immediately and admire your extrasensory ability.

You can also tell your clients that you can see the ghosts of their departed loved ones hovering around them. Approach a person of a certain age and say that near him you see the shade of an old man or woman who died from a heart problem. The person has had two parents and four grandparents and, if you're lucky, some uncle, godfather, or godmother who was dear to him. If your client is getting on in years, these dear ones are probably dead, and out of six there should be at least one who died of a heart attack. If your client says no but is in the company of others interested in your paranormal powers, simply suggest that the spirit you see may be related to another member of the group. It's almost certain that someone present will say it's his father or mother, and now you're in charge. You can speak of the ghost's warmth, the love it feels for the person who has by now fallen for your seductive patter . . .

Many readers will have recognized this technique as the one used by some charismatic personalities on television shows. Nothing is easier than convincing a parent who has just lost a child, or a child who is still grieving for a dead parent, that the good soul has not vanished into nothingness but is sending a message from the beyond. The suffering and credulity of others are your allies.

Unless, of course, someone from Cicap is in the vicinity. Cicap is the Italian Committee for the Control of Alleged Paranormal Events, and its researchers are always on the prowl for such phenomena (from poltergeists to levitation, from spiritualist manifestations to crop circles, from UFOs to rhabdomancers, not to mention ghosts, premonitions, forks bent by the power of the mind, tarot readings, weeping Madonnas, saints with stigmata and so on). They take the mechanism apart, expose the trick, provide a scientific explanation, and often repeat the experiment to show that anyone who knows the trick can be a magician.

Two members of the Cicap team are Massimo Polidoro and Luigi Garlaschelli, who together have written a book (with essays by other members of the association) titled *Investigatori dell'occulto: Dieci anni di indagine sul paranormale,* in which (if you are not one of those who gets upset when people tell you that Santa Claus doesn't exist) you will find many amusing stories.

But I hesitate to talk of amusement. The fact that groups like Cicap have so much work to do means that more people are gullible than you would think. This book of mine will sell a few thousand copies, but when certain personalities appear on TV to play on the suffering of others, the event is broadcast to millions of people. And who am I to say that such shows are harmful? The ratings are the ratings.

Believing in the Templars

Establish an ecclesiastical and military order and make it become powerful and rich. Find a king who wants to get rid of this state within a state. Pick inquisitors who know how to gather scattered rumors into a terrible pattern: plots, heinous crimes, unmentionable heresies, corruption, and a generous dollop of homosexuality.

Arrest and torture the suspects. Those who confess and repent

---

"Believing in the Templars" appeared in L'espresso, *December 2004.*

will save their skins; those who declare their innocence will die. The first to legitimize the inquisitorial apparatus will be the victims, especially if innocent. Finally, confiscate the order's immense assets. This is basically what we learn from the case brought against the Templars by King Philip the Fair of France.

The legend of the Templars follows from this. As you may imagine, many contemporaries were shocked by this trial, as well as remarking on the injustice of it, as Dante did. They were fascinated by the secret doctrines attributed to the Templars and struck by the fact that most of the knights did not die at the stake. Furthermore, when the order was disbanded, its members seemed to vanish into thin air.

The skeptical interpretation (that they quietly tried to make a life elsewhere) could not compete with the occult, romantic one: they went underground, where they remained active for seven centuries. And they are still among us.

There's nothing easier than finding books about the Templars. The only problem is that ninety percent of them (pardon me, 99%) are hot air because no subject has inspired mediocre thinkers, of all times and all places, so much as the story of the Templars. Hence their continual rebirth and their constant presence behind the scenes of history, what with Gnostic sects, satanic brotherhoods, spiritualists, Pythagorean orders, Rosicrucians, Freemasons, and the Priory of Sion.

Sometimes the nonsense is so glaring, as in *The Holy Grail*, by Baigent, Leigh, and Lincoln, where the authors' bad faith is both manifest and unconscionable, that the reader of good sense can see the work as an amusing example of fantastic literature. As is happening now with *The Da Vinci Code*, which is a crib of all the earlier works. But we should watch out, because thousands of credulous readers will go visit the village of Rennes-le-Château, the scene of another historical fabrication connected with the Templar legend and the Priory of Sion, among other things.

The only way to tell if a book on the Templars is reliable or not is to see if its account ends in 1314, the date on which their grand master was burned at the stake. One book that stops at that date is Peter Partner's *The Murdered Magicians: The Templars and Their Myth* (1993).

Now the Italian publisher Mulino has published *I templari*, by Barbara Frale, a scholar who has devoted years of work to her task and has published other books on this topic. It is less than two hundred pages long and a pleasure to read. It also has a lavish—and authoritative—bibliography.

Frale isn't scandalized by aspects of the Templar myth; in fact she is sympathetic to certain fictional developments of it (although she devotes only two pages to them in her conclusion), but only because they might stimulate new scholarly research on the many obscure aspects of the "true" story of the Templars.

For example, was there any connection between the Templars and the cult of the Grail? A possibility, since a contemporary of theirs, Wolfram von Eschenbach, wrote some fabulous yarns about this. But I would observe that poets, as Horace bears witness, have their poetic license. And a scholar of the next millennium who saw a film of our time that attributes the discovery of the Ark of the Covenant to a certain Indiana Jones would have no reason to draw historical conclusions from that entertaining fiction.

As for the fact that parts of this ancient story are not yet wholly clear, Frale mentions some recent discoveries she made in the Vatican archives, which cast in a different light the Church's role in the trial. But she has bad news for those people who still occasionally produce personal calling cards in which they describe themselves as Templars. When the order was disbanded, she points out, Pope Clement V outlawed any attempt to revive it without papal consent, while anyone using the names and insignia of the Temple does so on pain of excommunication.

Then again in 1780, Joseph de Maistre employed similar arguments to liquidate the neo-Templars of his day. The Order of the Templars existed insofar as it was recognized by the Church and the various European states, and as such it was formally dissolved in the early fourteenth century. Period. From that moment, since no one owns the copyright anymore, everyone has the right to reestablish it, in the same sense that anyone can declare himself a high priest of Isis and Osiris, the Egyptian government doesn't give a damn.

Believing in Dan Brown

I come across a new commentary on Dan Brown's *The Da Vinci Code* every day. I can only speak of those books that come out in Italy; providing a bibliography of everything that has appeared on this subject on the world market would be quite beyond me. Recent titles I have seen include *Truth and Fiction in the Da Vinci Code,* by Bart Ehrman; *Breaking the Da Vinci Code,* by Darrell L. Bock; and *Secrets of the Code,* by Dan Burstein; plus a few locally produced efforts. If you want updated information on all the articles on this topic, try visiting the Opus Dei Web site. You can trust it, even if you are an atheist. The real question is why the Catholic world is trying so hard to demolish Brown's book. One thing's for sure though: when Catholic writers say that all the information it contains is false, you can take their word for it.

The Da Vinci Code is a novel, so the author has the right to invent as much as he wants. The book is written particularly well, and you can read it in a flash. Nor is there anything reprehensible in Brown's telling us that what he is about to relate is historical fact. The experienced reader is accustomed to these narrative appeals to truth; it's part of the fictional game. The trouble is that a great many inexperienced readers believe this statement—much as when spectators at traditional Sicilian puppet shows insult the perfidious Gano di Maganza.

"Believing in Dan Brown" appeared in L'espresso, *August 2005.*

Demolishing the alleged historical veracity of the *Code* doesn't take much. All you need is a fairly short article (and some excellent pieces have been written on this) that points out two things: first, the whole story about Jesus's marriage to Mary Magdalene, her journey to France, the foundation of the Merovingian dynasty and of the Priory of Sion is all nonsense that has been circulating for decades, in a plethora of books and booklets written for devotees of the occult sciences (from de Sèdes's book on Rennes-le-Château to *The Holy Grail,* by Baigent, Leigh, and Lincoln).

That all this material is tall tales has been pointed out and demonstrated for some time now. But Baigent, Leigh, and Lincoln have threatened (or actually filed) a lawsuit against Brown, accusing him of plagiarism. What? If I write a biography of Napoleon (relating real events), I cannot then sue someone who has written another biography of Napoleon, one that contains the same historical events but with invented details. No theft has taken place.

The second thing is that Brown's book is littered with historical errors, such as the search for information about Jesus (which the Church allegedly censored) in the Dead Sea Scrolls—which deal not with Jesus but with Jewish matters such as the sect known as the Essenes. Brown has confused the Dead Sea Scrolls with those of Nag Hammadi.

To fill the number of pages needed to make a book, most of the works that appear on the Dan Brown phenomenon, especially the well-written ones, list all the things that he has plundered, down to the smallest detail. And so, perversely, even though these books were written to unmask falsehoods, they contribute to the ongoing circulation of all this occult material. If we accept the interesting idea—which has actually been suggested—that the *Code* is a satanic plot, every confutation of it reproduces and amplifies the insinuations it contains. As plots go, it's a good one. Why, even when this book is refuted, does it continue to reproduce itself?

Because people are hungry for mysteries (and plots). All you need do is offer them another one. Even when you tell them that it was all cooked up by a couple of con men, they'll swallow it right away.

I think that this is what is worrying the Church. The belief in the *code* (and in another Jesus) is a symptom of dechristianization. When people stop believing in God, as Chesterton used to say, it's not that they no longer believe in anything, it's that they believe in everything. Even the mass media.

As an immense crowd stood in St. Peter's Square waiting for the news of Pope John Paul II's death, I was struck by the sight of a young man of doubtful intelligence. With his cell phone glued to one ear and a big grin, he was waving happily at the TV camera. Why was he there? (And why were there so many others like him, while millions of true believers were sitting in their homes praying?) As he awaited a media-inspired supernatural event, wasn't he perhaps prepared to believe that Jesus married Mary Magdalene and was linked by some mystical and dynastic bond between the Priory of Sion and Jean Cocteau?

Believing in the Tradition

Many readers probably don't know exactly what black holes are. Frankly, the best I can do is to imagine them as being like the pike in "Yellow Submarine" that devours everything around it until it finally swallows itself. But to understand the news item that is my point of departure, all you need to know about black holes is that they are one of the most controversial and absorbing problems in contemporary astrophysics. Recently I read in the papers that the celebrated scientist Stephen Hawking (perhaps better known to the general public for the strength and determination with which he has worked all his life despite a terrible illness that would have reduced a lesser person to a vegetable) has made a sensational statement. He made an error in his theory of black holes (published back in the

---

"Believing in the Tradition" appeared in L'espresso, *July 2004.*

1970s) and is now preparing to put the necessary corrections before a meeting of fellow scientists.

For those involved in sciences there is nothing exceptional about this, apart from Hawking's fame, but I feel that the episode should be brought to the attention of young people in every nonfundamentalist or nonreligious school, so that they may reflect upon the principles of modern sciences.

Science is frequently criticized by the media, which accuses it of a devilish pride that is leading humanity to possible destruction. They are evidently confusing science with technology. It is not science that is responsible for atomic weapons, the hole in the ozone layer, global warming, and so on. Rather, science is that branch of knowledge still capable of warning us of the risks we run when, in applying its principles, we put our trust in irresponsible technologies. The problem is that in many critiques of the ideology of progress (or the so-called spirit of the Enlightenment), science is often identified with certain idealistic philosophies of the nineteenth century, according to which history is always moving on to better things, forever marching toward Optimal Ends. But many people (of my generation, at least) had doubts on reading idealist philosophy, which says that every thinker understands better what was discovered by those who came before (a bit like saying that Aristotle is smarter than Plato). It is this concept of history that the Italian poet Leopardi challenged when he waxed ironic about "magnificent and progressive fate."

These days, in response to a whole series of ideologies in crisis, some people are flirting with a school of thought according to which the course of history is not leading us closer and closer to the truth. According to them, all that there is to understand has already been understood by long-vanished, ancient civilizations; it is only by humbly returning to that traditional and immutable treasure that we may be reconciled with ourselves and with our destiny. In the most overtly occultist versions of this school, the truth was cultivated by civilizations we have lost touch with: Atlantis engulfed by the ocean, the Hyperboreans, hundred-percent pure Aryans who lived on an eternally temperate polar icecap, the sages of ancient India, and other yarns that, being indemonstrable, allow third-rate philosophers and writers of potboilers to keep churning out warmed-over versions of the same old hogwash for the amusement of summer vacationers.

Science does not hold that what is new is therefore right. On the contrary, it is based on the principle of "fallibilism" (enunciated by the American philosopher Charles Peirce, elaborated upon by Popper and many other theorists), according to which science progresses by continually correcting itself, disproving its hypotheses by trial and error, admitting its mistakes, and considering that an experiment that doesn't work is not a failure but worth as much as a successful one, because it proves that a certain line of research was wrong and we should either change direction or start from scratch. This is what was proposed centuries ago in Italy by an institute of learning known as the Accademia del Cimento, whose motto was "provando e riprovando," which would normally translate into English as "try and try again"—but there is a subtle difference. In Italian *riprovare* usually means to try again, but here it is to "reprove" or "reject" that which cannot be maintained in the light of reason and experience.

This way of thinking is the opposite of all forms of fundamentalism, all literal interpretations of holy writ—which are also open to continuous reinterpretation—and all dogmatic certainty in one's own ideas. Science is that good "philosophy," in the everyday and Socratic sense of the term, that ought to be taught in schools.

Believing in Trismegistus

Until now, whoever wished to study the *Corpus Hermeticum* (in a critical edition, with the original on the facing page, and not through the countless trashy confections circulating in bookstores that specialize in the occult) had at his disposal the classic Belles Lettres

---

"Believing in Trismegistus" appeared in L'espresso, *May 2005.*

edition, edited by Nock and Festugière, which appeared between 1945 and 1954 (a previous edition was that of Scott, in an English translation [Oxford, 1924]).

In an admirable publishing venture, the Italian house Bompiani has picked up the Belles Lettres critical edition, but with the addition of things that Nock and Festugière couldn't have known. These include some hermetic texts from the Nag Hammadi codices, complete with—for those who feel like checking it out—the original Coptic text on the facing page. These 1500 pages are available at a mere 35 euro, but obviously this is not bedtime reading for all. It is an irreplaceable and valuable study tool, but those who wish merely to get a taste of hermetic writings might content themselves with the *Poimandres*, a hundred-page edition published in Italian by Marsilio in 1987.

The story of the *Corpus Hermeticum* is a fascinating one. It is a series of writings attributed to the legendary Hermes Trismegistus—the god Thoth for the Egyptians, Hermes for the Greeks, and Mercury for the Romans, the inventor of writing and language, of magic, astronomy, astrology, and alchemy, and later identified with Moses, no less. Naturally these treatises were the work of various authors, living in a Grecian cultural environment nourished by some Egyptian spirituality and a veneer of Platonism, between the second and third centuries after Christ.

That the authors were different is amply demonstrated by the numerous contradictions to be found among the various pamphlets, and that they were Hellenizing philosophers and not Egyptian priests is suggested by the fact that these little treatises do not contain references consistent with Egyptian theurgy or any form of Egyptian worship. The appeal of these texts to many minds athirst for a new spirituality is, as Nock points out in his introduction, that they represented "a mosaic of ancient ideas, often formulated through brief allusions . . . and as devoid of logical thought as they were devoid of classical linguistic purity." As you can see (this hap-

pens with modern philosophers too) the mumbo jumbo is deliberately concocted to trigger the drift of infinite interpretation.

These little treatises (except one, *Asclepius,* which circulated
for centuries in Latin) had been forgotten for a long time until a
manuscript of one of them cropped up in Florence in 1460, during
the humanist period, precisely when people were turning to an ancient, pre-Christian wisdom. Fascinated, Cosimo de' Medici ordered
it translated by Marsilio Ficino, who titled the work *Pimandro,* from
the name of the first treatise. Ficino then presented it as an authentic work of Trismegistus, the wellspring of the most ancient wisdom
from which not only Plato but revealed Christianity itself had drawn
ideas. *Pimandro* marks the beginning of the extraordinary success
and cultural influence of these writings. As Frances Yates remarked
in her book on Giordano Bruno, this was an enormous historical
blunder destined to produce surprising results.

In 1614, the Swiss philologist Isaac Casaubon came up with ir-
refutable arguments to demonstrate that the *Corpus* was no more
than a collection of late-Hellenic writings—a fact we don't doubt
these days. Extraordinarily, Casaubon's exposé remained confined
to scholarly circles; it didn't dent the authority of the Corpus in the
slightest. Consider the development of all the occult, cabalistic,
mystical and—of course—hermetic literature of the centuries that
followed (down to modern authors, who are otherwise above suspicion): people have continued to consider the *Corpus* a product, if not
exactly of the divine Trismegistus, at least of an archaic wisdom that
can be sworn on as if it were the Gospel.

The story of the *Corpus* came to mind some time ago, when Will
Eisner's *The Plot* was published (New York: Norton). Eisner, one of
the geniuses of the modern comic strip (who died while the book
was still in the proof stage), uses words and images to tell the story
of *The Protocols of the Elders of Zion.* The interesting part of his tale
is not so much the story of the creation of this anti-Semitic fake as

what happened afterward, in 1921, when the London *Times*—followed by serious scholars everywhere—demonstrated that the *Protocols* were a fake. The circulation of the *Protocols* began to increase worldwide at exactly that moment, and they have been taken ever more seriously (just surf the Net a bit).

It's a sign that, whether it's Hermes or the Elders of Zion, the difference between true and false holds no interest for those who start from prejudice, or from a desire for or an anxiety about the revelation of a mystery, some omen of heaven or of hell.

Believing in the Third Secret

On recently reading the document written by Sister Lucia on the third secret of Fatima, I had a feeling of déjà vu. Then I understood: that text, which the good sister wrote not as an illiterate girl but in 1944, when she was an adult nun, is full of perfectly recognizable quotations from the Revelation of St. John.

Lucia saw an angel with a fiery sword who seemed to want to set the world ablaze. In the passage about the angel of the second trumpet, Revelation (9.8) speaks of angels spreading fire throughout the world. True, that angel does not have a fiery sword, but we'll see later where the sword might come from (apart from the fact that traditional iconography offers a wealth of archangels with fiery swords).

Then Lucia saw the divine light as if in a mirror: here the image comes not from Revelation but from the first epistle of St. Paul to the Corinthians (we see celestial things now *per speculum* and only after will we see them face-to-face).

After that we have a bishop dressed in white: he is alone. In Revelation there are frequent mentions of the Lord's servants dressed in white and sworn to martyrdom (in 6.11, 7.9, and 7.14), but not to worry.

"Believing in the Third Secret" appeared in L'espresso, *July 2000.*

Then bishops and priests are seen scaling a steep mountain, and we are in Revelation 6.12, where the powerful of the Earth hide in the caves and among the boulders of a mountain. The holy father arrives in a "half-ruined" city, and on his way he meets the souls of the dead: the city is mentioned in Revelation 11.8, corpses included, while it collapses into ruin in 11.3 and again, in the form of Babylon, in 18.19.

Let's go on: the bishop and many other faithful are killed by soldiers with arrows and firearms. Although Sister Lucia is inventive regarding the firearms, massacres with pointed weapons are carried out by armored locusts in 9.7, when the fifth trumpet is sounded.

Finally we come to two angels pouring blood out of a sort of crystal watering pot (*regador* in Portuguese). Now the Apocalypse is chock-full of angels pouring blood, but in 8.5 they do it with a thurible, in 14.20 the blood flows from a tub, and in 16.3 it is poured from a chalice.

Why a watering pot? I thought: Fatima isn't far from the Asturie region, where in the Middle Ages they made splendid Mozarabic miniatures of the Apocalypse, reproduced many times. These miniatures portray angels holding roughly made goblets from which issue jets of blood, as if they wanted to rinse the world with it. That this traditional iconography had an influence on Lucia's memory is suggested by the angel with the fiery sword mentioned at the beginning, because sometimes in those miniatures the trumpets held by the angels look like scarlet blades.

If we don't limit ourselves to reading the newspaper summaries and instead read Cardinal Ratzinger's theological commentary, we can see that while this honest man endeavors to remind us that a private vision is not a subject that regards faith and that an allegory is not a prophecy to be taken literally, he explicitly points out analogies to Revelation.

What's more, he explains that in a vision a person sees things "with the modalities of representation and knowledge accessible to him," and so "the image can appear only according to his criteria and possibilities."

Put in a somewhat more secular way (but Ratzinger titles the section after the "anthropological structure" of the revelation), this means that Jungian archetypes may not exist, but each prophet sees what his culture has taught him.

Relativism?

It's probably not so much the coarseness of the media as the fact that these days people, when they talk, worry about how they will appear in the media, but you certainly get the impression that debates (even between people with some knowledge of philosophy) are unsubtle exchanges in which delicate expressions are used like cudgels. A typical example is the current debate in Italy between the so-called *teocons,* who accuse secular thinkers of "relativism," and some secular thinkers who label their adversaries as "fundamentalists."

What does "relativism" mean in philosophy? That our representations of the world do not exhaust its complexity but are always perspectives, each of which contains a grain of truth? This thesis has been upheld by many Christian philosophers past and present.

That these representations should be judged not in terms of truth but in terms of their correspondence to historical and cultural exigencies? This is the position of Richard Rorty, a philosopher of stature, in his version of pragmatism.

That what we know is relative to the world the subject knows? Which brings us to good old Kantianism.

"Relativism?" appeared in L'espresso, *July 2005.*

That all propositions are true only within the framework of a given paradigm? This is known as "holism."

That ethical values are relative to cultures? We began to realize this in the seventeenth century.

That there are no facts, only interpretations? Nietzsche said that.

Are we thinking of the idea that if there is no God, then everything is permitted? That's Dostoyevskian nihilism.

Are we thinking of the theory of relativity? Please, no jokes.

It ought to be clear that if someone is a relativist in the Kantian sense, he can't be one in the Dostoyevskian sense (Kant believed in God and duty). Nietzschean relativism has little in common with the relativism of social anthropology, because the former doesn't believe in facts and the latter takes them for granted. The holism of Quine is firmly anchored in a healthy empiricism that has a lot of faith in the stimuli we receive from the environment, and so on.

In fact, the term *relativism* can refer to forms of modern thought that are often in opposition. Deeply realist thinkers are sometimes considered relativists, and "relativism" is used with the contentious heat once reserved by nineteenth-century Jesuits for "poisonous Kantianism."

If all this is relativism, then only two philosophies completely elude this accusation: radical neo-Thomism and Lenin's theory of knowledge in *Materialism and Empiriocriticism*.

Strange bedfellows.

VI

THE DEFENSE
OF THE RACE

Are the Italians Anti-Semites?

When a Jewish cemetery in Rome was recently desecrated, someone contentiously recalled a remark made by the exponent of the parliamentary center-right, Pier Ferdinando Casini, according to whom in Italy anti-Semitism is less deeply rooted than in other countries. I think we need to make a distinction between intellectual anti-Semitism and popular anti-Semitism.

Popular anti-Semitism is as old as the Diaspora. It springs from an instinctive reaction of the common people toward people who are different, people who speak an unknown tongue redolent of magical rites. A people accustomed to the culture of the Book, Jews learned to read and write, practiced medicine, engaged in commerce and money lending, hence the resentment toward these "intellectuals." The anti-Semitism of the Russian peasantry had such roots.

The Christian condemnation of these "deicides" certainly played a part, but even in the Middle Ages there was a (private) relationship between Christian and Jewish intellectuals characterized

"Are the Italians Anti-Semites?" appeared in L'espresso, *July 2002.*

by mutual interest and respect. This holds for the Renaissance too. The crowds of wretches that followed the Crusades and laid waste to the ghettos were not interested in fundamental doctrines but prompted by the lust for plunder.

The intellectual anti-Semitism we know today arose in the modern world. In 1797, Abbé Barruel wrote the *Mémoires pour servir à l'histoire du jacobinisme* to show that the French Revolution was a plot hatched by Templars and Masons, and later a certain Captain Simonini (an Italian) pointed out to him that those who pulled the strings were the perfidious Jews. After that began the polemic about international Jewry, a theory that the Jesuits made their own and used as an argument against the Carbonaro movement.

Throughout the nineteenth century this debate raged all over Europe, but it found the most fertile ground in France, where they singled out Jewish financiers as the enemy. The polemic was fed by Catholic legitimism, but in lay circles (and in the secret services) it slowly began to take shape, based on a fake, the notorious *Protocols of the Elders of Zion*. This sham spread to Russian Tsarist circles and was later adopted by Hitler.

The *Protocols* were made up of recycled material worthy of the feuilletons, and their unreliability is self-evident, because it is hardly credible that the bad guys would have talked about their wicked plans so openly. The Elders even declared that they would encourage sports and visual communications to dumb down the working classes (this last part seems more in harmony with Berlusconi's ideas than Jewish thinking). Yet, unsophisticated as it may have been, this was intellectual anti-Semitism.

One might agree with Casini and say that popular anti-Semitism was less strong in Italy than in other European countries (for various social, historical and demographic reasons), and that the common people did oppose racial persecution by helping the Jews. But Italy provided fertile ground for the doctrinal anti-Semitism of the

Jesuits (think of the novels of Father Bresciani) as well as the bourgeois variant, which was to produce those well-known scholars and
writers responsible for the infamous magazine *La difesa della razza*
(The Defense of the Race) and the edition of the *Protocols* published
in 1937 with an introduction by Julius Evola.

Evola wrote that the *Protocols* had "the value of a spiritual stim-
ulant" and "above all in these decisive hours in Western history
they cannot be ignored without seriously jeopardizing the front
made up of those who are fighting in the name of the spirit and the
tradition of true civilization." According to Evola, international
Jewry lay at the roots of the main breeding grounds of the perver-
sion of Western civilization:

> Liberalism, individualism, egalitarianism, free thinking, an-
> tireligious enlightenment, with all the various concomitant
> ideas that lead to the rebellion of the masses and to commu-
> nism itself. . . . It is a duty, for the Jew . . . to destroy all sur-
> viving vestiges of true order and differentiated culture. . . .
> Freud is a Jew, and his theory aims at reducing inner life to un-
> conscious instincts and forces; Einstein is a Jew thanks to
> whom we have the fad for "relativism" . . . Schoenberg and
> Mahler, the principal exponents of decadent music, are Jews.
> As is Tzara, the father of Dadaism, the extreme expression of
> the degradation that is so-called avant-garde art. . . . It is race,
> it is instinct at work here. . . . The time has come for forces to
> rise up everywhere in arms, because now the destiny to which
> Europe was about to succumb has shown its face. . . . May the
> hour of the "conflict" . . . find them together as one solid, iron-
> shod bloc, indestructible and irresistible.

Italy has made its contribution to intellectual anti-Semitism.
But today a number of developments point to a new popular anti-
Semitism, as if the ancient hotbeds of anti-Semitism had found a

new source of energy in other, crude, neo-Celtic forms of racism. Proof of this is that the doctrinal sources are always the same: all you have to do is visit certain racist Internet sites, or take a look at anti-Zionist propaganda in Arab countries, and you will see the same old recycling of the *Protocols*.

The Plot

The extraordinary thing about the *Protocols of the Elders of Zion* isn't the story of their production but that of their reception. How this fake was produced by secret services and the police of at least three countries, through a collage of diverse texts, is now well known—and Will Eisner tells the whole story, complete with references to the latest research. In an article I once wrote[1] I mentioned other sources that experts have paid scant attention to: the Jewish plan for the conquest of the world is copied, sometimes almost verbatim, from the Jesuitical plan recounted by Eugène Sue first in *Le juif errant* and later in *Les mystères du peuple,* and in fact one is tempted to think that these novels inspired Maurice Joly himself (whose story is fully recounted in Eisner's book). But there's more. Experts on the *Protocols*[2] have already reconstructed the story of

---

1. "Fictitious Protocols" in *Six Walks in the Fictional Woods* (Harvard University Press, 1994).
2. See, for example, Norman Cohn's *Warrant for Genocide* (London: Eyre and Spottiswoode, 1967), chapter 1.

"The Plot" was written as an introduction to Will Eisner's The Plot: The Secret Story of the Protocols of the Elders of Zion *(New York: Norton, 2005).*

Hermann Goedsche, who in his novel *Biarritz,* written in 1868 under the pseudonym Sir John Retcliffe, tells how representatives of the twelve Tribes of Israel met in a Prague cemetery to lay the groundwork for the conquest of the world. Five years later the same story was passed off as a real event in a Russian pamphlet (*The Jews, Masters of the World*). In 1881, *Le contemporain* republished it, asserting that it came from an authoritative source, the English diplomat Sir John Readcliff. In 1896, François Bournand used the Chief Rabbi's speech (under the name John Readclif) in his book *Les juifs, nos contemporains.* People didn't notice that Goedsche had done no more than copy a scene from *Joseph Balsamo,* by Dumas (1849), in which there is a description of a meeting between Cagliostro and other Masonic plotters to plan the Queen's necklace affair and to use this scandal to pave the way for the French Revolution.

This patchwork of mostly fictional texts makes the *Protocols* an incoherent text whose fictional origins are clear. It is not credible to have the bad guys say, if not in a *roman feuilleton,* or an opera, that they are driven by "boundless ambition, an all-consuming greed, a ruthless desire for revenge, and an intense hatred."

The *Protocols* were taken seriously at first, presented as a scandalous discovery coming from sources felt to be reliable. Amazingly, this fake is born again from the ashes every time someone comes up with the cast-iron proof of its falseness. The "romance of the *Protocols*" itself has the feel of fiction.

After the revelations in the *Times* in 1921, whenever an authoritative source reiterates the spurious nature of the *Protocols,* someone republishes them as authentic. This is going on today on the Internet. As if, after Copernicus, Galileo, and Kepler, people continued publishing school books that said the sun revolves around the Earth.

How can we explain this resistance to the evidence, and the continuing perverse fascination of this book? An answer may be found in the work of Nesta Webster, an anti-Semitic writer who spent her life defending the idea of the Jewish conspiracy. In her *Secret Societies and Subversive Movements,* she seems informed about the story that Eisner tells, yet she concludes:

> The only opinion I have committed myself to is that, whether genuine or not, the *Protocols* represent the programme of a world revolution, and that in view of their prophetic nature and of their extraordinary resemblance to the protocols of certain secret societies of the past, they were either the work of some such society or of someone profoundly versed in the lore of secret society who was able to reproduce their ideas and phraseology.[3]

The reasoning is impeccable: "since the *Protocols* say what I say in my story, they confirm my words." Or: "the *Protocols* confirm the story I have drawn from them, and hence they are authentic." Or again: "the *Protocols* might be false, but they say exactly what the Jews think, and so they must be considered authentic." In other words, it is not the *Protocols* that engender anti-Semitism; it is the profound need to identify an enemy that prompts people to believe in them.

So despite Eisner's courageous work, the story isn't over. But it's worth opposing yet again the great lie and the hatred it continues to foment.

---

3. Nesta H. Webster, *Secret Societies and Subversive Movements* (London: Boswell, 1924), pp. 408–09.

Some of My Best Friends

In the course of the recent uproar about the former Italian parliamentary undersecretary Stefano Stefani's attack on the Germans, Stefani pointed out—as proof of his good intentions—that his first wife was German. A poor argument: if she had been his present wife, that would have meant something, but as she evidently left him or he left her, at least this is a sign that he has probably never been able to get along with Germans. If my memory serves me well, Céline's wife was Jewish, and Mussolini had a Jewish mistress for many years, but this didn't stop either man from being anti-Semitic.

There is an expression that has become proverbial in English: "Some of my best friends." People who start off by declaring, say, that some of their best friends are Jewish, usually come to a "but" or "however," followed by an anti-Semitic tirade. In the 1970s there was even a play about anti-Semitism called *Some of My Best Friends* (running in New York). Those who begin with this expression are immediately labeled as anti-Semites—and in fact some time ago, paradoxically, I decided that the best way to begin any dis-

---

"Some of My Best Friends" appeared in L'espresso, *August 2003.*

course against racism would be to start off with: "Some of my best friends are anti-Semites . . ."

The phrase is an example of what classical rhetoric calls *concessio* or concession: you begin by speaking well of your adversary and showing that you agree with one of his theses, and then you move on to the demolition job. If I began a speech with "Some of my best friends are black," then it would be clear that I was angling for the KKK prize.

While it is less common, the opposite device works just as well: I have no good friends in Termoli Imerese, Canberra, or Dar-es-Salaam (and that's pure coincidence), but if I began a speech with "I have no friends in Canberra," I would probably be expected to sing the praises of the Australian capital.

Suppose there is a political argument in which we begin by citing statistics to prove that the vast majority of Americans are against Bush and the vast majority of Israelis are against Sharon, proceeding from this to criticize the two administrations. But a single example will not suffice; it's not enough to point to Amos Oz in Israel or Susan Sontag in the United States. Rhetoricians would call this an *exemplum*, which has psychological value but no argumentative weight. Reference to a particular, whether it is represented by Sontag or any other of my best friends, does not enable me to draw general conclusions. That someone steals my wallet in Amsterdam doesn't justify my saying that the Dutch are all thieves (only racists argue this way), though it's a greater sin to argue by starting from the general (all Scots are stingy, all Koreans smell of garlic), conceding at most that curiously all the Scots I have known have always generously paid for the drinks and that my Korean friends happen to smell only of expensive aftershave.

It is always dangerous to indulge in fancy footwork with general statements, proof of which is the paradox of Epimenides the Cretan, who said that all Cretans are liars. Obviously, if this statement is made by a Cretan, a liar by definition, then it is a lie to say that all Cretans are liars; but if therefore all Cretans are honest, then Epimenides is telling the truth when he says that all Cretans are liars. And so on, ad infinitum. St. Paul fell into this trap, arguing that the Cretans were liars because a Cretan had admitted this.

These are amusements for students of logic or rhetoric, but they teach us that we should always distrust those who begin with a concession. It is interesting, especially these days, to analyze the various forms of concession heard in the political arena, such as professions of respect (in general) for the judiciary, acknowledgment of the goodwill shown by many non-EU citizens in the workplace, admiration for the great Arab cultural tradition, professions of the utmost esteem for the president of the Republic, and so on.

So if someone begins with a concession, watch out: the sting will be in the tail.

Some of Her Best Friends

In the early 1960s, when some colleagues and I were invited to Spain for a series of cultural debates, our first reaction was to refuse, like the good democrats and beautiful souls we thought we were, saying that we would never go to a country run by a dictator. Then some Spanish friends had us think again: they explained that our visit would lead to dialogue, and it would be a fairly free one, because we were foreigners. In addition, our presence would increase the possibility of dissent for those Spaniards opposed to Franco's regime. After that, we went to Spain every time they invited us, and I recall that the Italian Institute of Culture under the direction of Ferdinando Caruso became an oasis of free discussion.

Since then, I have learned to distinguish between the policies of a government (or even the constitution of a state) and the cultural ferment at work in that country. This is why I later attended cultural meetings in countries whose politics I didn't agree with. Recently I was invited to Iran by some young, open-minded scholars who are fighting for the development of a modern culture there, and I agreed, asking only for the visit to be postponed until the situation in the

"Some of Her Best Friends" appeared in L'espresso, *January 2003.*

Middle East became clearer, because it didn't strike me as sensible to find myself on a plane that might get caught in missile crossfire.

If I were American, I certainly wouldn't vote for Bush, but this doesn't stop me from having continuous and cordial relations with various American universities.

I have just received a copy of *The Translator*, a specialist English magazine to which I have contributed articles in the past. It has an excellent international editorial committee and is run by Mona Baker, the esteemed editor of *Encyclopaedia of Translation Studies*, published by Routledge in 1998.

In the latest issue, Baker opens with an editorial in which she says that many academic institutions (in protest against Sharon's policies) have signed petitions calling for a boycott of Israeli universities (in agreement with certain Internet sites): "Call for a European Boycott of the Research of Israeli Scientific Institutions" and "Call for a European Boycott of the Research of and Cultural Links with Israel." Accordingly, Baker has asked Miriam Schlesinger and Gideon Toury (both well-known Israeli academics) to resign from the board of *Translation Studies Abstracts*.

Baker (fortunately) admits that she made this decision without asking the consultants and contributors to her magazine and that the academics she wishes to exclude have on various occasions expressed strong disapproval of Sharon's policies. She specifies that the boycott is not *ad personam* but against institutions. But this makes things worse, because it means your belonging to a certain racial group is more important than your individual position on a matter.

The consequences of such a principle are obvious: Italians who think Bush is a warmonger should work to block all contact between the Italian research establishment and its American counterpart; all foreigners who think Berlusconi is a man bent only on establishing his own personal power should break off all contact with that august academic body the Accademia dei Lincei; those against Arab terrorism should have Arab scholars expelled from all European cultural institutions, no matter whether those scholars are in agreement or not with fundamentalist groups and their principles.

Over the centuries, despite atrocious episodes of intolerance and state-sponsored ferocity, a community of learned people has survived, a community that has tried to foster understanding among the people of all countries. To sever this universal bond would be a tragedy. I'm sorry that Mona Baker doesn't understand this, especially considering that an expert in translation studies is by definition interested in a continuous dialogue between different cultures. You cannot condemn an entire country, no matter how much you disagree with its government, without taking into account the contradictions and divisions existing there.

As I write, I learn that an Israeli commission has blacked out a televised press conference called by Sharon, because it was held to be unfair electoral propaganda. So we can see that in Israel there is an interesting and ongoing dialectic between diverse positions, and I don't understand how this can be ignored by those who seem to think that the embargo against Iraq is unjust, because it is maintained at the expense of the people suffering under Saddam's dictatorship.

Nowhere in this world are all cats gray in the dark, and saying that they are is called racism.

VII

THE TWILIGHT OF
THE NEW MILLENNIUM

A Dream

When someone says, "I dream of . . ." or "I dreamt," he usually means that his desires have materialized, or were revealed, in a dream. But a dream can also be a nightmare, in which we see things that no one would ever wish for. Or it may be prophetic, requiring the help of an authorized interpreter.

My dream is of this third type, and I'll recount it just as I dream it, without asking myself beforehand whether it expresses my desires or my fears.

I dream that a global blackout has paralyzed the entire civilized world. This blackout is followed by a desperate search for those responsible. Because nations feel threatened, a planet-wide conflict ensues: an all-out war, not a marginal incident like the Second World War, which cost a mere 55 million dead. A war made possible by modern technology, with entire areas of the planet turned into radioactive desert and at least half the world's population dead from friendly fire, starvation, and pestilence. In short, a job well done, carried out by competent, responsible generals abreast of the times.

"A Dream" appeared in L'espresso, *December 2003.*

Naturally (for we are selfish even in dreams) I dream that I, my dear ones, and my friends all live in a part of the world (possibly Italy) in which things have not gone so desperately badly.

We won't have television anymore, not to mention the Internet. All the phone lines are out. Some form of radio communication may be left, using old crystal sets. Electrical power lines are no more, but by cobbling some solar panels together, especially in country houses, we will have a few hours of light, and for the rest of the time we must buy fuel for paraffin lamps on the black market. No one will take the trouble to refine gasoline for cars anymore, because there are no roads left. At best there will be horse-drawn carts and gigs.

By this poor light, and possibly beside a frugal fire made of sticks gathered here and there, I will sit of an evening and amuse my grandchildren—by now bereft of television—by reading them old books of fairy tales found in the attic, or by telling them about the world before the war.

Then we will all gather around the radio and pick up distant transmissions, which tell us how things are going and warn us of any threats to our area. Communications will be handled by retrained carrier pigeons, and think how nice it would be to detach the latest message from a bird's claw to discover that Uncle's sciatica is bothering him but he is still alive and kicking, or to find a microfiche copy of yesterday's newspaper.

Perhaps, if we have taken refuge in the country, there might still be a school in the village, and in that case I would do my bit by teaching grammar and history—not geography, because the map will have changed so radically that talking about geography would be like talking about ancient history. If there is no school, I'll assemble my grandchildren and their friends and tutor them at home: first calligraphy, to train their wrists, not only for writing but for the many manual tasks they must do, and then gradually—if there are a few older students—I could give philosophy lessons.

Perhaps the parish courtyard will still remain, complete with a soccer field (the kids could play with a ball made of rags), and we might find an old pool table in the cellar. The priest will have the carpenter knock together a Ping-Pong table, which the youngsters will find more enjoyable and creative than the old video games.

We will eat lots of vegetables, provided our area isn't radioactive, and we'll learn to enjoy steamed nettles, which taste like spinach. Since rabbits are prolific by definition, there will be no shortage of them, and there might be a chicken for Sunday lunch: the breast for the little girl, a leg for her big brother, a wing each for Mum and Dad; and for Grandma, who isn't fussy, the neck, head, and parson's nose, which is the tastiest part of a free-range bird.

We will rediscover the pleasures of walking, the warmth of old-fashioned lumber jackets and woolen gloves, also useful for snowball fights.

And there will be the good old family doctor, with his reserves of aspirin and quinine. Of course, without hyperbaric chambers, CAT scans, and other technological devices, the average life expectancy will return to sixty, but that won't be so bad, given the average in other parts of the world.

Windmills will reappear in the hills. In the shadow of their huge sails, the old folk will tell the story of Don Quixote, and the youngsters will find it wonderful. People will make music, and everyone will learn to play some rediscovered old instrument. No matter how bad things are, you can always take a penknife and some canes and whittle out entire orchestras of flutes. On Sundays there will be dancing on the village green, and maybe some surviving accordionist will play a mazurka.

In the bars and the taverns they will play cards, while drinking lemonade and new wine. The village idiot, forced to quit politics, will make his reappearance. Unmotivated young people will console themselves by inhaling camomile infusions with towels over their heads and they will say that it is a real blast.

In the mountains, many animals will make a comeback: bad-gers, martens, foxes, and hares by the score. Even animal libera-tionists will occasionally agree to go hunting for protein-rich food, with an old shotgun if there is one, with bow and arrow in any case, or with a blowpipe.

At nights, down in the valley, we will hear the barking of dogs, well fed and held in great consideration, because people will dis-cover that they are a cheap replacement for expensive electronic alarm systems. No one will abandon dogs on the highways anymore, because highways no longer exist and even if they did no one would use them, for that way you risk arriving too quickly in places better avoided: *ubi sunt leones.*

Reading will become popular again, because with the exception of fire, books can survive all kinds of disasters. They will be discov-ered in abandoned rooms and removed from the great ruined city li-braries; they will be lent out and given as presents at Christmas; and they will keep us company in the long winter nights and in the sum-mer, as we answer nature's call beneath a tree.

Disquieting news may come through over the crystal set, but we will hope that the worst can be avoided and thank our lucky stars every day, because we're still alive and the sun is shining. The more poetic among us will begin to say that a new golden age is dawning.

The cost of these renewed pleasures would be at least three billion dead; the disappearance of the Pyramids, the Louvre, and Big Ben (and New York would reduced to one big Bronx); and I would have to smoke straw if I couldn't kick the cigarette habit. I awake from my dream feeling agitated and—to tell the truth—I hope that none of this happens.

But I went to someone who practices divination and can inter-pret the entrails of animals and the flight of birds, and he told me that my dream doesn't only foretell something horrible, it also sug-gests how that horror can be avoided: curbing consumerism, refraining from violence, avoiding getting worked up about the violence of others, and occasionally savoring age-old rituals and outmoded customs—because even today we can turn off the computer and the TV and, instead of taking a charter flight to the Maldives, tell a story around the fire. All you need is the will to do so.

But, my dream interpreter added, that is the real dream: that we might have the courage to stop for a moment to prevent the other dream from coming true. And so, he added (for he is wise but testy, like all prophets to whom no one listens), you can all go to the devil, it's your own fault too.

On the Shoulders of Giants

I chose the title of this speech not only by way of tribute to last year's theme but also because the story of dwarfs and giants has always fascinated me. Yet the historical dwarf-giant polemic is only one chapter in the age-old struggle between fathers and sons that has a close bearing on our lives today.

We don't need a psychiatrist to tell us that sons tend to kill their fathers—and if I use the masculine, it's only because I want to stick to the literature on the question, for I am well aware that bad relationships may be extended to mothers and sons. Nero and Agrippina spring to mind, as does a recent murder case here in Italy. Mothers get killed too.

The problem is rather, in symmetry with sons who attack their fathers, that fathers have always attacked their sons. Oedipus, albeit blamelessly, killed Laius, but Saturn devoured his children, and Medea is unlikely to have a kindergarten named after her. Not to mention poor Thyestes, who made a Big Mac out of the flesh of his own sons without knowing it. And for every heir to the throne of

"On the Shoulders of Giants" is a speech given during La Milanesiana-Letteratura Musica Cinema, July 2001.

Byzantium who blinded his father, there is a sultan in Constanti-nople who guarded against an overly rapid succession by slaughter-ing all his sons by his first wife.

The conflict between fathers and sons can be nonviolent but no less dramatic for that. Fathers can be opposed with ridicule, as in the case of Ham who couldn't find it in himself to forgive Noah a little wine after all that water. As we know, Noah reacted with an expulsion based on race, exiling his disrespectful son to the developing coun-tries. Thousands of years of endemic hunger and slavery for laugh-ing at Dad after he had one too many is, let's admit it, a bit much.

Even if we consider Abraham's willingness to sacrifice Isaac as a sublime example of submission to the divine will, I would say that by so doing Abraham showed that he considered his son his property (his son dies with his throat cut, and Abraham earns the benevolence of Yahweh—now tell me that the man was behaving according to our notion of morality). Yahweh was only joking, but Abraham didn't know that. That Isaac was unlucky can be seen from what happened to him when he became a father in his turn: Jacob didn't kill him of course, but he swindled him out of the rights of succession with a low trick, taking advantage of his blindness, ar-guably a ploy even more outrageous than out and out parricide.

Every *querelle des anciens et des modernes* is a symmetrical struggle. To come to the seventeenth-century French affair from which I have borrowed this phrase, Perrault and Fontanelle claimed that the works of their contemporaries, being more mature than those of their forebears, were therefore better (and so the *poètes galantes* and the *esprits curieux* preferred the new forms of narration and the novel), but the *querelle* broke out and grew, because the new trend was opposed by authoritative figures like Boileau and all those in favor of imitating the ancients.

When there is a *querelle*, the innovators are always opposed by those who praise times past, and very often the enthusiasm for the new and the breach with the past is a reaction to conservatism. The

Italian *Novissimi* school of poetry is a twentieth-century phenomenon, but two thousand years ago we had the *poetae novi*. In Catul-
lus's day the word *modernus* was yet to be coined, but the poets who
looked to Greek lyricism in order to oppose the Latin tradition were
known as the "new" poets. In his *Art of Loving* (3.120ff) Ovid said
prisca iuvent alios ("I leave the past to others"), *ego me nunc denique
natus gratulor, haec aetas moribus acta meis* ("I am proud to be born
today because this time suits me, for it is more refined and less rus-
tic than past days"). That the innovators annoyed the lovers of earlier traditions is clear from Horace (*Epistles* 2.1.75ff), who instead
of "modern" used the adverb *nuper* to say it was a shame when a
book was condemned not for a lack of elegance *sed quia nuper,* in
other words, only because it came out the day before yesterday.
Book reviewers today, who complain that people don't write novels
the way they used to, are taking the same position.

The term *modernus* came along at the end of what we now call
antiquity, around the fifth century AD, when all Europe was plunged
into the murk that preceded the Carolingian renaissance—a period
we see as the least modern of all. Precisely in those "dark" ages, in
which the memory of past greatness was fading, leaving only a few
run-down, burnt-out vestiges, innovation was taking root, even
though the innovators were quite unaware of this. It was then that
the new European languages began to make headway, arguably the
most original and powerful cultural event of the last two thousand
years. Simultaneously, classical Latin became medieval Latin.

The first sign of pride in innovation was the recognition that
people were inventing a Latin unlike that of the ancients. After the
fall of the Roman Empire, the old continent saw the crisis of agricultural society; the destruction of the great Roman cities, roads,
and aqueducts; and—in a territory covered by dense woodland—
monks, poets, and miniaturists saw the world as inhabited by monsters. Since 580, Gregory of Tours had been proclaiming the end of

literacy, and one Pope (I don't remember which) wondered about the validity of baptisms held in Gaul, where they had taken to baptizing *in nomine Patris et Filiae* (of the Daughter) *et Spiritus Sancti*, because even the clergy didn't know Latin anymore. But between the seventh and tenth centuries there developed what has been called the "Hisperic aesthetic," a style that took root in Spain and the British Isles, and to a certain extent in Gaul too.

The classical Latin tradition had described (and condemned) this style, labeling it first "Asian," then "African," in contrast with the balanced manner of the "Attic" style. The Asian style was criticized for what classical rhetoric called *kakozelòn*, or *mala affectatio* (an "ill affectation"). For an example of just how deeply the Fathers of the Church of the fifth century were scandalized by cases of *mala affectatio*, see this invective by Saint Jerome (in *Adversus Jovinianum* I):

> These days there are so many barbarous writers and so many discourses rendered so muddled by stylistic vices that one can neither understand who is talking nor what he is talking about. All expands and contracts like a diseased serpent that falls apart as it vainly essays to make its coils. All is entangled in inextricable verbal knots, and one has to agree with Plautus: "Here no one can understand anything except the Sybil." What's the use of this verbal witchcraft?

But what was a vice for the classical tradition became a virtue for Hisperic poetics. Hisperic writing no longer complied with traditional syntactic and rhetorical norms; the rules of rhythm and meter were broken to produce lists of a baroque flavor. Long series of alliterations that the classical world would have deemed cacophonic now produced a new music, and Adhelm of Malmesbury (*Letter to Eahfrid*, PL 89.159) enjoyed himself hugely by constructing sentences in which (almost) every word begins with the same letter:

*"Primitus pantorum procerum praetorumque pio potissimum pater-
noque praesertim privilegio panegyricum poemataque passim prosatori
sub polo promulgantes. . . ."*

The lexicon was enriched with incredible hybrids, the use of
loan words from the Hebrew and Greek, and the discourse became
dense with cryptograms. Where classical aesthetics saw clarity as
an ideal, the Hisperic aesthetic strove for obscurity. Where classical aesthetics saw proportion as an ideal, the Hisperic aesthetic favored complexity, the abundance of epithets and periphrasis, the
gigantic, the monstrous, the uncontrollable, the fathomless, and the
prodigious. The waves of the sea were defined as *astriferus* or *glau-
cicomus,* while much-appreciated neologisms include *pectoreus, pla-
coreus, sonoreus, alboreus, propriferus, flammiger, gaudifluus . . .*

These are the same lexical inventions praised in the seventh
century by Virgil the Grammarian in his *Epitomae* and *Epistolae.*
This mad grammarian from Bigorre, near Toulouse, quoted passages
from Cicero or Virgil (the other one, the real one) that those authors
would never have written, but then we learn, or sense, that he belonged to a group of rhetoricians each of whom had adopted the
name of a classical author and, under that false name, wrote in a
Latin that was anything but classical, and gloried in it.

Virgil of Bigorre created a linguistic universe that looks as if it
sprang from the imagination of the Italian poet Edoardo Sanguinetti,
even though the springing was probably vice versa. Virgil maintained that there were twelve types of Latin, in each of which fire
could have different names, like *ignis, quoquinhabin, ardon, calax,
spiridon, rusin, fragon, fumaton, ustrax, vitius, siluleus, aeneon*
(*Epitomae* 1.4). Battle was called *praelium* because it can happen at
sea, or *praelum* because its immensity has the primacy, or *praela-
tum,* of the marvelous (*Epitomae* 4.10). The very rules of Latin were
questioned, and it is said that the rhetoricians Galbungus and Te-
rentius debated for fourteen days and fourteen nights about the vo-
cative case of *ego*—and the problem was of the utmost importance,

because it was a question of establishing whether one could refer emphatically to oneself ("O I, have I done well?" *O egone, recte feci?*)

But let's move on to vulgar speech. Toward the end of the fifth century people had already dropped Latin in favor of Gallo-Roman, Italo-Roman, Hispano-Roman, and Balkano-Roman. These were spoken, not written languages, yet even before the Serment de Strasbourg and the Charter of Capua, this looks like a celebration of linguistic novelty. Given the multiplication of tongues, people went back to the tale of the tower of Babel, usually seen as a sign of a curse or catastrophe. But in the birth of the new vulgar languages some now dared to see modernity and improvement.

In the seventh century, some Irish grammarians tried to describe the advantages of vulgar Gaelic with respect to Latin grammar. In a work titled *The Precepts of the Poets,* they referred to the structure of the tower of Babel: just as nine materials had been used in the construction of the tower—clay and water, wool and blood, wood and lime, pitch, linen, and bitumen—so Gaelic had been formed from nouns, pronouns, verbs, adjectives, adverbs, participles, conjunctions, prepositions, and interjections. The parallel is revealing: we must wait for Hegel before the legend of the tower is again seen as a positive model. The Irish grammarians held that Gaelic was the first and only case in which the confusion of tongues had been overcome. Its creators, by means of an operation we would now call cutting and pasting, chose the best features of every language, and when there was something for which no language had found a name, they produced one—in such a way as to reveal a formal identity between the thing and the word.

Centuries later, armed with a completely different awareness of his own undertaking and dignity, Dante saw himself as the inventor of a new vernacular. Faced with the plethora of Italian dialects, which he analyzed with the precision of a linguist but with the hauteur and occasional disdain of a poet—one who never doubted that he was the greatest of all—Dante concluded that there was a need for a language that was illustrious (diffusive of light), cardinal (serving as a mainstay and a rule), regal (worthy of a place in the royal palace of the national realm, if the Italians were ever to have one), and courtly (the language of government, law, and wisdom). His *De Vulgari Eloquentia* outlines the rules of composition of the only true vernacular, the poetic language he proudly felt he had founded. Unlike the tongues of the confusion, it had rediscovered a primordial affinity with things, just like the Adamitic language. This illustrious vernacular, to which Dante gave chase as if it were a "perfumed panther," was a restoration of the Edenic language, hence a tongue capable of healing the post-Babelic wound. This bold concept of his own role as the restorer of the perfect language explains the fact that, rather than criticize the multiplicity of tongues, Dante emphasized their quasi-biological power to renew themselves and change over time. It was precisely on the basis of this claimed linguistic creativity that he was able to set himself the task of inventing a modern, natural, perfect language without chasing after such lost models as the original Hebrew. He set himself up as a new (and better) Adam. Compared to Dante's pride, Rimbaud's far more recent assertion, *il faut être absolument moderne,* looks dated. In the struggle between fathers and sons, the *Inferno* is much more patricidal than *Saison en enfer.*

Perhaps the first episode of the generational clash in which the word *modernus* makes an explicit appearance occurred not in the literary sphere but in the realm of philosophy. Whereas the early medieval period found its primary philosophical sources in late Neoplatonic texts, in Augustine, and in those Aristotelian writings called the *Logica Vetus,* scholastic circles in the twelfth century were gradually permeated by other Aristotelian texts (such as the *Prior* and *Posterior Analytics,* the *Topics,* and *On Sophistical Refutations*), which came to be known as the *Logica Nova.* This stimulus led to a shift from a merely metaphysical and theological discourse to an exploration of all those subtleties of reason that modern logic sees as the liveliest inheritance of medieval thinking, and hence to what was defined (clearly with the pride common to all innovative movements) as Logica Modernorum.

The nature of the novelty of the Logica Modernorum as compared to the theological thinking of the past is underlined by the fact that the Church glorified Anselm of Aosta, Thomas Aquinas, and Bonaventure but has not done the same for any proponent of modern logic. It's not that these men were heretics. Simply, with respect to the theological debates of past centuries, they were interested in other things. Today we would say that they dealt with the workings of the mind. These men were more or less consciously killing their fathers, just as the humanist philosophers would later try to kill them, outdated modernists that they were—but all the humanist philosophers managed to do was condemn them to hibernation in the university lecture halls, where contemporary (and here I mean today's) universities would eventually rediscover them.

In the cases I have mentioned, it nevertheless appears that every act of innovation, and of protest against the fathers, occurs through recourse to an ancestor, who is recognized as better than the father whom one is trying to kill. The *poetae novae* challenged the Latin tradition by imitating the Greek lyricists; the Hisperic poets and Virgil the Grammarian created their linguistic hybrids by adopting loan words from Celtic, Visigothic, Greek, and Hebrew; the Irish grammarians celebrated a language that was opposed to Latin because it was a collage of far more ancient tongues; Dante needed a strong forefather like Virgil (the classical Latin poet); and the Logica Modernorum was modern thanks to the rediscovery of Aristotle.

A frequent topos in the Middle Ages held that the ancients were taller and better-looking, a position that would be completely untenable today: all you need to do is consider the length of the beds Napoleon slept in. But in those days, perhaps, it was not entirely lacking in sense: not only because people's image of antiquity derived from commemorative statuary, which added many centimeters to the subject's stature, but also because the fall of the Roman Empire was followed by centuries of famine and depopulation, so those crusaders and knights of the Holy Grail that tower in today's celluloid epics were very likely much shorter than the horsemen of our day. Alexander the Great was notoriously a runt, but Vercingetorix was probably taller than King Arthur.

In contrast, another topos, frequent in the Bible and through late antiquity and beyond, was that of the *puer senilis,* a youngster who, along with the virtues of youth, had all those typical of the old man. Praise of the stature of the ancients may seem a conservative foible, and the model of the *senilis in iuvene prudentia* celebrated by Apuleius may seem innovative—but this is not the case. Praise of the ancients was the way in which innovators sought to justify their innovations; they drew on a tradition their fathers had forgotten.

Apart from the few cases mentioned, the greatest being the pride of Dante, in the Middle Ages, people assumed that the truth of things lay in the extent to which they were backed up by an earlier *auctoritas.* If it was suspected that the authority in question didn't really support the new idea, his writings were promptly manipulated until they did; because authorities, as Alain de Lille put it in the twelfth century, have noses of wax.

We must try to grasp this point because, from Descartes on, a philosopher was one who wiped the slate of previous knowledge clean and—as Maritain said—presented himself as a *débutant dans l'absolu.* Any thinker of our day (not to mention any poet, novelist, or painter) who wants to be taken seriously has to show in some way that he is saying something different from his predecessors, and even when he doesn't do so he has to pretend that he does. Well, the Scholastics did exactly the opposite. They committed the most dramatic patricides, so to speak, by stating and trying to show that they were repeating verbatim what their fathers had said.

Considering the times he lived in, Thomas Aquinas revolution-ized Christian philosophy, but he would have promptly replied to anyone who reproved him (and some did), that he was only repeat-ing what St. Augustine had said eight and a half centuries before him. This was neither mendacious nor hypocritical. The medieval thinker simply believed it was right to correct the opinions of his predecessors here and there when, thanks to them, he thought he had a clearer idea. Which brings us to the aphorism that inspired the title of this address, that of the dwarfs and giants.

Dicebat Bernardus Carnotensis nos esse quasi nanos gigantium humeris insidentes, ut possimus plura eis et remotiora videre, non utique proprii visus acumine, aut eminentia corporis, sed quia in altum subvehimur et extollimur magnitudine gigantes.

Bernard of Chartres said that we are like dwarfs standing on the shoulders of giants, and so we can see farther than they not because of our stature or because of the sharpness of our sight, but because—by standing on their shoulders—we are higher than they.

To review the origins of this aphorism, for the medieval period you may consult Edouard Jeauneau's book *Dwarfs on the Shoulders of Giants,* but a more joyfully crazy and exciting romp is *On the Shoulders of Giants,* written in 1965 by one of the greatest contem-porary theologian, Robert Merton. One day Merton was quite taken by the way Newton expressed the aphorism in a letter to Hooke, dated 1675: "If I have seen further it is by standing on ye sholders of Giants." Merton started tracing its origin, documenting its vi-cissitudes through a series of erudite divagations that grew from edition to edition as he added notes and other material. Having published an Italian edition (*Sulle spalle dei giganti* [Bologna: Mulino, 1991]) and having been so good as to ask me to write an introduction, he reissued it in English in 1993 as "the post-Italianate edition."

The aphorism of dwarfs and giants is attributed to Bernard of Chartres by John of Salisbury in *Metalogicon* (3.4). We are in the twelfth century. Bernard was not the first inventor, because the concept (if not the metaphor of the dwarfs) appeared six centuries before, in Priscian, and a middleman between Priscian and Bernard, William of Conches, talks of dwarfs and giants in his *Commentary on Priscian*, thirty-six years before John of Salisbury. After John of Salisbury, the aphorism was picked up pretty much all over: in 1160 it appears in a text attributed to the school of Laon, around 1185 it was used by the Danish historian Sven Aggesen, then by Gerard of Cambrai, Raoul de Longchamp, Egidio di Corbeil, Gerard of Auvergne, and in the fourteenth century by Alexandre Ricat, doctor to the kings of Aragon. It cropped up two centuries later in the works of Ambroise Paré and of the seventeenth-century scientist Richard Sennert, then finally reached Newton.

Tullio Gregory notes an appearance of the aphorism in Gassendi (*Setticismo ed empirismo: Studio su Gassendi* [Bari: Laterza, 1961]), but we could also cite Ortega y Gasset, who in his essay "Entorno a Galileo" (*Obras completas,* vol. 5 [Madrid: 1947], p. 45), discussing the succession of generations, says that men stand "one on the shoulders of the other, and he who is on top enjoys the feeling of dominating the others, but he should realize that at the same time he is their prisoner."

On the other hand, in Jeremy Rifkin's recent *Entropy* I found a quotation from Max Gluckman: "Science is any discipline in which even an idiot of this generation can surpass the point reached by a genius of the preceding generation." Eight centuries divide this quotation from that of Bernard, and something has happened: a saying that referred to the relationship with the fathers of philosophy and theology has become a saying that marks the progressive nature of science.

At the time of its medieval origin the aphorism became popular because it made it possible to solve generational conflict in an apparently nonrevolutionary way. The ancients are giants compared to us; but although we are mere dwarfs seated on their shoulders to take advantage of their wisdom, we can see better than they. Was this statement originally humble or proud?

Since one of the recurring themes in medieval culture is the progressive senescence of the world (*mundus senescit*), one might interpret Bernard's aphorism to mean that we young ones are older than the ancients: thanks to them we understand and do things that they didn't manage to understand or do. Bernard of Chartres put forward the aphorism in the context of a debate on grammar, concerning the concept of knowledge and imitation of the style of the ancients. But, again according to John of Salisbury, Bernard criticized those pupils who slavishly copied the ancients, saying that the point wasn't to write like them but to learn from them how to write well, so that in the future people would find inspiration in them as they had found inspiration in the ancients. And so, although not in the terms in which we understand it today, Bernard's aphorism contained an appeal for autonomy and the courage to innovate.

"We can see further than the ancients." Clearly the metaphor is a spatial one, implying a horizon. We cannot forget that history, as a progressive movement toward the future, from creation to redemption to the coming of Christ triumphant, is an invention of the Fathers of the Church—and so, like it or not, without Christianity (even on the shoulders of Jewish messianism) neither Hegel nor Marx could have talked about what the Italian poet Leopardi saw skeptically as "the magnificent and progressive fate."

The aphorism reappears in the early twelfth century. Only a century before, a key debate had finally subsided, one that had run through the Christian world from the first interpretations of the Apocalypse to the terrors of the year 1000—legendary as far as mass movements are concerned, but present throughout millenarian literature and in many more or less subterranean schools of heretical thought. When the aphorism was coined, millenarianism, in other words the neurotic expectation of the end of days, was the active inheritance of many heretical movements, but it disappeared from orthodox debate. The movement was toward a final *parousia* (The Second Coming of Christ), but it became the ideal end to a story seen as positive. The dwarfs became the symbol of this march to the future.

The medieval appearance of the dwarfs marked the beginning of the history of modernity as innovation that rediscovers models forgotten by the predecessors. Take for example the curious situation of the first humanists, and of philosophers like Marsilio Ficino and Pico della Mirandola. They were the leading lights in a battle against the medieval world, and it was more or less in this period that the word *gothic* appeared, with not entirely happy connotations. Yet what did Renaissance Platonism do? It set Plato against Aristotle, discovered the *Corpus Hermeticum* or the Chaldean Oracles, built a new knowledge upon an ancient wisdom that antedated Jesus Christ. Humanism and the Renaissance were cultural movements commonly seen as revolutionary, whose innovative strategy was nonetheless based on one of the most reactionary coups de main ever, if by philosophical reactionism we mean a return to an atemporal tradition. So we are faced with a patricide that eliminates the fathers by turning to the grandfathers, and it was on the shoulders of the grandfathers that the attempt was made to reconstruct the Renaissance vision of man as the center of the cosmos.

It is probably with seventeenth-century science that Western culture realized that it had stood the world on its head, thereby truly revolutionizing knowledge. But the starting point, the Copernican hypothesis, referred back to Platonic and Pythagorean thinking. The Jesuits of the baroque period tried to construct an alternative modernity in opposition to the Copernican model by rediscovering the ancient writings and civilizations of the Far East. Isaac de la Peyrère, an out-and-out heretic, tried to show (by killing off biblical chronology) that the word began long before Adam, in the China seas, and consequently that the Incarnation was merely a secondary episode in the history of our planet. Vico saw all of human history as a process that takes us from the giants of the past finally to reflection with a pure mind. The Enlightenment saw itself as radically modern, and as a spin-off effect it really did kill its own father, using Louis Capet as a scapegoat. But here too—just read the *Encyclopédie*—it made frequent reference to the giants of the past.

The *Encyclopédie* contains woodcuts full of machines, in celebration of the new manufacturing industry, but it does not disdain articles in which ancient doctrines are revisited; like an energetic dwarf, it reinterprets history.

All the great Copernican revolutions of the nineteenth century refer to earlier giants. Kant needed Hume to awaken him from his dogmatic slumbers; the Romantics had the *Tempest* and Sturm und Drang with which to rediscover the mists and castles of the Middle Ages; Hegel finally sanctioned the primacy of the new over the old (by seeing history as a perfective movement devoid of waste and nostalgia) with his reinterpretation of human history in its entirety; Marx developed his materialism starting from the Greek atomists, which he discussed in his degree thesis; Darwin killed off his biblical fathers by electing as giants the great apes, on whose shoulders men came down from the trees to find themselves, still full of wonder and ferocity, using that marvel of evolution that is the opposable thumb.

The second half of the nineteenth century witnessed the emergence of an innovative artistic movement based almost entirely on the repossession of the past, from the Pre-Raphaelites to the decadents. The rediscovery of remote fathers served as a rebellion against the immediate fathers, who had been corrupted by mechanical looms. And while Carducci made himself the herald of modernity with his *Hymn to Satan,* he continually sought reasons and ideals in the myth of the Italy of the communes.

The avant-garde of the early twentieth century represented an extreme expression of modernist patricide, which wanted to free itself of all deference to the past. This was the victory of the racing car over the *Victory of Samothrace;* the slaying of moonlight; the cult of war as the only form of hygiene in the world; the cubist decomposition of form; the progression from abstraction to the blank canvas; the substitution of music with sound, or with silence, or the substitution of the tonal scale with the tone row; the victory of the reflecting curtain wall that does not dominate but absorbs the environment, of the building as stele, pure paralellepiped, and of minimalist art; and in literature, the destruction of the discursive flow and narrative tenses in favor of collage and the blank page.

Here too, as the new giants rejected the legacy of the old giants, there reemerges the deference of the dwarf. I am not referring so much to Marinetti, who sought forgiveness for murdering the moonlight by becoming a member of the Accademia d'Italia, a body that looked upon moonlight with considerable affection. But Picasso began to disfigure the human face only after meditating on classical and Renaissance models, and he ended up by revisiting the ancient minotaur. Duchamp stuck a mustache on the *Mona Lisa,* but he needed a *Mona Lisa* to stick the mustache on; and in order to deny that he was painting a pipe, Magritte had to paint a meticulously realistic pipe. Finally, the great patricide committed on the historic body of the novel was the work of Joyce, who took Homeric narrative as his model. The ultramodern Ulysses sailed on thanks to the shoulders, or better still, to the mainmast, of an ancient tradition.

Which brings us to postmodernism. *Postmodern* is an all-purpose term, which can be applied to many—perhaps too many—things. But the various operations known as postmodern all have something in common: a reaction, perhaps an unconscious one, to the second of Nietzsche's *Untimely Meditations* ("On the Use and Abuse of History"), in which he denounces our excess of historical awareness. If this awareness cannot be eliminated even from the revolutionary activities of the avant-garde, we might as well accept the oppression of its influence, revisit the past as a form of tribute, and reconsider it from the distance permitted us by irony.

Finally we come to the last episode of generational rebellion, a clear example of protest by the "new" youth against adult society, those young people who warned one another not to trust anyone over thirty: 1968. Apart from the American flower children who drew inspiration from old Marcuse's message, the slogans chanted during Italian demonstrations (Viva Marx!, Viva Lenin!, Viva Mao Tse-tung!) tell us just how much the rebellion needed giants to use against the betrayal of the fathers of the parliamentary left. There was even a comeback for the *puer senilis,* in this case the iconic figure of Che Guevara, who died young but was transformed by death into the bearer of all ancient virtues.

But something happened between 1968 and today. We see this when we consider a phenomenon that some call a new 1968, I mean the antiglobalization movement.

The press gives more visibility to this movement's younger members, but they are not representative of it as a whole; apparently, it also includes elderly prelates. The year 1968 was a true generational phenomenon, to which only a few adult misfits adapted by abandoning ties and wearing sweaters, by throwing out aftershave and relishing liberated and redeeming perspiration. The antiglobalization movement, in contrast, is led by mature adults like Bové or veterans of other revolutions. It does not represent a clash between generations, or even between tradition and innovation, otherwise one would have to say (superficially) that the innovators are the technocrats of globalization and the demonstrators are merely *laudatores temporis acti,* with Luddite nostalgia.

What is happening, from Seattle to Genoa, represents a new form of political struggle, but this struggle is wholly transversal with regard to both generations and ideologies. It contains two opposing aspirations; two visions of the world's destiny; two powers, one based on possession of the means of production and the other based on the invention of new means of communication. In the battle between proglobalization and antiglobalization forces, young and old are equally distributed, and the rampant forty-year-olds of the new economy face the forty-year-olds of the left-wing social centers, both with older sympathizers on their sides.

The fact is that in the thirty-odd years between 1968 and the 1999 G8 conference, a process begun many years before has come to fruition. Let's try to understand its internal mechanism. In order to establish a dialectic between fathers and sons there has always been a need for a strong paternal model, and the provocation of the son had to be so radical that the father could not accept it; nor could the father accept the rediscovery of forgotten giants who under-pinned that provocation. The new poets could not be accepted *quia nuper,* as Horace said; the vernacular was unacceptable to the solemn Latinists of the universities; Aquinas and Bonaventure in-novated hoping that no one would notice, but enemies of the men-dicant orders, in the University of Paris, spotted this and tried to have their teachings banned. And so it went, all the way down to Marinetti's racing car, which could be compared to the *Victory of Samothrace* because and only because right-minded people still saw the automobile as an unlovely, snarling heap of scrap iron.

The models had to be generational. Fathers had to worship Cranach's anorexic Venuses before they could call Rubens's cel-lulitic Venuses an insult to beauty; fathers had to love Alma Tadema before they could ask their sons what the hell that scribble by Mirò or that piece of African art was supposed to mean; fathers had to rave about Greta Garbo before they could ask their sons what they saw in that monkey Brigitte Bardot.

The mass media of today, and their influence on museums (also visited by the uncultivated of old), have brought about the copresence and the syncretistic acceptance of all models, indeed of all values. When Australian supermodel Megan Gale appears in an ad in which she waltzes on a skateboard among the cupolas and spires of the Guggenheim in Bilbao, both the sexual and the artistic elements appeal to all generations: the museum is as desirable as Megan, and Megan is as much a cultural object as the museum, for both exist in the amalgam of a cinematic invention that unites the sensuality of the ad and the aesthetic boldness of vision that once would have qualified only for the Museum of Modern Art.

Among new proposals for and exercises in nostalgia, the television has made transgenerational models out of Che Guevera and Mother Teresa of Calcutta, Lady Diana and Padre Pio, Rita Hayworth, Brigitte Bardot, and Julia Roberts, not the mention the macho John Wayne and the meek Dustin Hoffman of the 1960s. The slender Fred Astaire of the 1930s danced in the 1950s with the stocky Gene Kelly, while the silver screen has us dream about sumptuously feminine outfits, like those seen in *Roberta*, side by side with the androgynous designs of Coco Chanel. For men who do not possess the refined masculine beauty of Richard Gere, there is the sensitive appeal of Al Pacino and the blue-collar charm of Robert de Niro. For those who cannot afford the majesty of a Maserati, there is the elegant utility of the Mini Morris.

The mass media no longer present any unified model. They can retrieve, for an advertising campaign destined to last only a week, all the experimental work of the avant-garde and at the same time rediscover nineteenth-century iconography: the fairy-tale realism of role games and Escher's quirky perspectives; the opulence of Marilyn Monroe and the anorexic charms of the latest fashion models; the dusky beauty of Naomi Campbell and the Nordic beauty of Claudia Schiffer; the grace of traditional tap dancing as in *A Chorus Line* and the chilling futuristic architectures of *Blade Runner*; the androgyny of Jodie Foster and squeaky-clean girls next door like Cameron Diaz; Rambo and Ru Paul; George Clooney (whom all fathers would like to have as a son newly graduated from medical school) and neocyborgs who paint their faces in metallic shades and transform their hair into forests of colored spikes.

In this orgy of tolerance, this absolute and unstoppable polytheism, where is the watershed that separates fathers from sons, driving the latter to patricide (which is both rebellion and tribute) and the former to the cannibalism of Saturn?

We are barely at the beginning of this new path, but think for a second of the arrival first of the personal computer and then of the Internet. The computer came into the home thanks to the fathers, for economic reasons if for nothing else; the sons didn't refuse it and went on to master it, surpassing the fathers in ability, but neither of the two saw it as a symbol of the rebellion or resistance of the other. The computer hasn't divided the generations; if anything it has united them. No one lays a curse on his son because he surfs the Net, and for the same reason no son opposes his father.

It's not that innovation is lacking, but it is almost always technological innovation, imposed by an international center of production that is normally run by older people and creates fashions accepted by the younger people. We talk today of the new youth language of telephone SMS and e-mail messages, but I could show you essays written ten years ago in which the very people who created the new instruments, and the older sociologists and semioticians who studied them, foresaw that they would engender the very language and formulas that are now so popular. Bill Gates was young at the beginning of all this (now he is a mature gentleman who tells young people what language to use), but as a young man he didn't advocate revolt; he came up with a shrewd offer designed to interest both fathers and sons.

Some people think that young social misfits are opposing their families by turning to drug abuse, but drug abuse is a model proposed by the fathers, since the days of the artificial paradises of the nineteenth century. The new generations get input from adult international drug traffickers.

It might be said that there is no clash of models but merely an accelerated replacement of them. This changes nothing. For a brief span of time a certain youth trend (from Nike shoes to earrings) may strike the fathers as outrageous, but the speed of its diffusion in the media ensures that it will soon be absorbed by the fathers too, at most with the risk that in an equally brief time it will strike the sons as ridiculous. But no one will have the time to notice this relay race, and the overall result will always be polytheism, the syncretistic coexistence of all values.

Was the New Age a generational invention? As far as its content goes, it is a collage of ancient esoteric elements. It may be that young people were the first to turn to these elements, as if they were rediscovered giants, but the diffusion of images, sounds, and beliefs typical of the New Age, along with all its recording, publishing, cinematic, and religious paraphernalia, was taken over and run by the old foxes of the mass media, and if some youngsters run off to the Far East, it is to throw themselves into the arms of an elderly guru with lots of lovers and even more Cadillacs.

Things that looked like the last frontier of diversity, such as tongue studs and blue hair, in the sense that they are no longer the inventions of a few individuals but universally accepted, were proposed to young people by the gerontocracy of the international fashion business. Soon the influence of the mass media will impose them on the parents too, unless at a certain point both young and old abandon them simply because they discover that ice cream is hard to eat when you have a metal stud in your tongue.

Why then should fathers still devour their sons, and why should sons continue to kill their fathers? The risk, for everyone, though the fault of no one, is that constant innovation constantly accepted by everybody will lead to ranks of dwarfs sitting on the shoulders of other dwarfs.

But let's be realistic. In normal times I wouldn't be here to round off a cultural event like the Milanesiana; at most, I would have attended it as a pensioner. I was rounding off events like this when I was thirty. The trouble is that even if this event were organized by twenty-year-olds, they would have invited Salman Rushdie and Terrence Malick all the same.

That's wonderful, you will say. We are entering a new era in which, with the decline of ideologies, the blurring of the traditional divisions between left and right, between progressives and conservatives, generational conflict is diminishing. But is it biologically advisable for the rebellion of the sons to be merely a superficial adjustment to models of rebellion provided by the fathers, or for fathers to devour their sons simply by giving them room for a colorful form of social marginalization? When the very principle of patricide is in question, *mala tempora currunt*.

But the worst diagnosticians of every epoch are its contemporaries. My giants have taught me that there are transitional spaces in which the coordinates are lacking and the future cannot be seen clearly. We still do not understand the artifices of reason or the imperceptible plots of the Zeitgeist. Perhaps the sound ideal of patricide is rising again in different forms. Perhaps, in future generations, cloned sons will rebel—in a way we cannot predict—against their legal fathers or sperm donors.

Perhaps in the shadows lurk giants, whom we know nothing about, ready to sit on the shoulders of us dwarfs.

On the Disadvantages
and Advantages of Death

Philosophy may have begun when people started thinking about the beginning—or the *arché*, as the pre-Socratics teach us—but it is equally probable that such reflections were inspired by the realization that things have not just a beginning but also an end. The classic example of a syllogism and therefore of an unshakable argument is, "All men are mortal, Socrates is a man, therefore Socrates is mortal." That Socrates is mortal is the result of an inference, but that all men are mortal is a premise you cannot argue with. In the course of history, many "incontrovertible truths" (that the sun revolves around the Earth, that there is such a thing as spontaneous generation, that the philosophers' stone exists) have been called into doubt, but not the fact that men are mortal. At most, the faithful believe that One Man rose again, but before that happened, he had to die first.

We who practice philosophy accept death as our normal horizon, and there was no need to wait for Heidegger to state that we (at least

---

"On the Disadvantages and Advantages of Death" first appeared as a conclusion to La mort et l'immortalité, *edited by Frédéric Lenoir and Jean-Philippe de Tonnac (Paris: Bayard, 2004).*

those of us who think) live for death. By "we who think" I mean "we who think philosophically," because I know many people, even cultured people, who when someone mentions death (and not even their death) make gestures to ward off misfortune. Philosophers don't do this. Knowing they must die, they live their lives industriously as they await the end. Those who believe in a life hereafter await death with serenity, but so do those who believe that, as Epicurus taught, when death comes, we won't have to worry about it, because we will no longer be here.

Certainly each of us (philosophers too) wishes to reach that point without suffering, because pain is repugnant to our animal nature. Some would like to reach the moment without realizing it; others would prefer a long, conscious approach to the end; others again would like to choose the date. But these are psychological details. The central problem is the ineluctability of death, and the philosophical stance is to prepare oneself for it.

There are many ways to prepare for the end. As I have a favorite, I will permit myself the luxury of quoting myself and reproduce here a few excerpts from a piece I wrote some years ago. It is a text that seems facetious at first, but I consider it very serious indeed:[1]

Recently a pensive disciple of mine (a certain Criton) asked me: "Master, how can we best approach death?" I replied that the only way to prepare for death is to convince yourself that everyone else is a complete idiot.

Seeing Criton's amazement, I explained. You see, I told him, how can you approach death, even if you are a believer, if you think that, as you lie dying, desirable young people of both sexes are dancing in discos and having the time of their lives, enlightened scientists are revealing the last secrets of the uni-

---

1. "Come prepararsi serenemanente per la morte," now in *La bustina di Minerva* (Milano: Bompiani, 2000).

verse, incorruptible politicians are creating a better society, newspapers and television are bent on giving only important news, responsible business people are ensuring that their products will not damage the environment and doing their utmost to restore a nature in which there are streams with drinkable water, wooded hillsides, clear, serene skies protected by a providential ozone layer, and fluffy clouds from which sweet rain falls once more? The thought that you must leave while all these marvelous things are going on would be intolerable.

So try to think, when you sense the time has come for your departure from this vale, that the world (six billion human beings) is full of idiots, that the dancers at the disco are all idiots, the scientists who think they have solved the mysteries of the universe are idiots, the politicians who propose panaceas for all our ills are idiots, the journalists who fill page after page with vacuous gossip are idiots, and the manufacturers who are destroying the planets are idiots. In that moment would you not be happy, relieved, and satisfied to leave this vale of idiots?

And then Criton asked me: "Master, when must I start thinking like this?" I told him that one mustn't start too soon, because a person of twenty or thirty years of age who thinks that everyone else is an idiot is an idiot himself who will never attain wisdom. We should begin by thinking that all the others are better than us and then shift bit by bit, having our first doubts around forty, revising our opinions between fifty and sixty, and attaining certainty as we aim for one hundred, ready to call it quits just as soon as the telegram containing the summons arrives. Convincing ourselves that everyone around us is an idiot is a subtle, shrewd art, not at the disposal of the first Cebes to come along with a ring in his ear (or nose). It requires study and toil. You mustn't go at it too quickly. You must get there gradually, just in time to die with serenity. Right up to the day before, you must still think that someone you love and

admire is not an idiot. Wisdom consists in recognizing only at
the right moment (and not before) that he too is an idiot. Only
then can you die.

The great art lies in studying universal thought a bit at a
time; scrutinizing changes in customs; monitoring the mass
media day by day, the statements of self-assured artists, the
apothegms of politicians who shoot their mouths off, the
philosophemes of apocalyptic critics, the aphorisms of charismatic heroes; studying theories, propositions, appeals, images,
and visions. Only then, in the end, will you experience the in-
sight that everyone is an idiot. And at that point you are ready
for death.

Until the end, you must doggedly insist that some people
say sensible things, that a certain book is better than others,
that a certain leader really desires the common good. It's natural, human, and proper to our species to resist the idea that
all people are idiots, otherwise why go on living? But at the
end you will understand why it is worth the effort and how it
can be a splendid thing to die.

Then Criton said to me: "Master, I wouldn't like to make
hasty decisions, but I suspect that you are an idiot." See, I
replied, you are already on the right track.

This text was intended to express the profound truth that preparation for death consists essentially in convincing yourself gradually that *Vanitas vanitatum, dixit Ecclesiastes. Vanitas vanitatum et
omnia vanitas.*

Yet (and here I move on to the first part of my argument), despite all
this, even the philosopher acknowledges one painful disadvantage
of death. The beauty of growing and maturing is in realizing that life
is a marvelous accumulation of knowledge. If you are not stupid or
chronically absentminded, you learn more as you grow. We call this

experience. In times gone by, the elders were considered the wisest of the tribe, and their task was to pass on their wisdom to their children and grandchildren. It is a wonderful thing to know that every day you learn something more, that your past errors have made you wiser, and that your mind (while your body perhaps gets weaker) is a library that grows larger every day with the addition of a new volume.

I am one of those people who don't miss their youth (I'm glad I had one, but I wouldn't like to start over), because today I feel more fulfilled than ever. But the thought that all that experience will be lost at the moment of my death makes me feel pain and fear. The thought that those who come after me will know as much as I do, and even more, fails to console me. What a waste, decades spent building up experience, only to throw it all away. It's like burning down the Library of Alexandria, destroying the Louvre, or sending the beautiful, rich, and all-wise Atlantis to the bottom of the sea.

We remedy this sadness by working. For example, by writing, painting, or building cities. You die, but most of what you have accumulated will not be lost; you are leaving a message in a bottle. Raphael is dead, but the way he painted is still at our disposal, and precisely because he lived it was possible for Manet and Picasso to paint the way they did. I wouldn't like this consolation to take on an elitist overtone, as if this way to cheat death were available only to writers, thinkers, and artists . . . The humblest creature can pass on his experience to his children, perhaps by spoken words or the strength of his example. We all talk about ourselves, sometimes forcing others to listen to our memories, simply so the memories won't be lost.

Yet, no matter how much I pass on by writing about myself, or just by writing these few pages, even if I were a Plato, Montaigne, or Einstein, I can never transmit the sum of my experience—for example, my feelings on seeing a beloved face or my revelation on watching a sunset. Not even Kant fully transmitted what he understood on gazing at the starry sky above him.

This is the true disadvantage of death, and it saddens even philosophers. So much so that each of us tries to devote his life to reconstructing the experience that others have squandered by dying. A vain opposition to the general curve of entropy. Not to worry, that's the way it goes, and there's nothing we can do about it. Philosophers too must admit that death is not pleasant.

How to get around this problem? By winning immortality, some say. It's not for me to discuss whether immortality is a dream or a possibility, however small; whether it's possible to live to over a hundred and fifty, whether old age is merely an illness that can be prevented. These are matters for scientists. I limit myself to admitting the possibility of a very long or an endless life, because only in that way can I reflect upon the advantages of death.

If I could choose and was sure that I would not spend my last years stricken in the flesh or the spirit, I'd want to live to a hundred or a hundred and twenty rather than seventy-five (in this, philosophers are like everyone else). But it is precisely on thinking of myself at a hundred that I begin to see the disadvantages of immortality.

The first question is whether I would be the only one privileged to live to such a ripe age or whether everyone would have that choice. If it were granted only to me, I would witness the disappearance, one by one, of my dear children and grandchildren. If these grandchildren gave me their children and grandchildren, I might become attached to them and console them on the loss of their parents. But the aftermath of suffering and nostalgia that would accompany me in this protracted old age would be unbearable, not to mention my remorse at having survived.

And then, if wisdom consisted, as I said earlier, in the growing conviction that I was living in a world of idiots, how could I stand to survive as the only wise man? Being the only one with memories in a world of scatterbrains who have regressed to prehistoric levels, how could I bear my intellectual and moral solitude?

But it would be even worse if, as is probable, the growth of my personal experience was slower than that of the collective experience and I had to live with my modest, dated wisdom in a community of young people who surpassed me in every intellectual way. Worse still, if immortality or an incredibly long life were granted to all.

First of all, I would be in a world crowded with people over a hundred (or a thousand) years of age who would rob the younger generations of vital space. I would find myself plunged into an atrocious struggle for life, in which my descendants would wish me finally dead. Yes, there would be the possibility of colonizing other planets, but at that point either I would have to emigrate, with people of my age, galactic pioneers all oppressed by an incurable nostalgia for Earth, or the younger ones would have to emigrate, leaving Earth to us immortals, and I would find myself a prisoner on an aging planet, mumbling away about my memories with other old men whose constant and unstoppable repetition of things already said would become intolerable.

And who can say I wouldn't get bored with all the things that in my first hundred years were a source of wonder, amazement, and the joy of discovery? Would I still take pleasure from reading the *Iliad* for the thousandth time or from listening uninterruptedly to the *Well-Tempered Clavier*? Would I still be able to bear a dawn, a rose, a meadow in bloom, or the taste of honey? *Perdrix, perdrix, toujours perdrix* . . .

I begin to suspect that the sadness that overcomes me when I think that, by dying, I would lose all my treasure of experience is much like the feeling I get when I think that, by surviving, this oppressive, *fanée*, and even moldy experience would begin to get on my nerves.

Perhaps it's better to carry on, for the years that might be granted me, leaving messages in bottles for those who will come after me, as I wait for what St. Francis called Sister Death.

Index